U^{The eye of the}NIVERSE

Brahmavidya Meditation
& its Upanishadic base

Devesan

The Eye of the Universe
Devesan

Published by the Author
First Published : April 2013
Cover Design : T. Sukumaran, Gulf Graphics
© *All rights reserved*

No part of this publication may be reproduced or transmitted in any form or by any means of information storage and retrieval system without permission in writing from the publisher.

Typeset at : Navaneet Computers, Jawahar Nagar, Tvpm-3
Printed at : St. Joseph's Press, Tvpm-14

Copies are available at leading book stalls
Copies can be had direct from the author also.
e-mail :   info@yogaspiritualretreat.com
           devesan40@gmail.com

USD : 15 (for print book)

PREFACE

Vedant-ists repeatedly assure us that the burden of Vedanta is not to prove the non-existence of the world (Maya), but to assert the Reality of Brahman. But in reality (in practice) I find 80 to 90 percent of the volume of discussions is devoted to the subject of Maya ..to say that the world is unreal.

With this whole book, my attempt is to assert the Reality of Brahmam / bodham /awareness, and define its role; and in this, I don't find any need to negate the world!

* *sahasra-shirsha ...paani paadam* (with a thousand heads, ...hands and legs).
* sees without eyes, hears without ears.
* moves not, but runs past others
* has unthinkable power
* the *Viswaroopa darsanam* presented in Bhagavad Gita – and the related pictures drawn by artists in Sivakasi –

...all these together have presented to the world a horrendous picture of a weird Super Being as God.

Put 'awareness' in place of this Super Being – and see how well it fits! How clear, how simple! Awareness, working through the intellects of all the beings ...becomes 'thousand-headed'. This is only a figure-of-speech – and people mistake it. Awareness acts with the hands and legs of all beings.

And 'shivam' (in 'shivohum') is made Siva/Sivan. It is not the Shiva sitting in the temples and at Kailas with snakes round the neck, that is meant. What is meant is a no-male no-female no-being SIVAM (neutral gender) ...meaning AUSPICIOUSNESS (*mangalam*). All other conclusions – ways of interpretation, explanation, understanding – are absurd, nonsense, childish and even less than that. Even children (of 3-4 years) are sensible now-a-days: seeing the lifestyles of animals in nature – the law of the jungle, children ask "why did the God create it this way?"

I have been listening to a lot of teachers from early childhood (3 years) for a long lifetime of 75 years[*]. Till now I have not seen anyone teaching anything perfectly clean ..in public. (Ramana Maharshi, Nisarga Datta, Swamy Vivekananda,Poojappura Gopala swamy and a few others from the southern tip of India ..Swaroopaananda[1], Tatwaraayar[2], Tandavarayar[3], for example, are exceptions ..as far as my knowledge goes. Their major writings are shown below[+]). I don't know whether anyone ..in private ..teaches anything close to truth. In them I find at the bottom an unreasoned reliance on Bhakthi ..and a reluctance ..incapacity to solidify in Jnanam ..the path of Knowledge. The truth is shining ..with dazzling brilliance ..in the Upanishads. But the teachers and their students want only Bhagavatham and Ramayanam ...the vast majority. Those who speak about the reality also get deflected at the end. They say "you seek out some competent guru, and follow him". If they know the reality properly, is it so much of a taboo to speak in public? Why, the Truth cannot be spoken in public? Only un-truth can be dispensed in public?

---

[*] I think I have the backing of a minimum of two more previous lives (revealed to me in a regression into past lives undergone at Osho centre, Haryana) –one looking like an avadhootha sanyasi and the other as a guide to a group of sanyasis in saffron robe.

+ [1] Swaroopasaaram
 [2] Ajnavadhai bharani, Paaduthurai
 [3] Kaivalya navaneetham

I felt this gap very much ...and this book ..with the included Brahmavidya Meditation, fills this gap. I have been introducing people to this meditation for more than a decade ..and a lot of people from very many countries have seen the light of reality. (Some responses are quoted at the end of this book.)

In olden times, in India, this Brahmavidya was preserved as a closely-guarded secret; and was given out only to super-mature seekers.

***   ***   ***

You may find that my approach does not fall in line with monistic Vedanta in toto —not in line with Samkhya theory in toto — and a deviation from the normally-accepted paths. Paths we straighten and widen (making highways) …. The old meandering roads are straightened and widened and ups and downs levelled constantly.

***   ***   ***

For those who grope in darkness, truths can be many. For those who see things in broad daylight, truth can be only one. All the ugly strife in the world in the name of religions and beliefs can end when things are seen in broad daylight. And this book contains only Upanishadic thoughts, sharply focusssed. This is a spirituality acceptable to the sharpest of intellects, also. Here it is not a matter of faith. This is tangible ...can be touched, felt, experienced most directly. This is a way out from the spiritual pauperity with which the world is flooded.

Understand Brahmam to be your own awareness ..pure and simple. Don't get frightened by the big word.

This book does mainly four things:-

**   With the help of Upanishads, relieves Brahmam of the 'omnipotence and omniscience' imposed on it – and helps you understand It as clean awareness.

**   Then there will be absolutely no difficulty in understanding that this Awareness and the awareness in each one of us is just the same. (The Brahmavidya Meditation included in the book also gives a strong boost in this direction).

**   Solidifies in your mind that this Awareness (your awareness) is eternal.

**   Helps you undertand that, though seemingly mixed-up with the universe (and your body), Brahmam (your Awareness) is not really mixed up; it is clean, free, eternal.

With this book, I introduce you to your Reality - Eternal Reality.

Wish you a purposeful reading …..clear understanding …and enlightenment.

                Shivohum   …shivohum.

                                    Devesan

ACKNOWLEDGEMENTS

I am thankful to the numerous teachers – from ancient times to the present day – for feeding into me their brilliant ideas. Maharshi Valmiki, Maharshi Vyasa, Sage Vasishta, God Death (through his appearance in Kathopanishad), Yajnvalkya (through Brhadaranyakam), Sage Ashtavakra, King Janaka, Sri Suka Brahmarshi, Devarshi Narada ...... Jagadguru Sankaracharya, Swami Vidyaranya (Pancadasi) ...Swami Ram Tirtha, Swami Vivekananda, Swaroopaa-nanda, Tandavarayar, Tatwarayar, Vallalar ...... Swami Vaikuntanathan, Narayana Guru, Chattambi Swami, Pooajappura Gopalaswami, ... Ramana Maharshi, Nisarga Datta ... (and I had the opportunity to interact with Swami Brahmasuthan, Swami Chinmayananda, Swami Bodhananda, ...and lastly, but very importantly, Prof. G. Balakrishnan Nair.) (...the list is not exhaustive) ... These luminaries adorn the firmament of my teachers.

I have benefitted from the advices and consultations with Sri PN Subramanian (former Dy. Director, ISRO), Sri Ajithkumar (Bodhananda Ashramam), Maya (Madam Rosmarie Walthert) from Switzerland, and Sri Haridasji (for Sanskrt language). I am indebted to Madam Rimma Korneeva from Russia for her many-sided attention to this book, including proof-reading, and to Sri T. Sukumaran of Gulf Graphics, Venganoor for the cover design, Sri Premnath of DEVA VIDYA for his all-round assistance and guidance in logistics, and to Navaneet Computers for the effiient typesetting and the immense patience shown towards me .... and to Sri Sunish of Bensun Creations for the efficient production of the audio CD (meditation), and St. Joseph's Press, Thiruvananthapuram for the efficient printing of this book.

I am deeply indebted to a couple from Germany (Mr Hans J. Feucht and Madam Gudrun Feucht) who made the printing of this book possible, by providing the finance, even without my asking!

I am very much thankful to a neighbour boy (Shejin S. Ravi); but for his constant prompting, progress assessment, and support with computer and its idiosyncracies, this book would not have been ready even now.

Devesan

Words of Swami Vivekananda:

"To teach dualism was a tremendous mistake made in India and elsewhere, because people did not look at the ultimate principles but only thought of the process which is very intricate indeed. To many these tremendous philosophical and logical propositions were alarming. They thought these things could not be made universal. ....But I do not believe at all that monistic ideas preached to the world would produce immorality and weakness. On the contrary I have reason to believe that it is the only remedy there is. If this be the truth, at this moment *why let people drink ditch water when the stream of life is flowing by? Why not teach it to the whole world? Why not teach it with the voice of thunder to every man that is born* ...to saints and sinners, men and women and children, to the man on the throne and to the man sweeping the streets? ...*We have listened to words of weakness from our childhood."
(THE COMPLETE WORKS OF SWAMY VIVEKANANDA Vol.2/8 p199)*

CONTENTS

1	What I am and what I am not	11
2	The Path	103
	Mulla's camel	117
	Impediments	124
	The attitude / sadhana	126
3	Jivanmukthi — The goal	174
4	Confusions & Conflicts	199
	Kindergartens in spirituality	206
	Spiritual nonsenses	207
	Hard nuts	211
	One-time meal?	214
	How valuable are the siddhies?	239
5	Some related thoughts	242
	Illusion	256
	Bhakthi	265
	Whatever exist, exist	272
	Astral beings	273
	Some straight thinking	276

	Some unrelated thoughts:	280
	Bull story	281
	Cockroaches	282
	One language	282
	Apples well-preserved	282
	Noise pollution	283
6	**Conclusion**	285
	Appendix : Tejobindu Upanishad	308
	Glossary	313
	Some responses	316

1
WHAT I AM and WHAT I AM NOT

The air we breathe is one single great mass all over the world. The water in the oceans, lakes, rivers, ice-caps of mountains, in the clouds, in the wells, pipelines, cups and pots and bottles—all together is one great mass of a single entity. The earth we stand on is a single land mass; a continuum through the ocean beds. *Kathopanishad* contributes one more thing along this line: "The fire is a single entity round the world—(in un-manifest form) *Agnir yathaiko bhuvanam pravishto...*" And the space is a single entity – endless. Similarly the Awareness is a single entity. No two.

You are essentially the Awareness. Except awareness, everything in you – the body-mind-intellect combine ...is simply matter/material, which is not capable of knowing even its own existence! The core of your being....the essence of your personality....is this awareness. In fact, *you are the Awareness.*

At the outset I would like that my readers undergo the meditation. 'BRAHMA-VIDYA MEDITATION' is the name I assign to this meditation. Brahmam is another name of *prajna*. *(prajnanam Brahma)*. *Prajnanam*... Awareness... is the theme of this meditation, and the subject matter of this book.

[Meditation script – somewhat condensed – is provided here; but that is no substitute for the full-fledged version in the audio record/CD]. To download the audio record please visit www.eyeofuniverse.in

With this much of an introduction, ...now please play the audio record and undergo the meditation.

***   ***   ***

MEDITATION SCRIPT

This meditation needs some introduction. During the introduction you will be sitting up. This meditation can be called BRAHMAVIDYA MEDITATION. The Upanishadic philosophy is fully utilised in this. It is mainly a soaking in the philosophy — a spiritual soaking .

The whole Vedantic philosophy –– is condensed into one verse by Shankara acharya. Eka sloki is the name .. meanig one verse .. in Question-answer form. *Kim jyothis'thava*.. What is your light? Sun is the light during day, and lamps etc. in the night. In the matter of seeing the sun and the lamps, what is the light? The eye is the light. If the eyes are closed? Then it is the intellect that sees. What is it that sees the intellect? I am the seer of the intellect. Yes, you are the seer ...the ultimate LIGHT ....the light of all lights. (*jyotishaam jyoti*). ...It is the AWARENESS that is meant here.

Awareness is the real seer; your eyes are its instruments. This awareness makes you the perceiver, feeler, thinker. Minus your awareness, you won't perceive anything, you won't feel anything, you won't think anything. Think of a computer, and the electricity that activates it. A computer is built with the efficiency to communicate with and guide a satellite that has been sent 14 years ago and now moving beyond saturn. But minus electricity the computer is of no use.

The body-mind-intellect equipment is not capable of knowing even its own existence. It is the awareness that provides the power of perception to this equipment. You are really this awareness – the knower; not the body. Close your

Ch.1 What I am and what I am not

eyes for a while and think: minus your awareness what do you find in you? Minus the awareness you are a big zero.

So, the core of your being – the essence of your personality – is the awareness. You are really the awareness; not the body-mind-intellect equipment. This is point No.1 to be understood

Now, ..this awareness, your own awareness, is the cosmic consciouness. Pot-space is seemingly limited in the pot – contained by the pot. But there is only one space – the entire, vast, endless space. The endlessly vast space occupies the pots, the caves, and the rooms. The limitless space and the pot-space is just the same ..nothing different, nothing smaller.

(1) You, minus your body-mind-intellect equipment : is awareness, pure and simple.

(2) The universe plus the related Cosmic consciousness .. minus the universe: is awareness, pure and simple.

These two are just the same; not that one is big and the other is small. Cosmic consciousness and your own consciousness — divested of all contents — purged clean of elements — are nothing different, nothing separate, not two ..they are just the same.

This is Point No.2 to be borne in mind — pot-space is the vast space; not a part or piece of the space. So firm it up: space is one, awareness is also one. Space is not in the pot; pot is in space. Awareness is not in the body, body is in the awareness.

So point No.1 is ...You are really the Awareness, not the body.

Point No.2: Your own Awareness is the Cosmic Consciousness.

The one single awareness shines in the intellects of all creatures.

    ***   ***   ***

Now we proceed with the meditation. All of you please lie down on your back, comfortably ..fully relaxed. (...the preliminaries start: ...tensing ..instant relaxation ...auto suggestion ...setting aside the body, setting aside the mind, getting rid of the universe.) (these are there in the Meditation audio CD...not reproduced here in writing).

***   ***   ***

With the body relaxed and set aside, mind cleared out, and the universe dissolved, ..you now remain as AWARENESS. Not aware of anything; but aware of awareness alone. The core of your being....the essence of your personality....is this awareness. In fact, **you are the Awareness.**

Your awareness is your closest ...most intimate experience. *swaprakasam, aparoksha*m; ... nothing distant, nothing different from you ...To see your awareness you don't need any other instrument of cognition. To see a burning lamp, you don't need another lamp. When the sun rises, everyone sees it, no announcement is necessary. Similarly, your awareness is there always ...it needs no introduction.

This awareness is not a product of the body/ or body-chemistry, or brain chemistry. – This awareness – your own awareness – is something supreme. It continues in your physical body, and thereafter in the astral body, and is still beyond the bodies. The space is a single entity ...endless, vast. ...Space remains as a single unit; ...it fills the pots also. Don't mistake. ... Don't confuse. Space cannot be divided.

Similarly, your own seemingly limited awareness is the cosmic consciousness, universal awareness ..not part of it. It is never born; and it never dies. It is infinite, eternal.

Now repeat, along with me, mentally ... resounding in the brain. Repeat mentally:

Ch.1   What I am and what I am not

"I am not the body; I don't have a body. I am not the possessor or owner of a body. I am pure awareness. I am not a man or a woman or a eunuch. I am not a human being either; nor any being.

I am pure awareness. I have no name, I have no form. Name and form are of the body. Awareness has no name, no form. Formlessness is my only form. I am endless, and beginningless. I am never born. I have no mother or father. Mother and father are irrelevant to me, since I am not born. It is a challenge: nobody can point out my date of birth ….because I am not born.

Since I am not the body, I have no diseases, disasters, calamities and death.
Since I am not the mind, I have no miseries, desires and fears.
Since I am not prana … I have no hunger and thirst.
I am neither old nor young;   neither healthy nor unhealthy.
I have no body, no mind, no intellect …and no botherations.
I am in peace   … always, eternally.

If I travel along with the sun always – at a comfortable distance – it will be light and heat always; no night no day; no morning no evening. Similarly I am beyond time. As awareness I don't do anything …and so no karma binds me. I have no duties cast upon me; and I have never done anything …and so no past histories, no past to me   …no past in me. I am in the Present, always – in an ever continuing present – the point through which the endless future flows back into the infinite past.

I stand at the centre of time …eternally …like the midday sun at the centre of the firmament. I am beyond time, beyond space. Infinity and eternity are my real dimensions.

There is no moment when I feel that I do not exist. Awareness and existence is one and the same thing ...like a word and its meaning. Awareness is existence. Existence is known by awareness – characterized by awareness. Awareness is the reality that always exists. I am existence absolute. I am reality absolute. *I am reality-awareness-bliss absolute.* Saturated ecstasy is my nature. There is no room for any misery in saturated ecstasy. Diseases, disasters, calamities, death – these words hold no meaning to me ..I am AWARENESS, ETERNAL.

Give due weight to the word eternity – never, never never ending. The distance from here to the sun is eight minutes travel of light. Though this is a very very great distance, since it is a specific distance, 1 mm can have a microscopic relation to this enormous distance. But in front of my ETERNITY, even the duration of millions of universes cannot hold a microscopic relation. I am something really grand, glorious, bright, brilliant, beyond words, beyond any imagination. God Death salutes me from a respectful distance. What else can Death do to me? It cannot touch me, it cannot come close to me. What can death do to ETERNAL AWARENESS? Think. ... ...

I am smaller than an atom. I don't need any space to exist. It is a comfortable situation. You don't have to imagine anything big, and get confused. This is a great helpful reassurance from the Upanishads: I am smaller than an atom: *anoraneeyan*, (anu= means atom); and *mahato maheeyan*. I am larger than the universe ...because as awareness I hold the universe in me ...

(Now all of you please gently roll to a side and sit up ...and assume some comfortable sitting posture)

Ch.1 What I am and what I am not

Softly focus your closed eyes at the eyebrow-centre; (with picture, or no picture) and continue to hold it so till the end of medittion.

As you converge a beam of light onto a point with a lens, now converge all this philosophy into the word *Shivoham* ...Shivam=means auspicious, all-good; aham=means Me. Shivam aham = I am eternal, all-good, auspicious; and chant this *pregnant* shivoham in a pitch that vibrates through you. ....Shivam Aham, Shivohum, ..louder and still louder. I am auspicious, all-good, eternal ... shivohum ...... *I am reality awareness bliss absolute* ...... shivohum ...shivohum ...shivohum ... ...

Now taper off the chanting. Reduce it to a humming, by closing the lips and chanting *shivohum. hum* ...*hum* ...*hum* And slowly, very slowly, fade out the sound.

......Now silently chant shivohum. Carry all the philosophy with it. And in the final phase, I leave you alone for 10 minutes. Go on mentally chanting *shivohum.* Let the philosophy keep thundering in the brain. The mental chanting and breathing gradually slow down. The metabolism slows down. With a corner of the mind watch the slowing down of the breath. Soon you reach a stage where breathing is not really necessary for a long long time ...a *kevala kumbhakam* state. Let this mental chanting of *shivohum* with all its meaning, combined with exhalation -- like waves in the sea -- carry you forward and forward to a shore of thoughtless stillness and rapturous silence.

Shivohum ....'hum, ...'hum ....hum ...hum ...hum ....hum ....

(plus the tail end ..in the CD)

***   ***   ***

Now that you have undergone this meditation (or at least heard it through), I am presenting here the supportive material spread over the Upanishads, Yoga Vasishtam, Ashtavakra Gita, Sankara Acharya's writings and many more such, that uphold the validity of the thoughts used in this meditation.

Let us begin with Sankaracharya where he sums up the whole Upanishadic philosophy in one verse....*Eka Sloki.*

किंज्योतिस्तव भानुमानहनिमे
रात्रौप्रदीपादिकं
स्यादेवं रविदीपदर्शनविधौ
किं ज्योतिराख्याहिमे
चक्षुस्तस्यनिमीलनादि समये
किं धीर्धियोदर्शने
किं तत्राहमतोभवान् परमकं
ज्योतिस्ततस्मि प्रभो

kim jyothis'thava bhaanuman'ahani mae
raathrou pradeepadikam;
syaadevam ravi'deepa'darsana vidhou
kim jyothi'rakhyahi mae
chakshus'thasya nimeelanaadi samaye
kim dhir dhiyo darsane
kim thathra'ahamatho bhavaan paramakam
jyothis'thath'asmi prabho.

What is your light? Sun is the light during day, and lamps etc. in the night. In the matter of seeing the sun and the lamps, what is the light? Eye is the light. If the eyes are closed? Then it is the intellect that sees. What is it that sees the intellect? I am the seer of the intellect. Yes, you are the

Ch.1 What I am and what I am not

seer ..the ultimate LIGHT .....the light of all lights. (*jyotishaam jyoti*).

.. चतुर्मुखेषु देवेषु मनुष्याश्वगवादिषु
चैतन्यमेकं ब्रह्मातः प्रज्ञानं ब्रह्म:मय्यपि॥

(*Suka rahasyopanishad*) Upa-112 p49

chathurmukheshu deveshu
manushyaswa'gavadishu
chaithanyam ekam Brahmaatha:
prajnanam Brahma mayyapi.

... The (power of) perception—consciousness—in the four-headed Brahma, lord Indra, and in all the gods, the man, the horse, the cow and in all other living organisms is BRAHMAM+ —the Infinite Reality; and that is the consciousness in me also.

.. येनेक्षतः तत् प्रज्ञानमुदीरितं ॥

enekshatha ...thath prajnanamudeeritham.

The sensitivity that enables the living organisms to see, to hear, to smell, to taste and to express is called perception .. ..*prajnanam*. The power of perception.

It exists in the intellect as witness (*saakshi*) – and the ego (the sense of 'I' – I-ness) arises out of it. (Suka rahasya upanishad - 31, 32, 33)

+ Brahmam: In Malayalam we have done away with the ambiguities and clashes with the spelling of the word Brahma/ Brahman. There is a god Brahma (one among the trinity). There is a caste called Brahman or Brahmana. This Brahmam, the subject of this discussion – the ultimate Reality – has no gender (no male, no female). It is purposely denoted by a sound that is neutral in gender. This is achieved in Malayalam by pronouncing it B r a h m a m. ... with an 'm' at the end.

•• *Sarvakalpanajalarahita'jnanajneya'nirvrtthi'svabhavam, sivam, paramartha'svabhavam.* (*Chandrakirti*) Quoted by Dr Radhakrshnan in Ind.Phil. p702

The Real ... transcends all distinctions of experience and knowledge. ... without the observed and observance (ie. without the act of seeing or the objects seen).

** अवबोधैकरसोहं *(avabodhaika rasoham)*

I am nothing but Awareness; ie Awareness, simple and pure.

— Awareness is simply the witness of prakrti
(*Sarvasaaropanishad*)

** निस्त्रैगुण्यपदोहं *(nis-thrigunya padoham)*
I am without the three gunas[1]
(*Atmaprabodha Upanishad 2.4*)

The changes are in *Prakrti* (nature), not in Brahmam. The thing that brings about changes is *Apara-Brahmam* not *Para-Brahmam*, it is claimed. So, In *Para-Brahmam* there is never any transformation, there is never any form (*roopam*) nor the activity/ tendency/ propensity of producing the forms. *Parabrahmam* is *Kutastha* (unchanging). (Vedanta Prabodh P.146 by Swamy Paramanand Bharati)

•• कालत्रये यथासर्पो रज्जौनास्ति तथा मयि
अहङ्कारादि देहान्तं जगन्नास्त्यहमद्वयम् ॥
(*Atmaprabodha Upanishad 2.29*)

kaala thraye yatha sarpo
rajjou naasthi tatha mayi
ahamkaraadi dehantham
jagan-nasthi-aham-adwayam.

---

[1] Satwa, Rajas, Tamas – with which all the visible world is made.

Ch.1 What I am and what I am not

Just as a serpent does not exist in the rope in the three periods of time (past, present and future), the universe – from *ahamkaram* down to the body – does not exist in Me; I am non-dual.

.. न भूमिर्नतोयं न तेजो न वायुर्-
न खं नेन्द्रियं वा न तेषां समूहः   *(Dasasloki 1)*

> *na bhoomir na toyam na tejo na vaayur-
na kham na indriyam va na theshaam samooha.*

I am not earth, water, fire, space; or the sense organs, nor a combination of all these.

.. न वर्णा नवर्णाश्रमाचारधर्मा
न मे धारणा ध्यानयोगादयोपिः
अनात्माश्रयाहं ममाध्यासहानात्-
तदेकोवशिष्ट शिवःकेवलोहम् ॥   *(Dasasloki 2)*

> *na varna na varnashrama achara dharma
na mae dharana dhyana yoga aadaya api
anatmashrayaham mama adhyasa hanaath
thath eko-avashishta shiva kevaloham.*

No caste to me, and no *varnaasrama*[1], and no *dhaarana-dhyana-yoga* and all. On dissolution of the mistaken identity with the body that is not Athma ...I remain as *Sivam* ...the auspiious, single ..lone ..absolute Reality.

.. न सांख्यं न शैवं न तत् पाञ्चरात्रं
न जैनं न मीमांसकादेर् मतं वा
विशिष्टानुभूत्या विशुद्धात्मकत्वात्
तदेकोवशिष्ट शिव केवलोहं ॥   *(Dasasloki 4)*

---

[1] *brahmacharyam, gaarhasthyam, vanaprastham, sanyasam.*

*na samkhyam na shaivam na thath pancharaathram
na jainam na mimamsakader matam va
vishishtaanubuthya vishudha-atmakatwath
thath eko-avashishta shiva kevaloham.*

Samkhyam, Saivism, Bhaagavatham, Jainism, Mimamsa – none of these elucidate the Reality that is your own Self.

That which remains when everything other than the Self is negated and discarded ... that which is then clearly experienced as the non-dual glorious auspicious Awareness (*Bodham*)...I am that.

• • अरूपं तथाज्योतिराकारकत्वात्
तदेकोवशिष्ट शिवः केवलोहं ॥   (*Dasasloki 6*)

*........na hrswam na dirkham
aroopam thatha jyothir-aakaarakatwaath
thath eko-avashishta shiva kevaloham*

....not long or short; I am formless, still with the form of light – light of awareness. That remaining independent *bodha-athma* ...I am that.

• • न शास्ता न शास्त्रं न शिष्यो न शिक्षः
न च त्वं न चाहं नचायं प्रपञ्चः
स्वरूपावबोधो विकल्पाऽसहिष्णु-
स्तदेकोवशिष्ट शिवः केवलोहं ॥   (*Dasasloki 7*)

*na sashtha na shastram na shishyo na shiksha
na cha thwam na cha aham na cha ayam prapancha
swaroopa avabodho vikalpa-asahishnu-s
thath eko-avashishta shiva kevaloham.*

Ch.1 What I am and what I am not

No knowledge, no producer of knowledge; no disciple, no teaching. Neither you nor I nor the universe exist. Awareness (Self) does not provide any room in it for anything.+

The one that then remains— alone (*kevalam*) I am that – *shivam* (auspicious ...reality-awareness-bliss).

Prof.GB's commentary: "I am Bodha-Atma, free of everything. How? Because there is no room in Me (bodham) for anything other than Me (bodham). In my experience of 'I' ...when I experience 'me' ...when I cognize 'me / I', is there anything other than me in it? The cognitions of my body, the house, the sun and all the things around are added on to the basic cognition 'I am'. If the add-on's are removed, I remain, alone. Why speak more; if you purify the cognition / experience 'I am (I exist)', the component 'I' in it will also fall off; and pure existence will remain shining." ..."This is the brilliant finding of Vedanta"..says Prof GB.

... If you think you have known the Supreme (Brahmam), then you know mighty little—you know nothing about It (*Keno*.2.1) **"He who knows It as separate from himself knows It not**; while he who knows It as his Self knows It in truth. He who sees his consciousness as separate from It, is ignorant of consciousness itself". (*Swami Gabhirananda, Advaita Ashram explaining Keno.2.3; SRUTIGITA p96*)

A poet saint exclaims: "Strange! That itself remains unknown to us, because of which we know everything". (*Pancadasi* p7)

+ Asahishnu = intolerant. Like the eye doesn't tolerate any foreign body in it. – Irrelevant, incompatible – with no place in it for any vikalpam (vividha kalpana), multiplicity.

- - रज्जुवज्ञानादहिर्भाति
  तज्ञानादूभासते नहि ॥
  rajjwajnanad'ahir bhathi
  thath jnanath bhasathe nahi

  Snake in the rope is a delusion. No snake in proper light ... when the rope is known.

  ... Unmoving, this One is swifter than the mind;

  ... The sense powers reach It not.

  ... Speeding on before, past others running,

  ... This goes standing. *(Anejadekam manaso ....)*

  (Isavasyam 4)

- - तदेजति तन्नैजति तद्दूरे तद्वन्तिके...
  thadejati tannaijati thath doore tad'vanthike
  thath antarasya sarvasya thath sarvasyasya baahyatha

  It moves. It moves not. It is far and It is near. It is within all this. It is outside all this.

- - दूरात् सुदूरे तदिहान्तिके चः *(Mundaka Upa. 3.2.7)*
  doorath sudoore thadiha'anthike'cha

  It is very very distant (farther than the farthest), yet very close too.

- - अपाणिपादोहं ..पश्यामचक्षु श्रुण्वामकर्ण
  (Kaivalyopanishad 22) & *(Swetaswatara Upa.3.19)*

  apaani'paadohum.....
  ...pashyaam'achakshu   ...srnuvaam'akarna

  I have neither hands nor feet. I see without eyes, hear without ears.

Brahmam causes?

Brahmam, Pure Atma, is the cause of causes? Then that points to something beyond just a witness – showing up – power of perception. Does it cause? Like the sunlight causes growth on earth?! Let it be cause or no cause; it is a matter for closer investigation. Reduce it to Awareness – simple; and see how clearly we can understand things now. Minus the causation also it is a great Reality. ...good enough – great enough.

•• दृश्यदर्शननिर्मुक्तः केवलामलरूपवान्।
नित्योदितो निराभासो द्रष्टा साक्षी चिदात्मकः ॥
चैतन्यनिर्मुक्त चिद्रूपं पूर्णज्योति स्वरूपकं ॥

drsya darshana nirmuktha
kevala'amala'rupavan.

nithyoditho[+] niraabhaaso
drshtaa sakshi chidatmaka
chaithya'nirmuktha chid'roopam
poorna'jyothi'swaroopakam (Mahopanishad VI.80)

Relieved of the observed and observance...the observer remains...un-perceivable, yet ever-present[1]... independent of everything... as the pure (power of) perception only (kevalam)... as the witness, in the form of Awareness (chid-roopam). Perceiver.. witnesss ....Consciousness ...complete, whole ..in the form of Light. (*jyothi-swaroopam*).

•• तत् ब्रह्मानन्दमद्वन्द्वं निर्गुणं सत्यचिद्घनं
विदित्वा स्वात्मनोरूपं न बिभेति कदाचन ॥

---

[1] the word used is *nithyoditho*. It carries some compelling brilliance, not just ever-present. It denotes a sun that stays risen... never setting.

thad 'brahmaanandam'adwandvam
nirgunam sathya'chid'khanam
viditva swaathmano'roopam
na bibhethi kadaachana (Mahopanishad IV.70)

Coming to know the splendorous, non-dual, blissful, *nirguna* Brahmam (without the three gunas that cause the prakrti) – the essence of Awareness – as your own Reality... your own formless form....you become absolutely fearless.

* Without a perceiver, there is no perception.
* Let the **drsyam** (things that are seen) exist or not exist, without a **drk** (seer) **drsyam** has no relevance.
* Without you the world cannot exist; but you exist without the world. (Brahmavidya..poem - verse-171 - Vidyananda Tirthapada Swami)

•• अहं भोजनं नैव भोज्यं न भोक्ता
चिदानन्दरूपः शिवोहं शिवोहं ॥

aham bhojanam naiva bhojyam na bhoktha
chidanandarupa sivohum sivohum

I am not the objects of the world *(bhogyam=useables)* nor the utiliser of the objects *(bhoktha)*. I am blissful Awareness...glorious...auspicious.

•• न कर्तास्मि न भोक्तास्मि
सर्वं शान्तमजंशिवं

na kartha'asmi na bhoktha'smi
sarvam shantham ajam shivam

I am not the doer nor the one who reaps the consequences of doings. I am peaceful... unborn... auspicious.

•• अहं कर्तेत्यहंमान महाकृष्णाहिदंशितः
नाहं कर्तेति विश्वासामृतं पीत्वा सुखीभव ॥ *(Asht. Gita I.8)*

Ch.1 What I am and what I am not

aham karthe'thyaham maana-
maha krshnaahi'damsitha:
naaham karhethi viswasa-
amrtham peethwa sukhi'bhava.

You are bitten by the great black-serpent of egoism "I am the doer". Drink the nectar of faith "<u>I am not the doer</u>"— and be happy. (When one is not a doer, no omnipotence is required. 𝒟ₙ)

•• That in whom (which) reside all beings and that which resides in all beings, which gives grace to all (which lends reality to all) ...that Supreme Soul of the universe, the limitless being—I am that. (*Amrthabindu Upanishad*)

•• That which permeates all, which nothing transcends and which, like the universal space, fills everything completely from within and without, that Supreme non-dual Brahmam – that thou art. (Sankaracharya)

***   ***   ***

•• भास्यं मेघादिकं भानुरू भासयन प्रतिभासते
यथा स्थूलादिकं भास्यं भासयन् प्रतिभात्ययं ॥

(Adwaitaanubhuthi 61)

bhaasyam mekhaadikam bhaanur
bhaasayan prathibhaasate
yatha sthulaadikam bhaasyam
bhaasayan prathibhaathyayam

Illumining — showing up – throwing light on—the clouds and all, the sun proclaims its existence. So too, illumining the objects (illumining the physical body and all ..making the physical body aware of its existence) the Awareness declares its existence.

•• सर्वप्रकाशको भानुः प्रकाश्यैर् न दूष्यते
सर्वप्रकाशको ह्यात्मा सर्वैस्तद्वन्नदूष्यते ॥
(Adwaitaanubhuthi 62)

sarva'prakaasako bhaanu:
prakasyair'na dushyathe
sarva'prakaasako'hyaathma
sarvais'thathvath'na dushyathe.

The sun that throws light on everything, is not contaminated by the things it shows up. Similarly, the Athma that cognizes everything is not contaminated by the things it cognizes.

•• अयः काष्ठादिकं यद्वद् वह्निवद् वह्नियोगतः
भाति स्थूलादिकं सर्वमात्मवत् स्वात्मयोगत॥

aya:kaashtaadikam yadvad
vahnivad'vahniyogatha:
bhaathi sthoolaadikam sarvam'
aathmavath swathma'yogatha. *(Adwaitaanubhuthi 20)*

Iron, wood etc. seem to be fire itself, infused with fire. Infused with Athma (awareness) the un-athman objects (physical body etc.) also look to be aware.

•• केवलं साक्षिरूपेणः विना भोगं महेश्वरः

kevalam saakshi'roopena
vinaa bhogam maheswara. *(Rudrahrdayopanishad 42)*

Maheswara (God) is witness only ...seer, illuminator; no role of enjoyer (*bhogam*).

•• "With the blessings of (aided by) the sun, fire, air and all, the Athma grasps the sense stimuli through the sense organs" (*Sarvasaropanishad*-3; p.834 Upa-108)

Ch.1   What I am and what I am not   29

It may be noted that the Upanishad agrees here that the power comes from Prakrti.

.. अवस्तात्रयभावाभावसाक्षी   स्वयं भावरहीतं
avasthaa'thraya bhaava'abhaava'saakshi
swayam bhaava'rahitham   (*Sarvasaropanishad*-4)

Witness of the three states... witness of existence and non-existence of things and attitudes....and itself devoid of any attitude!

Setting aside all such Upanishadic teaching, how do people assert that It is self-willed?

.. सर्वोपाधि विनिर्मुक्त सुवर्णवद् विज्ञानघनः
चिन्मात्र स्वरूप आत्माः स्वतन्त्र   (*Sarvasaropanishad* 8)
sarvopaadhi vinirmuktha,
suvarna'vath vijnana'ghana:
chinmaathra swarupa athma: swathanthra

I am free from all adjuncts –- containers – apparatus – and uncontaminated by the world and its contents... like burnished gold[1]. I am Pure Awareness condensed – of the form of Awareness alone   ..free from everything.

.. ब्रह्मादि पिपीलिकान्तं
सर्वप्राणि बुद्धिस्थं   (*Sarvasaropanishad*-10)
Brahmaadi pipeelikantham
sarva'praani buddhistham

Seated (located) in the intellect of all creatures — from Brahma down to the ants.

.. देशकालवस्तुनिमित्तेषु अव्यभिचारी
पदार्थाद्युपाधिकादिलक्षणः

---

[1] Purified in fire, it has nothing else in it except gold.

आकाशवत् सर्वगतः सूक्ष्मा केवलः
सत्तामात्रोसि स्वयंज्योतिरात्मा सत् चित् ॥

(Sarvasaropanishad-8)

*desa'kaala'vasthu'nimittheshu avyabhichaari
padaartha'dyupaadhikad'vilakshana:
aakaasavath sarvagatha: sukshma'kevala:
satthamaathrosi swayam'jyothir'athma sath'chith.*

Athma is '<u>unadulterated</u>' by time, space, <u>matter or causation</u>. It is different from matter and (limiting) adjuncts (containers) etc. It pervades everywhere and everything...is subtle and single (one only), everlasting (eternal) and therefore Real...and it shows itself (*swayam jyothi*)...is Awareness, the Reality.

.. नाहंकर्ता नवैभोक्ता प्रकृते : साक्षिरूपकः
मद्सान्निद्ध्याद् प्रवर्तन्ते देहाद्या अजडा इवः

(Sarvasaaropanishad-11)

*naham kartha na vai bhoktha
prakrte saakshi'rupaka:
mad'saannidhyaath pravarthanthe
dehaadya ajada'iva*

I am not the doer, nor do I reap the consequences—I am witness, by nature. (I am only witness of nature —explains Dr NP Unni also in *108 Upanishads)*. In my presence the body and all work on as if they are not-*jadam* — as if they are aware—as if endowed with awareness.

I am tempted to include one more verse from this Upanishad (*Sarvasaropanishad*) – so that those who like it can include it among a collection of pregnant Sanskrt verses and record and hear – or chant themselves :

Ch.1 What I am and what I am not

- ब्रह्मैवाहं सर्ववेदान्तवेद्यं
  नाहं वेद्यं व्योमवातादिरूपं
  रूपं नाहं नाम नाहं न कर्म
  ब्रह्मैवाहं सच्चिदानन्दरूपं ॥

brahmaiva'ham sarva vedantha'vedyam
naham vedyam vyoma'vathaadi roopam
roopam naaham naama naaham na karma:
brahmaivaaham sadchidaananda roopam.

I am Brahmam— known all through the Vedanta — not a substance or object like air or space. I am formless, nameless, actionless. I am Brahmam, Sath-Chid-Ananda-roopam.

- त्रिषुधामसु यद्भोज्यं भोक्ता भोगश्च यद्भवेद्
  तेभ्यो विलक्षण साक्षी चिन्मात्रोहं सदाशिवः

(Kaivalyopanishad 18)

thrishu dhaamasu yad'bhojyam
bhoktha bhogaccha yath'bhaveth
thebhyo vilakshana saakshi
chin'maathro'ham sadasiva.

I am shivam—the auspicious eternal ...other than the aspect of enjoyer (*bhoktha*), enjoyed or enjoyment in the three seats (bodies) ...I am the witnessing awareness *only* (*maathram*).

- सूक्ष्मात्सूक्ष्मतरं नित्यं
  तत् त्वमेव त्वमेवतत् *(Kaivalyopanishad 16)*

sukshhmaath sukshma'tharam nithyam
thath'twameva twameva thath

(The base of everything) and subtler than subtle ..and eternal. That you are....You are that.

- जाग्रद् स्वप्न सुषुप्त्यादि प्रपञ्चं यद् प्रकाशते
  तद् ब्रह्माहमिति ज्ञात्वा सर्वबन्धैः प्रमुच्यते ॥
  jaagrad swapna sushupthyaadi
  prapancham yad'prakaasathe
  thad'brahmahamithi jnathwa
  sarva'bandhai pramuchyathe (Kaivalyopanishad 18)

  That which shows up the world in waking, dream and sleep states ...is Brahmam. Knowing this, one is freed from all bondages.

- ज्ञानमस्ति किं ज्ञातुमन्तरं ॥
  jnanam'asthi'kim jnathum'anthram

  How can knowledge exist.. without the knower?

- वेद एव परंज्योतिः ज्योतिषामा ज्योतिरानन्दमयत्वेवमेव
  तत्परं यत् चित्तं परमानन्द आनन्द यतिः
  veda eva param'jyothi
  jyothishaamaa'jyothir'aanandamayathwevameva
  thath'param yath chittham
  paramaananda aananda yathi.

  One who is conscious that he is the light of lights...is in ecstatic bliss.

- सद्वस्तु जन्मक्षयशून्यमेकं
  sadvasthu janma'kshaya'soonyam'ekam

  The Real....is birthless, deathless, single (one only).

- निखिलान्तराल निवासिनं
  ....उज्ज्वलं परमंपदं
  nikhila'antharaala nivaasinam
  .... ujjwalam paramam padam

Ch.1 What I am and what I am not

Seated ...situated.. in everything
.... Its state is brilliant and ultimate.

[Think ...Think ...ponder over ...meditate ...on this POWER OF PERCEPTION ...seated, situated in every being.]

•• कूटस्थं बोधःमद्वैतमात्मानं परिभावयः
आभासोहंभ्रमं मुक्त्वा भावंबाह्यमथान्तरं ॥ (Asht.Gita I.13)

*kootastham bodham'advaitham
aathmaanam paribhaavaya
aabhaso'ham bhramam'muktwa
bhaavam baahya'mathantharam*

Giving up external and internal self-modifications and the illusion 'I am the reflected (individual) self' meditate upon the Self as immutable Consciousness that transcends all limitations.

•• सर्व भूतस्थमेकंवै
नारायणं कारणपुरुष-
मकारणंपरब्रह्मः ओं ॥

*sarva'bhoothastham'ekam'vai
naaraayanam kaaranapurusham'
akaaranam parabrahma om*

Narayanan is the cause; <u>Parabrahmam is not the cause</u>.

•• एकमेवाद्वितीयं सन्-
नामरूप विवर्जितं   (Suka'rahasyo'panishad)

*ekameva'adwitheeyam san-
naana'roopa vivarjitham*

The lone one is ...without another... existent-absolute (sath) ....devoid of names and forms.

कार्योपाधिरहं जीवः कारणोपाधिरीश्वरः
कार्यकारणतयां हित्वा पूर्णबोधोवशिष्यते॥

karyopaadhi'raham jiva
kaaranopaadhi'reeswara
kaarya'kaaranathayaam hitwa
poorna'bodho'vasishyate. (Suka'rahasyo'panishad)

Iswara (God) is the cause, and the jeeva (living soul) is the effect. ….., let go the cause, let go the effect; ….the awareness alone remains in its fullness.

न अन्तप्रज्ञं न बहिःप्रज्ञं नोभयप्रज्ञं
न प्रज्ञं नाप्रज्ञं अदृष्टमव्यवहार्य-मग्राह्य-मलक्षण-
मचिन्त्यमव्यपदेश्य-मेकात्मप्रत्ययसारं
…प्रपञ्चोपशमं शान्तं
शिवं अद्वैतं चतुर्थं मन्यते
स आत्मा स विज्ञेयः ॥

na anthaprajnam na bahi-prajnam nobhaya'prajnam
na prajnam na-aprajnam
adrshtam'avyavahaaryam'agrahyam'alakshanam'
achinthyam'avyapadesyam'ekatmaprathyaya'saaram
……prapanchopashamam shaantham
shivam advaitham chathurtham manyathe
sa athma sa vijneya. (Mandukya Upanishad)

Not inwardly cognitive, not outwardly cognitive, not both-wise cognitive, not a cognition-mass, neither cognition nor non-cognition……unseen (*a-drshta*), with which there can be no dealing {*a-vyavahaarya),* ungraspable (*a-grahya*), having no distinctive marks *(a-lakshana*), non-thinkable (*a-chinthya*), that does not fall under any designation/

Ch.1 What I am and what I am not 35

classification *(a-vyapadesyam)*......where the universe dissolves.....in the fourth state...is the Athma (Self)... the one to be discerned.

The Upanishad here tries ...in its inimitable style ...to drive home the idea in unmistakable terms that *It* is not a mass of knowledge, but is simply the power of perception... pure *(shuddha bodham)*.

prapanchopa'shamam'shaantham. ... Mark it. Universe subsides.

.. सद्घनं चिद्घनं नित्यमानन्दघनमक्रियं

(Vivekachudamani-466)

*sad'khanam chid'khanam nithyam
aananda'khanam'akriyam*

The essence of Existence, the Essence of Knowledge, the essence of eternal Bliss, devoid of any activity *(akriyam)*.

.. प्रत्यगेकरसंपूर्णमनन्तम् .. *(Vivekachudamani-467)*
prathyag'ekarasam'poornam'anantham.

The Brahmam is not an object but is the very subjective core, the essence in each individual *(pratyak)*. It knows no change, and so remains for ever in the same nature *(eka rasam)* ...It is endless.

.. इदं सर्वं न मे किंचिदयंसर्वं न मे क्वचित् ।

(Tejo-bindu Upanishad IV.11)

*idam sarvam na mae kinchid'
ayam sarvam na mae quachith.*

I have none of these objects of the world; I am none of the objects of the world.

•• न त्वं विप्रादिको वर्णो नाश्रमी नाक्षगोचरः
असङ्गोऽसि निराकारो विश्वसाक्षी सुखी भव ॥

na twam vipraadiko'varno
na'asrami naaksha'gochara
asangosi niraakaaro
viswa'saakshee sukhee bhavah.

You do not belong to the Brahmana or any such caste. Nor do you belong to any station-in-life (*ashrama* = householder, *sanyasi* etc.). You are not perceivable by the senses. You are unattached (not sticking to anything), formless and 'witness'-of-all; be happy.

•• यथाकाशो हृषीकेशो नानोपाधिगतो विभुः
तत्भेदात् भिन्नवत् भाति तन्नाशे केवलोभवेत् ॥

(Atmabodham-9)

yadhaakaaaso hrshikesho naanaa'
upaadhi'gatho vibhu
thath'bhedath bhinnavath bhaathi
thannase kevalo'bhaveth.

The all-pervading space appears to be diverse on account of its association with various *upaadhis* (vessels); and it becomes one when the vessels are broken. Similar is the case with the Reality (*bodham*)...when the *upadhis* dissolve, *bodham* is one...not many.

•• नानारूप व्यतीतोहं चिदाकारोहमच्युतः
सुखरूप स्वरूपोह-महमेवाहमव्ययः ॥

(Brahmajnanavali'maala 8)

nana rupa vyatito'ham chidakaroham'achyutha
sukha rupa swarupoham ahameva'ham'avyaya.

Ch.1 What I am and what I am not

I am different from the multitudes of forms. ..I don't have these multiplicity of forms; ...undiminished, unadulterated ...undiluted Awareness is my form. ..in a happy state...without waxing and waning.

Avyaya: literally, unspent. It doesn't get spent-out, exhausted, at any time. No waning. "I am immutable. What is the proof? Since I remain as-I-am always.[1] *The awareness that we find clearly in every living being, is the direct, visible, tangible expression of Brahmam.* I (the awareness) exists eternally. So it is real ..it is the Reality, the Truth. "I exist" is the experience / feeling, always; nobody ever feels "I don't exist". You can wipe out whatever you see around; but you cannot wipe out your awareness. Even to experience "I don't exist", I have to be there, existing. This is absolute existence. Reality. The only thing that has this Reality in this world is 'chith' (meaning: awareness). Where this 'chith' (awareness) is experienced in its pristine purity, ..it becomes 'anandam' (bliss). When you experience this bliss, it carries along with it 'sath' and 'chith'. Thus, these three (sath-chith-anandam) put together is my form. In this form, I have no relation to anything else ..even to my body. If this fact is understood properly ..and it gets stabilised and solidified in your understanding, it paves the way to the Brahmic experience." (Prof. GB, Proudhanubhoothi p234).

.. माया तत्कार्य देहादि मम नास्त्येव सर्वदा
स्वप्रकाशैक रूपोह-महमेवाहमव्ययः ॥

(Brahmajnanavali'maala 9)

---

[1] There is never an end to this awarenes – this power of perception. Think. It is eternal. It continues through physical body, and astral body ..and continues still beyond. It is explained elsewhere in this book. *Dn*

maya thath'karya'dehadi mama nasthyeva'sarvada
swaprakasaika'rupo'ham ahameva'ham'avyaya

Maya and the things brought about by it ...the body and all...I don't ever have. Self-awareness alone is my form, and I am immutable...never waxing or waning.

- न तेजो न तमस्ततं ॥ .... *na tejo na thamas'thadam*
  I am not light – nor darkness.

  * I am light: "but not a light like sunlight or electric light" (Swami Chinmayananda)

  * Darkness I am not. *Aham irul alla* (Mal.)
  अहं इरुलल्ल (Narayana Guru)

- नैनं छिन्दन्ति शस्त्राणि   नैनं दहति पावकः
  न चैनं क्लेदयन्त्यापो   न शोषयति मारूतः ॥

  (Bh.Gita II.23)

nainam cchindanthi sastraani
nainam dahati paavaka
nachainam cledayanthyapo
na shoshayathi maarutha.

Weapons do not cut It, fire does not burn It, water does not soak It, wind does not dry It.

- निमित्तं मनःचक्षुरादिप्रवृत्तौ
  रविर्लोकचेष्टानिदानं यथा यः (*Hasthamalaka sthothram 3*)

nimittham manas'chashur'adi pravrtthau
ravir'loka'cheshta'nimittham yatha yah:

Causing the activities of the mind, eyes etc.   just as the world gets activated in the presence of the sun....

Ch.1   What I am and what I am not   39

Sankaracharya graciously inserts a line in-between—

· · निरस्ताखिलोपाधिराकाशकल्प,
nirastha'akhil'opaadhir'aakaasa'kalpa —

(*devoid of all limiting adjuncts,* — *like space*), so that we are not swept off the proper path – by the bringing in of 'cause/caused' and all . No cause, ... no causation. Presence, simple. Still, things happen in that presence.

Sakshi /observer

I look at a waterfall. I don't get my back broken because of that. It is the water that falls.., not me.

· · रवेर्यथा कर्मणि साक्षिभावो
वह्नेर्यथा दाहनियामकत्वं
रज्जोर्यथाऽरोपितवस्तुसङ्ग-
स्तथैव कूटस्थचिदात्मनो मे ॥   (*Vivekachudamani 507*)

ravair yatha karmani sakshi bhavo
vahner yatha daaha'niyaamakathvam
rajjaur yatha'aropitha vasthu'sanga-
sthathaiva kutastha'chidaathmano'mae.

The world comes alive in the presence of the sun; the sun plays no other role in this, except its presence.

Fire burns anything that comes in contact...no inhibition, no hesitation...no thought about what it burns. (It is *vasthu dharmam* that works—the intrinsic character of the stuff.)

The rope is not responsible if it looks to be a snake to you. (It is only its material characteristic—it has a shape that misleads.) The rope has nothing to do with the snake superimposed on it—it did not cause a snake, did not produce a snake, nor did it transform into a snake.

The sun, the fire, the rope....in their presence/because of them, many things happen. The doer-ship superimposed on them is really not in them. Similarly in my mere presence many things happen...that should not be construed to be my doing; I am the inactive Self, the Intelligence Absolute. [The POWER OF PERCEPTION]

***   ***   ***

- दृश्यैसंग विवर्जितो गगनवत्
  संपूर्ण रूपोस्म्यहम् ॥   (*Proudhanubhuti* p.179)

  *drsyai: sanga vivarjitho gaganavath
  sampoorna ruposmyaham.*

I have no connection to the world of objects (*drsyam* ...things seen)—like the space. I am complete in myself.

(The space exists with the world ...without the world also. Space is independent.) If the world is "My body" (from the stand-point of Brahmam) as many people choose to believe, then the one in the *proudha anubhoothi* (mature experience) cannot say 'I have no connection'.

- जगद्विलक्षणं ब्रह्म: (*Athma Bodham*-63)
  Jagad'vilakshanam Brahma:

Brahmam is different from *jagath*.

- *'siva: purusha ishaana
  nithyam'aathme'thi katthyathe'* (*Mahopanishad*)

Note that siva is a synonym of Atma here. ...Siva, Iswara, Eternal 'Purusha', Athma.

- न जायते म्रियते वा विपश्चिन्नायं कुतश्चिन्न बभूव कश्चित् ।
  अजो नित्य: शाश्वतोयं पुराणो न हन्यते हन्यमाने शरीरे ॥

Ch.1 What I am and what I am not

na jaayate mryate vaapi pacchin-
na ayam kutacchin na babhuva kaschith;
ajonithya saaswathoyam purano
na hanyathe hanyanane sarire. (Katho. II.18)

The all-knowing Bodham/ Self/ Awareness / chaithanyam (being what it is – being, by nature, Awareness) …is not born nor does it die. This one has not come from anywhere, has not become anyone. Unborn, constant, primieval, eternal… This is not slain when the body is slain. (*112 Upa.* p.21)

.. हन्ता चेन्मन्यते हन्तुः हतश्चेन्मन्यते हतं ।
उभौ तौ न विजानीतो नायं हन्तुः न हन्यते ॥

hantha chenmanyate hanthum
hatha chenmanyate hatham
ubhau tau na vijanitho
na aham hanthi na hanyate. (Katho.II.19)

If the slayer thinks he has slain; and if the slain thinks himself slain, both understand not. This One slays not, nor is slain.

.. अशब्दमस्पर्शमरूपमव्ययं तथारसं नित्यमगन्धवच्च यत् ।
अनाद्यनन्तं महतः परं ध्रुवं निचाय्यतन्मृत्युमुखात् प्रमुच्यते ॥
(Katho.U. III.15)

asabdam'asparsa'marupa'mavyayam
tatha'rasam nityam'agandhavacchayath
anaadyanantham mahata'param dhruvam
nichaayyatham mrthyumukhath pramuchyate.

What is soundless, touchless, formless ….likewise tasteless, constant, odourless …beginningless, endless

….higher than the great (Mahath)[+], stable—by discerning That, one is liberated from the mouth of death.

No swagatha bhedam

There are no differentiations — parts/ partitions/ components whatsoever in the Reality …It is One, without another. The differentiations in the world are categorized into three—

1. *Sajathiya bhedam*: Difference within the species or groups … eg. between man and man. One may be tall and fair, another may be short and dark.
2. *Vijatiya bhedam:* Difference of species or groups … eg. one is a rock; another is a tree.
3. *Svagatha bhedam:* Differences in the specimen in a species or group … eg. between head, legs and arms of a man.
   Or
   In a tree the difference is in the form of trunk, branches, roots, leaves, flowers, fruits.

In Brahmam all such possible differences are emphatically denied by the scriptures. (No *sajaatheeya-vijaatheeya-swagatha bhedam*). Mark it; no 'swagatha bhedam'; within Itself, there is no differentiation ..no component parts …It is an absolute Whole …single, undifferentiated, undivided. …like the space.

- - एष आत्मापहतपात्मा विजरोविमृत्युर्विशोको
  विजिघत्सोपिपासः   *(Chandogyam 8.1.5)*
  esha aathma apahatha'paapma
  vijaro'vimrthyur'vishoko vijikhatso'pipaasa

+ denotes the root cause of prakrthi.

Ch.1 What I am and what I am not

Atma is untouched by sin, beyond decay, death, and misery, without hunger and thirst.

•• सत्यं ज्ञानं अनन्तं ब्रह्मः *(Taithiriyopanishad 2.1.1)*
sathyam jnanam anantham brahma:
Reality-Awareness-Eternal...is Brahmam.

Atma is the seat of Peace, bliss, repose, serenity..... quietude—all rolled into one. Bliss Absolute. Anything else is a mix. ...as in the case of saturated sugar (undiluted), and sugar mixed with things—starch/flour and all ...cakes and the like. Anything other than Absolute Peace—is a reduction, diminution, step-down. Anything—anything—palatial houses, cars, cell phones, properties, wealth, sumptuous food. Even conjugal pleasure is a drag-down from the peak of Absolute Peace.[+]

•• सूक्ष्मात् सूक्ष्मतरं नित्यं तत् त्वमेव त्वमेवतत् ॥
(Kaivalyopanishad)
sukshmaath sukshma'tharam nithyam
thath twameva twameva thath.

Subtler than the subtle (*sukshmam*) and eternal ...you are that ...you alone are That. [This gross world cannot be said to be *sukshmam* (subtle)]

•• आत्मनो विक्रिया नास्ति बुद्धेर्बोधो न जात्विति ।
जीव सर्वमलं ज्ञात्वा ज्ञाता द्रष्टेति मुह्यति ॥
aatmano vikriya naasthi
buddhair bodho na'jathvithi
jeeva sarvam'alam'jnaatva
jnaatha drshteti muhyathi. (Athma Bodham 25)

[+] "Even the best of music also will be a disturbance" Prof. GB used to tell us; and I have experienced it at times.

Atman never undergoes change, and buddhi is never endowed with consciousness. But man believes Athman to be identical with *buddhi* and falls under the delusion that he is the seer and the knower.

Attitude in meditation:

।। अस्थूलमित्येतदसन्निरस्य
सिद्धं स्वतो व्योमवत्प्रतर्क्यं
अतो मृषामात्रमिदं प्रतीतं
जहीहि यत् स्वात्मतया गृहीतं
ब्रह्माहमित्येव विशुद्धबुद्ध्या
विद्धि स्वमात्मानमखण्डबोधं ।।   (*Viveka chudamani* 250)

asthoola'mithyetha'dasannirasya
siddham swatho vyomavath'apratharkyam
atho mrshaa'maathram'idam pratheetham
jaheehi yath swaathmathayaa graheetham
brahmaaha'mithyeva vishuddha buddhyah
viddhi swam'aathmaanam'akhandabodham

Eliminating all that is perceived - the gross - the not-Self, in the light of passages such as "It is not gross *(asthoolam)*" etc., one realises the Athman which is self-established, unattached like the sky and beyond the range of thought. So dismiss this phantom of a body which you perceive and accept as thy own Self. With a purified understanding that "I am Brahmam", realise thy own Self ...the Knowledge Absolute / Awareness Absolute.

।। स्वप्रकाशपरोक्षत्वं अयमित्युक्तितो मतम्
अहंकारादि देहान्तं प्रत्यगात्मेति गीयते ।।

Ch.1 What I am and what I am not   45

swaprakaasa'aparokshathwam
ayamithyukthitho'matham
ahamkaaraadi dehaantham
prathyagaathmethi geeyathe. (Mandukya ka.7)

Swa-prakaasam = self-shining, self-luminous, self-effulgent. Aparoksham = direct, closest, ... the most intimate.

The self is the direct, closest, most intimate experience, ...and self-shining. (No other light is necessary to see your own awareness).

And when the feeling of "I"...I-ness (*aham-kaaram*, the feeling that 'I am an individual entity, limited in the body) gets superimposed, It becomes *Pratyagathma*. (*pratyeka athma*= limited Athma...*jiva bhavam*)

As the flowing rivers disappear in the ocean, discarding names and forms ....so too the Knower of reality, being liberated from names and forms, goes to the supreme Purusha, higher than the high. (*Mundakopanishad* 7)

He who knows that Supreme Brahmam, verily becomes the very Brahmam. (*Brahma-veda Brahmaiva bhavathi*) (*Mundakopanishad* 9)

.. निमित्तं मनश्चक्षुरादिप्रवृत्तौ
निरस्ताखिलोपाधिराकाशकल्प
रविर्लोकचेष्टानिमित्तं यथाय: *(Hasthamalakam 3)*

nimittham mana-chakshuraadi'pravrtthou
nirasthaakhilopaadhir'aakaashakalpa
ravir'loka'cheshtaa'nimittham yadhaa'ya.

"Just as the sun is the cause of all worldly activities ... I am that ever-existing Athman which is the cause of the activities of the mind, eyes and all, ...devoid of all limiting adjuncts ....like space".

Though this verse has only a few words in it, it speaks volumes; listen to it – ponder over.

.. येन शब्दं रसं रूपं गन्धं जानासि राघव
ततात्मानं परब्रह्म जानीहि परमेश्वर:

yena shabdam rasam rupam
gandham jnaanaasi Raaghava
thathaathmaanam parabrahma:
jaaneehi parameswara.

That because of which you know sound, sight, taste and smell ...know that to be the Self, para-Brahmam, the lord of everything, oh Raghava.

.. यथाकोशस्तथा जीव:
यथाजीव: स्तथा शिव:

yadha koshas'thathaa jiva
yadhaa'jivasthatha siva.

The consciousness of jivan and the cosmic consciousness – are (is) just the same consciousness.

.. सविकारस्तथाजीवो निर्विकारस्तथा शिव:॥
savikaarasthatha jivo nirvikaarsthatha siva.
(Thrisikhi brahmano'panishad.13) Upa.108-p470

Jivan is in a state of constant flux – changing, moving, pulsating. Not in a state of flux ...it is Sivam.

If anyone has any doubt about the meaning of 'Siva': (and the meaning I attach to it), have a close look here (above).

Ch.1   What I am and what I am not   47

•• Sivam (bodham / Prajnanam / Awareness). It pervades everything :-
1) Like butter permeates every drop of milk.
2) Like salt in sea-water.
3) Like the juice/pulp pervades the whole of a big fruit. (*Thrisikhi...*)

(यथा महाफले सर्वे रसा सर्वप्रवर्तकः
तथैवान्नमयेकोशे कोशास्तिष्ठन्तिचान्तरे ॥

yadhaa maha bhale sarve
rasaa sarva pravarthaka
thadhaiva'annamaye koshe
koshas'thishtanthi'chaanthare.)

•• सर्वदृश्यविहीनोहं दृग्रूपोस्म्यहमेवहि
सर्वदा पूर्णरूपोस्मि नित्यतृप्तोस्म्यहं सदा ॥

(*Tejobindu Upanishad 15 Upa.112 p507*)

sarva drsya viheenoham
drgrooposmyahamevahi
sarvadah purnarooposmi
nithya'thrptho'smyaham sadah

All the sense objects are not in me...I am only the seer of the objects. I am always complete in myself, and contented in myself.

•• I am of the nature of all-void ... I am the primeval consciousness alone.... without even the state of witness... the supreme nectary essence... (all from *Tejobindu upa.*)

•• यथाऽमृतं विषादुभिन्नं विषदोषैर्नलिप्यते
न स्पृशामि जटाद् भिन्नं जटदोषाऽप्रकाशतः ॥

> *yatha amrtam vishaad bhinnam*
> *visha doshiir na lipyate*
> *na sprsami jadaath bhinnam*
> *jada dosha-aprakasata (Atmaprabodhopanishad-2.27)*

Amrtham (elixir/ nectar / ambrosia) is one thing; poison is another. And the gruesome efficiency attached to the poison does not defile the Amrtam (is not transposed on Amrtham). I who am different from *jadam* (inert, matter), am not defiled by the stigma of *a-prakasata* (non-luminosity) of jadam.

•• The all-pervading space, being subtle, is not contaminated. So too the Self, located in every body, is not contaminated. The embodied soul illumines all bodies, just as the sun illumines the whole world.

> *(yadtha sarvagatham soukshmyath*
> *aakaasam nopalipyathe*
> *Sarvathra'vasthitho'dehe*
> *thath'athma no palipyathe*
> *......... lokamimam ravi...)*   (Bh.Gita XIII. 32, 33)

•• अनात्माश्रयाहं ममाध्यासहानात्-
तदेकोवशिष्ट शिवः केवलोहम् ॥ *(Dasasloki-2)*

anatma'ashraya'aham mama'adhyasa'haanath-
thath'ekovashishta shiva kevalo'hum.

When all the hallucinations (false visions) dependent upon the un-Atma vanish, I shine as the remaining, One and only, Atma – Auspicious, Awareness, Absolute.

•• दृश्यै संगविवर्जितो गगनवत्   *(Proudhanubhooti 4)*
drsyai'sanga vivarjitho gagana'vath

Ch.1 What I am and what I am not

Without any connection to anything that is seen (drsyam), I remain in my Reality – like the space without any objects.

•• पूर्णोस्मि द्वयवर्जितोस्मि
विपुलाकाशोस्मि नित्योस्म्यहम ॥ *(Proudhanubhoothi-6)*
poorno'smi dvaya'varjito'smi
vipula'akasos'mi nithyo'smyaham.

I am complete, without duality, I am the all-pervading ..eternal ..light of awareness (*bodham*).

What we see here is the emphasis on avoidance/ discarding /getting rid of (*varjitham*) everything... Not holding everything in ... or keeping latent in (like salt in water, or like a seed).

A person seeking *mukti* has to let go of all names and forms. A bird on a flight to the high peaks...how will it carry all the eggs under its wings? If eggs are its concern, it must sit over them and brood; no soaring to high peaks.

•• '*Nanaa roopa vyatheetho'ham*' I am different from the names and forms ...all the names and forms are not me. (*Brahmajnanavali maala*)

Here also I don't find any loophole to interpret that 'everything is me—everything is in me in a seed-form'. No such shade or shadow is found. It emphatically says "I am different from names and forms".

•• This is a peace/ tranquility/ bliss experienced without the participation of the body, while in the body. (P.230 *Proudhanubhoothi*)...GB

•• न साक्षिणं साक्षिधर्मा : संस्पृशन्ति विलक्षणं
अविकारमुदासीनं गृहधर्मा प्रदीपवत् ॥

na saakshinam saakshidharma:
samsprshanthi vilakshanam
avikaara'mudaaseenam
grha'dharmaa pradeepavath. (Kuntikopanishad 27)

The witness is not affected by the event; it is unconcerned, just as a lamp in the house is unconcerned in the household activities.

(Vilakshanam: different. The witness is not a partner in the event; it stands apart.)

.. नाहं विलिप्ये तद्धर्मैर्
घटधर्मैर् नभो यथा ॥ *(Kuntikopanishad-28)*
naaham vilipye thadharmai-
khada dharmair nabho yadha.

(Whatever happens to the body) ..I am unconcerned, unaffected. The quality or contamination of the air in a pot does not contaminate the pot-space.

.. न मे देहेन संबन्धो   मेघेनेव विहायसः
अतःकुतोमे तद्धर्मा   जाग्रत्स्वप्नसुषुप्तिषु॥
na mae dehena sambandho
mekheneva vihaayasa
atha kutho mae thath dharma
jaagrath-swapna-sushupthishu (Kuntikopanishad-19)

I have no relation to the body ...I am not conditioned by the body ....The cloud is no botheration to the space. The vicissitudes attendant on the body in waking dream and sleep ..how can they affect me?

Kuntikopanishad-30:-
.. सर्वात्मकोहं सर्वोहं
sarvaatmakohum sarvohum ..

I am everything (let it be; don't bother)

Ch.1 What I am and what I am not

सर्वातीतोहमद्वयः
sarvaatheethoham'advyaya ..
I am beyond everything (listen to this!)

.. केवलाखण्ड बोधोहं ॥
kevala'akhanda bodhohum
I am the single, unfragmented Awareness (nothing else..*kevalam*)

.. असङ्ग पुरुषप्रोक्तः बृहदारण्यकेपि चः
अनन्तमलसंकृष्टः कथं स्यादेहकःपुमान् ॥
(*Aparokshaanubhuthi 36 p441*)

*asanga purusha'proktha
brhadaaranyake'pi'cha
anantha'malasamkrshta:
katham'syad'dehaka'pumaan*

Brhadaranyakam also states that *Purusha* (the Self) is independent of everything – unattached to anything. Then how can the body –composed of a multitude of impurities— be the Self?

.. लिङ्गं चानेकसंयुक्तं चलं दृश्यं विकारि चः
अव्यापकमसद्रूपं तत् कथं स्यात् पुमानहं ॥
(*Aparokshanubhoothi-39*)

*lingam cha'anekasamyuktham
chalam drsyam vikaari cha
avyaapaka'masad'roopam
thath katham'syath pumaanahum*

The subtle body is also a combination of many components ... is in a state of agitation ... is an object observed by the seer (the Atma) ... is always in a state of flux ...is limited in a spot ...is not capable of knowing its own existence. Then how can the *linga sariram* be me, the *Purusha* (*Pumaan*) — the Self?

•• एवं देहद्वयादन्य आत्मा *evam deha'dvayad'anya athma.*

If thus the thought proceeds and gets stabilised, then you will know that Atma is different from physical body and astral body.

•• सर्वातीतोऽहमव्ययः

sarva'atheethohum'avyaya (Aparokshaanubhoothi-40)

I am beyond everything, and changeless.

•• अहं विकारहीनस्तु देहोऽनित्यं विकारवान्
इति प्रतीयते साक्षात् कथंस्याद्देहकः पुमान् ॥

(Aparokshaanubhoothi-33)

*aham vikara'heenasthu
deho'anithyam vikaaravaan
ithi prathiyathe sakshath
katham'sya'ddehaka: pumaan?*

I am always changeless. We experience this always. (I remain I... always, from birth to death). Body is always changing. Then how can I be the body?

•• यदर्केन्दुविद्युतप्रभाजालमाला
विलासास्पदं यद् स्वभेदादि शून्यं ... ... तदेवाहमस्मिः

*yad'arkendu-vidyuth prabhajaalamaala-
vilaasaaspadam yath: swabhedaadi'sunyam.
............thath'evahamasmi:*   (Nirvanamanjari 10)

Depending on which the sun moon and the lightning shine – the light that lends reality to the sunlight, moonlight, and lightning – and that in which there are no other entities other than itself (that in which there are no *swagtha bhedam, sajaatiya bhedam or vijaateeya bhedam* ...differences)... That I am. (*thath evaahum'asmi*)

"It is the pure basic consciousness by the light of which everything shines."

.. तमेवभान्तमनुभातिसर्वं तस्यभासा सर्वमिदं विभाति:
(*Swetaswatara upanishad VI.14*)

*thameva bhaantham anubhaathi sarvam;
thasya bhaasaa sarvamidam vibhaathi.*

It alone shines; everything shine after it ... shine because of it. This whole world is illumined by Its light.

The self-luminous light of the world. ... It shines of itself; it doesn't shine in reflection. (in its light...with its light...everything shine). (It is the 'POWER OF PERCEPTION' of the world; understand it clearly; and it is YOUR OWN POWER OF PERCEPTION also).

.. The sun shines not there (the sun is incapable of showing up this Awareness —the light of lights ...*jyotishaam jyothi*) ... nor the moon and the stars. The lightnings shine not ... much less this (earthly) fire.
After Him ..as He shines, do everything shine. The whole world is illumined with Its light. (*na thathra suryo bhaathi....*) (*Kathopanishad*)

.. अहं नामरो नैव मर्त्यो न दैत्यो
न गन्धर्वयक्ष: पिशाच प्रभेद:
पुमान्नैवनस्त्री तथानैव षण्ड:
प्रकृष्टप्रकाश: शिव केवलोहम् ॥ (*Nirvanamanjari 1*)

> *aham na'amaro'naiva marthyo'na daithyo-*
> *na gandharva yaksha: pisacha'prabheda*
> *pumaan naiva na-sthree thatha'naiva shanta-*
> *prakrshta prakasha siva kevalohum.*

I am not a *deva* (deathless celestial being) nor a human being that dies. Nor am I a Gandharva nor demon nor of any such categories. I am neither a man nor a woman nor a eunuch. I am the one and only Awareness that distinctly knows its auspicious existence.

> ·· अहं नैववालो युवानैववृद्धो
> नवर्णी न च ब्रह्मचारी गृहस्थः
> वनस्थोपि नाहं न सन्यस्थधर्मो
> जगज्जन्मनाशैकहेतुःशिवोहं ॥ *(Nirvaanamanjari 2)*
>
> *aham naiva baalo'yuvaa'naiva vrddho-*
> *na varni na'cha brahmachari'grhastha:*
> *vanasthopi'naaham'na sanyastha'dharmo*
> *jagat-janma'naasaika hethu: shivohum.*

I am not a boy, nor a youth nor an old …I don't fall under any of the caste classifications (*brahmana-kshatriya-vaisya-sudra*) …I don't fall under any category of *ashrama dharma* (*brahmacharya, garhasthyam, vanaprastham, sanyasam*) …I am the only reason for the birth and death of the world… I am shivam (the auspicious awareness-absolute).

> ·· अहं नैव मन्ता नगन्ता नवक्ता
> नकर्ता नभोक्ता न मुक्ताश्रमस्थ
> यथाहं मनोवृत्तिभेदस्वरूपः
> स्तथा सर्ववृत्तिप्रदीपः शिवोहम् ॥ *(Nirvaanamanjari 4)*

Ch.1   What I am and what I am not   55

aham naiva'mantha na-gantha na-vaktha
na kartha na-bhoktha na-mukthashramastha
yatha'ham manovrthi'bheda'swarupa-.
sthatha sarva'vrthi'pradeepa: shivohum.

I am not one that thinks, not one that goes, not one that speaks, not one that does. I am the one that shows up ..reveals (makes aware of) everything.. I am *shivam* (the auspicious Awareness-Absolute).

•• Also Tejobindu Upanishad says: "In Awareness there is no mind" And so no thinking; but in combination with *prakrti* (nature) it is awareness that makes the living beings perceive, feel and think. Think.

•• It is declared here that the thinking faculty is not me… that I have no business of thinking. Then how can people assert that "It thought …to become many" … "created the universe"…."*kreedartham*"…for the sake of fun… (Is there a desire for fun possible where no thinking is possible — where no thinking faculty is present?) Also it is declared in this verse that "I am not one that does anything".

•• निर्द्वैतोस्यहमस्मि   निर्मलचिदा-
काशोस्मि पूर्णोस्म्यहं
निर्देहोस्मि निरीन्द्रियोस्मि नितरां
निष्प्राणवर्गोस्म्यहं ॥   (Proudhanubhoothi 5)

nir'dwaitho'smyahamasmi nirmala'chidaa-
kaasosmi poornosmyaham
nirdehosmi nireendriyosmi nitharaam
nishpraana'vargosmyaham

I am the single (only) reality…without another. Complete in myself. The sky of awareness *(chid-aakaasam)* …without body, without sense organs, without the *praana* pulsations.

.. निर्मुक्ताशुभमानसोस्मि विगलद्-
विज्ञानकोशोस्म्यहं ।
निर्मायोस्मि निरन्तरोस्मि विपुल-
प्रौढप्रकाशोस्म्यहं ॥   *(Proudhanubhoothi 5 contd..)*

nirmukthaashubha'maanasosmi
vigalath vijnaana'kososmyaham
nirmaayosmi nirantharosmi vipula
proudha prakaasosmyaham.

Devoid of the inauspicious mind ...with the intellect erased with the collection of its knowledge... without a tinge of Maya in me... I am the dense, saturated grand glorious light ... the power of perception ...THE POWER OF PERCEPTION.
(Why can't we take it in its face value ...that there is no Maya in Brahmam?)

.. प्रौढानन्द चिदेक सन्मयवपु:
शुद्धोस्म्यखण्डोस्म्यहं ॥   *(Proudhanubhoothi-2)*

proudhaananda chideka sanmaya vapuh:
shuddhosmyakhandosmyaham.

I am the pure un-fragmented light of awareness ...in saturated bliss.

.. अशरीरं शरीरेषु अनवस्थेष्ववस्थितं
महान्तं .... आत्मानं
मत्वा धीरो न शोचति ॥

asariram sarireshu
anavasthe'shwavasthitham
mahaantham vibhum'athmaanam
mathva dhiro na sochathi.

Ch.1 What I am and what I am not

That which dwells bodiless in bodies – that which shines/revels changeless in changing forms – that all-pervasive Conscious Reality, is my own form, my own Self, MYSELF. One who knows and experiences this, is free from grief. (*Kathopanishad* II.22) Prof GB vol.1 p206

'Atman is all-Spirit, and has been experienced by the seers as Action-less, Change-less, stain-less, attribute-less, part-less, un-manifested, in-comprehensible, and free from all other traces of matter.' (*Atmabodham E*/ Self knowledge: Chinmaya p152)

- न तत् अश्नाति किंचन
  न तत् अश्नाति कश्चनः
  na thath asnathi kinchana;
  na thath asnathi kaschana. (Brh.upa. 3.8.8)

It doesn't eat anything; nor is It eaten up by anything.

- निर्गतोपाधिराकाश एक एव यथाभवेत्
  एक एव तथात्मायं निर्गतोपाधिकः सदा ॥

  (*Adwaitanubhoothi-9*)

  nirgatopaadhi'raakaasha
  eka eva yatha bhaveth
  eka eva thadha'atmaayam
  nirgathopaadhika: sadah.

When all the limiting factors (pot, cave, well, walls) are gone, the space remains one...single...whole. Similarly awareness shines as One..single...whole in the absence of limiting factors.

- आकाशादन्य आकाश आकाशस्य यथा नहि
  एकत्वादात्मनोनान्य आत्मा सिद्ध्यतिचात्मनः

  (*Advaithanubhoothi-10*)

aakaasadanya akasa akasasya yadha nahi
ekatvad'atmanonanya atma sidhyati'cha'atmana

The space has no other space. Similarly the Self.. Athma... has no other Athma, Athma being one ...single ...whole.

•• यथा बुद्बुदनाशेन जलनाशो न कर्हिचित्
तथा प्रपञ्चनाशेन नाशःस्यादात्मनो नहि॥

(*Advaithanubhoothi*-15)

yadha budbuda nasena jala naaso na karhichith
thatha prapancha nasena naasasya'datmano nahi.

When the bubble bursts nothing happens to the water. When the universe dissolves nothing happens to Awareness ...Athma.

•• अहिनिर्ल्वयनीनाशादहेर्नाशो यथानहि
देहत्रय विनाशेन नात्मनाशस्तथाभवेत् ॥

ahinirlvayani nasadahernaso yadha nahi
dehatraya'vinasena naatmanaasa'sthatha bhaveth

(*Advaithanubhoothi*-18)

When the snake-skin falls off, the snake does not die. The falling off of the three bodies does not affect the *athman*.

•• यथाधटेषु नष्टेषु घटाकाशो न नश्यति
तथा देहेषु नष्टेषु नैव नश्यामि सर्वगः ॥

yadha khadesu nashteshu
khada'akaso na nasyati
thatha deheshu nashteshu
naiva nasyaami sarvaga. (*Advaithanubhoothi*-29)

When the pot breaks up, nothing happens to pot-space. So too, the dissolution of the body does not make any difference to the all-pervading Athma.

Ch.1   What I am and what I am not

·· तथा देहेषुनष्टेषु देही नित्यमलेपकः॥
   thadha deheshu'nashteshu dehi nithyamalepaka

   ..so too, when the body falls off, the eternal Self stands unaffected.

·· सर्वं जगदिदं नाहं विषयत्वादिदं धिय *(Advaithanubhoothi 39)*
   sarvam jagadidam naaham
   vishayathwaad idam dhiya

   The whole world is not me...since I see the world. (That is, I am the seer that sees the world—the object. ... Think.)

With limitless mercy to mankind, Sri Sankara continues:-

·· The pots are of countless shapes (pot-space), but the shape (or rather, the shapelessness) of the endless space is unaffected.

·· Rice flour, wheat flour, etc. become sweet by mixing with sugar. So too, that which has no awareness looks to be aware, by a fusion with awareness.

·· If the pot, the water, and the rice – all are hot, it is clear that fire provided this heat. So too, if the five-elements and the bodies that manifest with these elements appear to be aware, where else the awareness can come from, other than the Awareness?

·· Good and bad flowers are strung on a central thread. Similarly, higher forms of bodies and lower forms of bodies are strung in Me—the Awareness... And the string is not affected by the quality of flowers.

·· The one sunlight, passing through the holes of the woven matrix of the cot, appears in countless forms. So too, the One and Only Awareness appears as many.

•• The dust and dirt sticking on to the holes (of the woven matrix-cot) do not contaminate the sunlight. So too Awareness is not contaminated by the births and deaths of the bodies.

I am stopping here; but Sankara Acharya pours forth 84 brilliant verses along these lines (in Adwaithanubhoothi).

Acharya Sankara could have uttered these only on the firm understanding and conviction that, even though seemingly mixed up, Awareness is something always unmixed and pure − not mixed integrally with anything (irrevocably) / not transformed into the bodies and the universe.

•• माया तत्कार्य देहादि मम नास्त्येव सर्वदा
maaya thaath kaarya dehaadi
mama naasthi'eva sarvada (*Brahmajnanavalimaala*)

Maya, and the body and all brought about by it ...are not mine at any time.

•• "**He is the Soul of the universe**. With this knowledge alone man attains immortality. He pervades all creations, and yet transcends it. He is detached from it. This knowledge ... frees one from the cycle of births and deaths. ...unmanifest". (*Yajur Veda*): Q p3 *Kriya yoga.*

"Unmanifest" says Yajur Veda..... Then why do people insist that Brahmam manifests into the universe?

•• The sun holds the efficiency to show (to throw light on), even while there is nothing around to show. (*kevala jnanam* ..pure awareness ..is also similar). (*Vedanta prabodh* p.8)

•• The sun is one; reflections are many.

(ओन्नाणु सूर्यन् पलतु प्रतिबिंबं) *(from a Malayalam film song)*

•• ज्ञानं ज्ञेयं ज्ञानगम्यादतीतं
शुद्धं बुद्धं मुक्तमप्यव्ययं चः
सत्यं ज्ञानं सच्चिदानन्दरूपं ॥ *(Sukarahasyopanishad 24)*

Ch.1 What I am and what I am not

jnanam jneyam jnana'gamyaadatheetham
shuddham buddham muktham'apyavyayam cha
sathyam jnanam satchidaananda'roopam...

Beyond the knowable, the knowing ..and the knowledge; pure, enlightened, liberated ...and without any diminution/waning, is the Reality ..the faculty of cognition ...Reality-Awareness-Bliss.

•• नित्यानन्दं परमसुखदं केवलं ज्ञानमूर्तिं
द्वन्द्वातीतं गगनसदृशं तत्त्वमस्यादिलक्ष्यं
एकं नित्यं विमलमचलं सर्वधीसाक्षिभूतं
भावातीतं त्रिगुणरहितं .. ..॥ *(Suka'rahasyopanishad 21)*

nithyaanandam parama sukhadam
kevalam jnanamoorthim
dwandwaatheetham gagana'sadrsam
thattwamas'yadi lakshyam
ekam nithyam vimalla'machalam
sarva'dhee saakshi'bhootham
bhaavaatheetham thriguna'rahitham.....

Bliss eternal ..is comfort supreme, lone, (alone) knowledge personified, non-dual, space-like ...pointed out by Thath-Twam-Asi..., the one and only, stainless, unmoving ...witness of all intellects ...beyond all attitudes (conditionings), without the three-gunas.

•• *nischala Brahma prakasam* ... (*Bhakthi deepika*, Mal.)
(..Gaining sight of) the unmoving light of Awareness...

•• Except this Imperishable there is no seer, no hearer, no thinker, no knower. [THE POWER OF PERCEPTION] Undoubtedly, O Gargi, the sky exists woven in this (awareness) ... as woof and weft.   (Br.3.8.11).

.. *sthree parirambhanam thadha:*

In the embrace of a sweet-heart, a man knows nothing that goes on outside, nothing that goes on inside. Similarly, when you see your Reality you see nothing external, nothing internal. *Br.*4.3.21 (p.412 Kailas)

(Note that the Upanishad does not say here that you become all-knowing... on Self-Realisation.) This is Its desire-fulfilled, desire-less, grief-less self-desiring form (*aptha-kama, athma-kama, akama, shoka-rahitha swaroopam*).

***   ***   ***

- .. नित्ये परे निर्मले । *nithye pare nirmale*
  In the eternal, ultimate, pure
- .. सर्वं शान्तं अजं शिवं । *sarvam shaantham ajam sivam*
  .. all-calm, unborn, auspicious

To me these do not point to any omnipotence.

* In me there are no five elements.
* Untainted and *Adwiteeyam* (without another)
* Witness of all
* Neither existent nor non-existent.
* Clean, untarnished, unblemished
* Birthless and deathless
* Action-less, desire-less, fear-less
* Without any thought pulsations
* Eternal — beyond time, beyond space
* Known by the name of 'jnanam'...bodham ...power of perception ..cognizance.

These epithets / labels do not suit the body and the universe. (and also to its creator-controller, if any).

And these descriptions unquestionably fit well with Awareness ...pure and simple. Try to see it this way. This is the proper angle of vision.

WHERE THIS MANY POINTERS SHOW THE RIGHT DIRECTION ...people prefer to take wrong routes!?

Needs courage

It needs some courage to imbibe this view. The weakness fed into our blood for very many millenniums – the dependence on the unknown supernatural – needs to be cleansed, shaken off. That is why the Hindu scriptures call them *'dheera'* (valiant, brave, fearless, adventurous) who see the validity of this view and follow it. Walking without a stick ...independent. *(na'ayamathma balahinena labhyo ...na cha pramaada'thapaso...) (Mundakopanishad 3.2.4)*

•• समस्तसाक्षिं सदसद्विहीनं
प्रयाति शुद्धं परमात्म रूपं ।

*samastha saakshim sadasadviheenam
prayaathi shuddham paramaathma roopam.*

Witness to everything... ...the *Parama Athma* has nothing in it ...real or unreal. Wow! Look at this ...closely. Try to understand every syllable of this couplet. This alone is enough to wipe out all the misconceptions commonly prevalent.

•• सत्यं ज्ञानमनन्तं ब्रह्मः ...

sathyam jnanam anantham Brahma

Reality-Awareness-Eternal ...is Brahmam.

•• निरामयो निराभासो निर्विकल्पोहमाततः
नाहं देहो ह्यसदरूपो ज्ञानमित्युच्यते बुधैः *(Aparoksha. 26)*

*niraamayo niraabhaso
nirvikalpohamaathatha
naaham deho'hyasadroopo
jnaanamithyuchyathe budhai*

I am the all-pervading Reality ...having no reason to be down-hearted, without a tinge of duality, with no thought vibrations ... I am not the body that has no absolute reality ... I am known by the name of *'Jnanam'*.

•• निर्मलो निश्चलोऽनन्तः शुद्धोहमजरोमरः
नाहं देहो ह्यसदरूपो ज्ञानमित्युच्यते बुधैः *(Aparoksha. 28)*

*nirmalo nischalo'nantha
shuddhoham'ajaromara
naaham deho'hyasadroopo
jnaanamithyuchyathe budhai*

I am uncontaminated, immobile, eternal, pure, birthless, deathless. I am not the unreal body...I am known by the name of *'Jnanam'*.

•• If awareness becomes non-awareness, then there is no experiencing ...no cognition! Think. (GB *in Proudha. p 438*)

•• **Awareness...is the eye of the world.**
प्रज्ञानेत्रो लोकः *(prajna nethro loka).*
(Aatmaprabodhopanishad I.6)

The world has Awareness as its eyes. This is not just for reading. Look at the brilliance of this statement!

Think, think, think ...and assimilate it. AWARENESS IS THE EYE OF THE WORLD.

* * येनेक्षतः —तत् प्रज्ञानमुदीरितं ॥
  enekshatha ...thath prajnanamudeeritham.

The sensitivity that enables the living organisms to see, to hear, to smell, to taste and to express is called perception ....*prajnanam*. (This was introduced earlier; still I want to repeat it here also).

***   ***   ***

* * छायया स्पृष्टमुष्णं वा शीतं वा सुष्ठु दुष्टु वा
  न स्पृशत्येव यत्किञ्चित् पुरुषं तद्विलक्षणं ॥ (Vivekachudamani 505)
  chhayayaa sprshta'mushnam va
  sheetham va sushtu dushtu va
  na sprsatyeva yath'kinchith
  purusham thath'vilakshanam

If your shadow falls on something hot (be it a blast furnace) or something cold, or on something good or something filthy, it affects you not in the least; you are not the shadow.

* * न मे प्रवृत्तिर्नच मे निवृत्तिः
  सदैक रूपस्य निरंशकस्य ।
  एकात्मको यो निबिडो निरन्तरो
  व्योमेव पूर्णः स कथं नु चेष्टते ॥ (Vivekachudamani 503)
  namaepravrthir'nacha'mae'nivrthi:
  sadaikarupasya'niramsakasya
  ekaathmakoyo'nibido'nirantharo
  vyomeva purna: sa katham nu cheshtathe.

For me who is always the same and devoid of parts, there is neither engaging in work nor cessation of work. How can that which is One, saturated, continuous (without a break or gap anywhere), homogenous, and infinite like the space, ever strive?

> मय्यखण्डसुखांभोधौ बहुधा विश्ववीचयः
> उत्पद्यन्ते विलीयन्ते माया मारुत विभ्रमात् ॥
>
> mayyakhanda sukhaambhodhou
> bahudhaa viswa'veechaya
> uthpadyanthe vileeyanthe
> maaya'maarutha'vibhramaath. (Vivekachudamani 497)

In me, the ocean of infinite bliss, the waves of the universes emerge and dissolve by the play of the wind of Maya.

> पुण्यानि पापानि निरीन्द्रियस्य
> निश्चेतसो निर्विकृते निराकृते
> कुतो ममाखण्ड सुखानुभूते ॥ *(Vivekachudamani 504)*
>
> punyani paapaani nireendriyasya
> nis-chethaso nirvikrthe nirakrthe
> kutho mama'akhanda sukhanubhuthe

I am mindless, organs-less, formless, and always... continuously.. in saturated ecstasy; how can there be *punya* or *paapa* (merit or sin) to me?

> नाहमिदं नाहमदोऽप्युभयोरवभासकं
> बाह्याभ्यन्तरशून्यं पूर्णं ब्रह्माद्वितीयमेवाहं
>
> naaham'idam naahamado'
> pyubhayo'ravabhaasakam
> baahyaabhyanthara'shunyam purnam
> brahmaadwitheeyamevaaham
>
> *(Vivekachudamani 493)*

Ch.1 What I am and what I am not

I am neither ***this*** nor ***that*** but the supreme Illuminator of both. I am pure. I have neither an interior nor an exterior. (There is no 'matter-content' in me.) I am infinite[1]. I am the non-dual Brahmam.

.. असङ्गोहमनङ्गोहमलिङ्गोहमभङ्गुरः
प्रशान्तोऽहमनन्तोऽहममलोऽहं चिरन्तनः॥

asangoha' manangoha'
malingoha' mabhangura
prashaanthoha' mananthoha'
mamaloham chiranthana   (Vivekachudamani 490)

I am not related/ connected/ attached to anything. I am bodiless, eternal , serene, unsullied...and endless.

.. अकर्ताहमभोक्ताहमविकारोऽहमक्रियः
शुद्धबोधस्वरूपोहं केवलोहं सदाशिवः ॥

akarthaha'mabhokthaha'
mavikaaroha'makriya
shuddha'bodha swaroopoham
kevaloham sadaasiva   (Vivekachudamani 491)

I am not the doer (activities are not mine... not in my lot ..no such portfolio to me) ..I am not the experiencer, I am without any modification, and without activity. I am embodiment of pure knowledge (the power of perception—simple). I am Absolute (*kevalam* = one and only) and I am Auspiciousness eternal.

---

[1] purnam...complete...is the word.

• • द्रष्टुःश्रोतृर्वक्तुः कर्तुर्भोक्तुर्विभिन्न एवाहम्
नित्यनिरन्तरनिष्क्रिय निःसीमासङ्गपूर्णबोधात्मा ॥
drshtu'shrothru-vakthu-
karthru-bhokthr-vibhinna eva'aham
nithya'niranthara'nishkriya
nisseema'asanga'poorna'bodhaathma
(Vivekachudamani 492)

Indeed I am other than the seer, hearer, speaker, doer, and experiencer. I am unborn, eternal Athma, beyond activity, boundless, unattached and infinite ...the essence of Knowledge.

(Sankaracharya shouts at the top of his voice with hands raised ...but nobody hears. The jagath-guru places the word 'inactive/actionless ...*akriyam/akartha*' in three places in four successive lines; but nobody has the eyes to see it.)

Very many sign boards at closer distances so that people will not deviate from the directed path ... but people prefer not to look at them ...and want to proceed only along the paths their feet lead them (not led by the eyes or the head).

This imposition of all-doership on Athman ...and therefore Brahmam ... is like the police trying to impose the responsibility of crimes committed by many people on someone whom they can easily book.

• • कर्तापि वा कारयतापि नाहं ....
....सोहं स्वयंज्योतिरनीदृशात्मा ॥ *(Vivekachudamani 508)*
karthaapi'va kaarayathaapi naaham
soham swayam'jyothi'raneedrshaathma

Here again is another solid pointer: I don't do anything; nor do I get anything done. **(I do not act; nor do I activate.)**

Ch.1   What I am and what I am not

I am neither the experiencer nor do I make others experience. I am the self-luminous Athma   ...(*swayam jyothi*)   ..the light of perception.

•• जलैवापि स्थलैवापि लुठत्वेष जटात्मकः
नाहं विलिप्ये तद्धर्मैर्घटधर्मैर्नभो यथा ॥

> *jalaivaapi sthalaivaapi*
> *ludhatwesha jadaathmaka*
> *naaham vilipye thath'dharmair*
> *khada'dharmair'nabho'yadha*
>
> (Vivekachudamani 510)

Whether in water or on land, let the inert body drop down; I am not affected by what happens to the body...like the **space is not affected by whatever happens to the pot.**

•• "*Yathra naanyath pasyati naanya-chrunoti nanyath-vijanaati sa bhooma*" (*Suthra bhaashyam* 2.1.1.4)

Where nothing else is seen, nothing else is heard, nothing else to know ...that is *Bhooma* (totality, fullness, alone-ness, complete).

•• सर्व दृश्य विहीनोहं दृग्रूपोस्म्यहमेवहि ।
सर्वदापूर्णरूपोस्मि नित्यतृप्तोस्म्यहं सदा ॥

> *sarva drsya viheeno'ham drg'roopo'smyahameva hi*
> *sarvadah purna'ruposmi, nityatrpto'smyaham sadah.*
>
> (Tejobindu Upa. III.15 p507 Upa.112/I)

I am without all the sense-objects (ie, objects are not in me); I am always complete and ever-contented.

- द्रष्टारमात्मानमखण्डबोधं
  सर्वप्रकाशं सदसद्विलक्षणम् ॥   *(Vivekachudamani 220)*
  drstaram'atmaanam'akhanda bodham
  sarva prakasam sad'asad'vilakshanam.

The Athman ..is the one who sees ...the continuous ever-existent Awareness that shows up/reveals everything ...distinct from the gross and the subtle.

- क्षीरयोगात् यथानीरं क्षीरवद्दृश्यते मृषा
  आत्मयोगादनात्माय-मात्मवद् दृश्यते तथा ॥

  ksheera yogaath yadha neeram
  ksheeravath'drsyathe mrsha
  aathmayogaad'anaathmaaya-
  maathmavad'drsyathe thadha.

  (Advaitanubhoothi 75)

Just as water added to milk looks like milk .. in combination with Athma (awareness) the things that are not endowed with awareness look as if they are aware.

देहत्रय विलक्षण: deha'thraya vilakshana.

- different from the three bodies.
  जाग्रदादि विलक्षण: jaagradaadi vilakshana.

- different from jagrat-swapna-sushupthi.
  विश्वादिक विलक्षण: viswaadika vilakshana.

- different from the world etc. *(Advaitanubhoothi 81,82,83)*

•• यथाकाशो घटाकाशो महाकाश इतीरितः
तथा भ्रान्तैर्द्विधा प्रोक्तो ह्यात्मा जीवेश्वरात्मना ॥
yadhaakaaso khadakaso
mahaakaasha itheeritha
thadha bhraanthair dwidha proktho'
hyaathma jiveswaraathmana. (Jabaladarsana Upa.X.4)

Just as pot-space is considered as a different entity from the single endless vast space, jiva and Iswara are considered as two different entities by mistake.

•• एकमेवाद्वितीयं सन्नामरूपविवर्जितं ॥ *(Sukarahasyopanishad)*
ekameva'adwitheeyam san-naamaroopavivarjitham

I am one only, without another – the Reality (sath), divorced/divested of all names and forms.

It doesn't say here that 'I hold everything in me' or 'I am the universe myself' or 'the universe is my body'. *Namarupa vivarjitham*: divorced of everything... devoid of everything.

••   jneya'vasthu parithyaagath
   jnanam thishtathu kevalam.
       (Sadacharaanusandhanam-37 by Sankarachaarya)

Relieved of the sense objects, the object-less (power of) perception remains ... alone.

•• The illumining principle behind BMI PFT OET is the pure Self—the Consciousness.

•• The Awareness envelops everything together as a light does its surroundings.   (*Pancadasi* p429)

•• It (Brahmam/Awareness) is not He or She....so It. No male, no female. When it is He or She, we personify it; and that is a pitfall.

              ***   ***   ***

- यथा दर्पणाभाव आभासहानौ
  मुखं विद्यते कल्पनाहीनमेकं
  तथा धीवियोगे निराभासकोय:
  स नित्योपलब्धि स्वरुपोहमात्मा ॥ (Hasthamalakam-6)

  yatha darpana'abhava' aabhasa'haanau
  mukham vidyate'kalpana'hinam'ekam
  thatha dhi'viyoge niraabhasa'ko'ya.
  sa nithyopalabdhi swaroopoham'aathma'

When the mirror is removed, the image vanishes and the (original) face remains. When dissociated from the intellect, pure awareness alone remains ... I am of the nature of that ever-existing Athman.

- निष्कलं निष्क्रियं शान्तं निरवद्यं निरञ्जनं
  अमृतस्य परं सेतुं दग्धेन्धनमिवानलं ॥

  nishkalam[+] nishkriyam shaantham
  niravadyam niranjanam
  amrthasya param sethum
  dagdhen'dhana'mivaanalam.

It is part-less[+], action-less, tranquil, eternal, uncontaminated ... ocean of saturated bliss... as a fire subsides when the fuel runs out.

- एकस्मिन्नव्ययेशान्ते चिदाकाशेऽमले त्वयि
  कुतो जन्म कुत कर्म: कुतोऽहंकार एव च: ॥

  ekasmin'avyase'santhe chidakase'amale'tvayi
  kuto janma kutah karma kuto'hamkara eva ca?

  Asht.gita XV.13

[+] Partless, component-less, not divided, single, whole, without anything else other than Itself (Akhandam).

Ch.1 What I am and what I am not

In you – the single, immutable, serene, uncontaminated Pure Consciousness – how can there be birth, activity, and ego-sense?

•• Can we consider this 'I-feeling' (I-ness) as the Reality? That 'I' is also not the Reality. The awareness as a witness— that shows up the 'I-ness' is the real stuff / reality. (Prof GB in his commentary to *Proudhanubhoothi* .. p.354)

***   ***   ***

•• निषिध्य निखिलोपाधीश्नेति नेतीति वाक्यतः
विद्यादैक्यं महावाक्यैर्जीवात्मपरमात्मनोः ॥ *(Atma Bodham 29)*

nishiddhya nikhilopadhin'
neti-neti'ti vakyata
vidyaat'aikyam mahavakyai
jeevatma-Paramatmano.

Negating all *upadhis* (conditioning/limiting) using the scriptural pointer 'not this, not this', realize the oneness of the soul and the Supreme Soul by means of the great Vedic *maha vakyas*.

•• स्वबोधे नान्यबोधेच्छा बोधरूपतयात्मनः
न दीपस्यान्यदीपेच्छा यथा स्वात्मप्रकाशने ॥

swabodhe na'anya bodheccha
bodharupataya'atmanah
na deepasya'anya deepeccha
yatha swatma'prakaasane. *(Atma Bodham 28)*

Atman being Consciousness itself, does not need another instrument of cognition to reveal Itself. To see a burning lamp, you don't need another lamp.

•• अनाद्यविद्यानिर्वाच्या कारणोपाधिरुच्यते
उपाधित्रितयादन्यमात्मानमवधारयेत् ॥ *(Atma Bodham 13)*

anaady'avidya'anirvaachya
kaaranopaadir'uchyate
upaadhi thrithayaad'anyam
aathmaanam avadhaarayeth.

Avidya (ne-science)...indescribable and beginning-less... is said to be the Causal Body. Know for certain that the Athman is other than these three* conditioning bodies (*upadhi-s*).

•• पञ्चकोशादियोगेन तत्तन्मय इव स्थितः ।
शुद्धात्मा नीलवस्त्रादियोगेन स्फटिको यथा ॥

pancha'kosaadi yogena
tath'thanmaya'eva'sthitha
shuddhaatma neela'vasthraadi
yogena sphatiko'yatha.   (Atma Bodham 15)

In its identification with the five sheaths the immaculate Athman appears to have borrowed their qualities upon Itself; as in the case of a crystal which appears to gather unto itself colour of its vicinity (blue cloth etc).

•• पञ्चकोश गुणत्रयादि समस्तधर्मविलक्षणं ।
panchakosa guna thrayaadi
samastha dharma vilakshanam

(Gurupaaduka sthothram)

Different from five sheaths, three gunas and all such ..and all their functions.

•• *janthu deha nivaasinam* (Gurupaaduka sthothram)

Stationed/situated in the living beings. -

•• सदा सर्वगतोप्यात्मा न सर्वत्रावभासते ।
बुद्धावेवावभासेत स्वच्छेषु प्रतिबिम्बवत् ॥

---

* Physical body, astral body, causal body.

Ch.1 What I am and what I am not 75

sadaa sarva'gatho'pi'aatma
na sarvatra'avabhaasathe
buddhaveva'avabhaasetha
swacche'shu pratibimba'vath   (Atma Bodham 17)

Although the Athman is all-pervasive, it manifests only in the intellect (*buddhi*), just as the objects reflect only in a clean mirror.

देहेन्द्रियमनोबुद्धिप्रकृतिभ्यो विलक्षणम् ।
तद्-वृत्तिसाक्षिणं विद्यादात्मानं राजवत्सदा ॥

dehendriya mano buddhi
prakrthibhyo vilakshanam
thad vrthi'saakshinam vidyaad'
aathmaanam rajavath sadaa (Atma Bodham 18)

The Athman is distinct from the body, senses, mind and intellect—all of which are constituted of matter (*prakrthi*)—and is the witness of their functions, like a king.+

व्यापृतेष्विन्द्रियेष्वात्मा   व्यापारीवाविवेकिनाम् ।
दृश्यतेऽभ्रेषु धावत्सु   धावन्निव यथा शशि ॥

vyaprteshu-indriyeshu-Athma
vyaapaareena avivekinam
drsyathe-abhreshu dhavatsu
dhaavanniva yatha sashi   (Atma Bodham 19)

The Athman appears to be active when it is observed through the functions of the sense organs...just as the moon appears to be running when the clouds move.

आत्मचैतन्यमाश्रित्य देहेन्द्रियमनोधियः
स्वक्रियार्थेषु वर्तन्ते सूर्यालोकं यथा जना ॥

+ Like a king observes/oversees the functioning of the officials.

> *aatma'chaithanyam'aasrthya*
> *dehendriya'mano'dhiya*
> *swakriyartheshu varthanthe*
> *suryaalokam yatha jana.* (Atma Bodham 20)

The body, senses, mind, buddhi etc. engage in their activities with the help of Consciousness, just as men work with the help of sunlight.

देहेन्द्रियगुणान्कर्माण्यमले सच्चिदात्मनि ।
अथ्यस्थन्ति अविवेकेन गगने नीलतादिवत् ॥

> *dehendriya'gunaan'karmaany-*
> *amale sacchidaatmani*
> *addhyasthanthi'avivekena*
> *gagane neelathaadivath*   (Atma Bodham 20)

Through non-discrimination people superimpose on the pure uncontaminated Athman— Existence and Consciousness Absolute — the characteristics and functions of the body and the senses ...just as blue colour and concavity are attributed to the sky.

अज्ञानान्मानसोपाधेः कर्तृत्वादीनिचात्मनि ।
कल्प्यन्तेम्बुगते चन्द्रे चलनादि यथाम्भस ॥

> *ajnaanaan'maanaso'paathe*
> *karthrthvaadeeni'cha'atmani*
> *kalpyanthe'mbugathe chandre*
> *chalanaadi yathaambhasa.* (Atma Bodham 22)

When the water shakes, the reflected moon appears to be shaking. Likewise, action, enjoyment and such other attributes which really belong to the mind are understood— under delusion—as the nature of the Self (*Athman*).

Ch.1   What I am and what I am not

•• प्रकाशोर्केस्य तोयस्य शैत्यमग्नेर्यथोष्णता ।
स्वभावः सच्चिदानन्द नित्यनिर्मलतात्मनः ॥

*prakasa'arkasya toyasya
shaithyam'agnair'yathoshnatha
Swabhava sacchidaananda
nithya'nirmalatha'athmanah.* (Atma Bodham 24)

The sun emits light, water is cool, fire is hot. This is *vasthu-swabhavam* (nature of the stuff). The nature of Athman is Eternal, Ever-Pure Reality-Awareness-Bliss.

•• आविद्यकं शरीरादि दृश्यं बुद्बुदवत्क्षरम् ।
एतद्विलक्षणं विद्यात् अहं ब्रह्मेति निर्मलम् ॥

*aavidyakam shariraadi
drsyam budbuda'vathksharam
ethath'vilakshanam vidyaad'
aham Brahmethi nirmalam.* (Atma Bodham 31)

The body and all (inclusive of the 'causal body' which is ignorance) are objects perceived...are perishable like bubbles. Realise through discrimination that I am the 'Pure Brahmam' ever completely different from all these.

•• देहान्यत्वान्नमेजन्म जराकार्श्य लयादयः ।
शब्दादि विषयैः सङ्गो निरिन्द्रियतया न च ॥

*deha'anyathvaath na mae janma
jaraa'kaarsya'layaadaya
shabdaadi'vishayai sango
nirindriyathaya na cha.*   (Atma Bodham 32)

I am other than the body, and so I am free from the vicissitudes attendant on the body (such as birth, wrinkling, senility, diseases, and death). And I have nothing to do with the sense objects such as sight, sound and taste ...as I am without sense organs.

•• **"Bodham stands as the Seer** (drk) of the astral body also." (*Vedanta Prabodh* p117).
Is it not clear then that all the components (elements/ *tathwas*) of the astral body are *drsya* (things seen / objects), and that the Seer (*drk*) is other than the things seen?

•• अमनस्त्वान्नमे दुःखरागद्वेषभयादयः ।
अप्राणो ह्यमनाः शुभ्र इत्यादि श्रुतिशासनात् ॥

> amanastvath na mae dukkha
> raaga'dvesha'bhayaadaya
> apraano'hyamanah shubhra
> ithyaadi'sruti'shaasanaath. (Atma Bodham 32)

I am other than the mind, and hence I am free from sorrow, attachment, malice and fear. "HE is without breath, without mind...Pure, etc." is the assertion of the great scriptures, the Upanishads.

•• अहमाकाशवत्सर्वं बहिरन्तर्गतोच्युतः ।
सदा सर्वसमशशुद्धो निस्सङ्गो निर्मलोचलः ॥

> aham aakaashavath sarvam
> bahi'ranthargatho'achyutha
> sadaa sarva'sama'sshuddho
> nissamgo'nirmalo'achala.   (Atma Bodham 35)

I fill all things...in and out...like the space. Changeless, and the same in all, at all times I am pure, unattached, uncontaminated and motionless.

नित्यशुद्धविमुक्तैकम् अखण्डानन्दमद्वयम् ।
सत्यं ज्ञानमनन्तं यत्परं ब्रह्माहमेव तत् ॥

Ch.1   What I am and what I am not   79

nithya'shuddha'vimukthaikam
akhandaananda'madvayam
sathyam'jnaana'manantham yath'
param Brahma'ahameva thath. (Atma Bodham 36)

I am verily that Supreme Brahmam itself, which is Eternal, Pure, Free, One only, Indivisible, Non-dual, Changeless Awareness-Infinite.

•• ज्ञातृज्ञानज्ञेयभेदः परे नात्मनि विद्यते ।
चिदानन्दरूपत्वात् दीप्यते स्वयमेव हि ॥

jnatr-jnana-jneya bheda:
parae na aathmani vidyate
chidananda rupathwath
deepyate swayameva hi. (Atma Bodham 41)

There are no distinctions as 'knower', the 'knowledge' and the 'object of knowledge' in the Supreme Self. On account of its being of the nature of Awareness-Bliss (chid-anandam) eternal, it does not admit of such distinctions within Itself. It shines alone by Itself.

•• "If you find yourself the Perceiver-Feeler-Thinker, then also you are wrong". Coming from Swamy Chinmayananda, this is a great pointer to pure Brahmam, Pure Awareness, *prakaasa maathram* (light/*jyothis* alone).

•• न भूमिरापो न च वह्निरस्ति नचानिलो मेऽस्ति न चांबरं चः
एवं विदित्वा परमात्मरूपं गुहाशयं निष्कलमद्वितीयं ।
समस्तसाक्षिं सदसद्विहीनं प्रयाति शुद्धं परमात्मरूपम् ॥

na bhumi'rapo na cha vahnir'asthi
nachanilo'mae'asthi na cha ambaram cha
evam viditva paramaatma rupam
guhasayam nishkalam adwitiyam

samastha'saakshim sad'asad'vihinam
prayaathi shuddham paramathmaroopam
(Kaivalya Upa. 23, 24)

There is no earth, no water, no fire, no sky..(to me)..in me. He who knows Paramathman as being in the cave (of the heart), as having no form, as being the one and only (without another), as being the witness of all, as being neither Sath nor Asath, ..attains the pure form of Athman.

एवमात्मारणौ ध्यानमथने सततं कृते
उदितावगतिर्ज्वाला सर्वाज्ञानेन्धनं दहेत् ॥

evam'athma'aranau dhyana-
madhane sathatham krthe
udithavagatir'jvaala
sarva'ajnana'indhanam daheth (Atma Bodham 42)

By constant meditation (like the rubbing of flint-wood), the flame of knowledge kindled, completely consumes the fuel of ignorance.

अरुणेनेव बोधेन पूर्वं सन्तमसे हृते
तथा आविर्भवेदात्मा स्वयमेवांशुमानिव ॥

aruneneva bodhena
purvam samthamase hrte
thatha aavirbhaved'athma
swayameva'amsumaniva (Atma Bodham 43)

As the sun appears rolling away darkness by dawn, so too Athman appears when knowledge rolls away the ignorance.

स्थाणौ पुरुषवद्भ्रान्त्या कृता ब्रह्मणि जीवता ।
जीवस्य तात्त्विकेरूपे तस्मिनदृष्टे निवर्तते ॥

sthanau purushavad'bhraanthya
krtha brahmani jeevatha

Ch.1 What I am and what I am not

jeevasya tathvike roope
thasmin drshte nivarthathe (Atma Bodham 45)

Brahmam appears to be a jiva through ignorance, as the stump of a tree appears to be a man. This jiva-hood vanishes when the real nature of jiva is understood.

.. यल्लाभान्नापरोल्लाभो यत्सुखान्नापरं सुखम् ।
यज्ज्ञानान्नापरं ज्ञानं तद्ब्रह्मेत्यवधारयेत् ॥

yallabhath'na'aparo'laabho
yath'sukhaath'naaparam sukham
yajnaanaath naaparam jnaanam
thath'Brahma'ityavadharayeth. (Atma Bodham 54)

<u>Realize that to be Brahmam, the attainment of which leaves nothing more to be attained ..the blessedness of which leaves no other bliss to be desired, and the knowledge of which leaves nothing more to be known.</u>

.. यज्ज्ञात्वा नापरं ज्ञेयं

yajnatwa naaparam jneyam (Atma Bodham 55)

Knowing which, nothing else remains worth knowing.

.. भिद्यते हृदयग्रन्थिश्छिद्यन्ते सर्वसंशयः
क्षीयन्ते चास्यकर्माणि तस्मिन दृष्टे परावरे॥

bhidyathe hrdaya'grandhi
chidyanthe sarva'samshaya:
ksheeyanthe chaasya'karmaani
thasmin'drshte paraavare. (Mundakopanishad II.ii.80)

The heart knot is rent asunder – all doubts are dispelled, and karmas roll away when the Supreme Self is seen by the seeker.

•• यद्युक्तमखिलं वस्तु व्यवहारस्तदन्वितः
तस्मात्सर्वगतं ब्रह्म क्षीरे सर्पिरिवाखिले ॥

yad'yuktham'akhilam vasthu
vyavahaaras'thadanvitha
tasmaath sarva'gatham Brahma
ksheere sarpiriva'akhile.   (Atma Bodham 59)

All objects are pervaded by Brahmam, all the actions are possible because of Brahmam ... Brahmam permeates everything, as butter permeates milk.

•• अनण्वस्थूलमह्रस्वम् अदीर्घमजमव्ययम् ।
अरूपगुणवर्णाख्यं तद् ब्रह्मेत्यवधारयेत् ॥

ananv-asthulam'ahrasvam
adirgham'ajam'avyayam
arupa'guna'varna'aghyam thath
brahmety'avadhaarayeth.   (Atma Bodham 60)

Realise that Brahman is neither subtle nor gross, neither short nor long; is birthless, changeless, formless, colourless, nameless, and without any traits of characteristics.

•• भास्वन्तंभानुमन्धवत्   (Atma Bodham 65)

bhaswantham bhanum andha'vath

...but one whose vision is obscured/hindered by ignorance does not see the radiant Atman, as the blind do not see the resplendent sun.

•• यद्भासा भास्यतेकोदि भास्यैर्यत्तु न भास्यते
येन सर्वमिदं भाति तद्ब्रह्मेत्यवधारयेत् ॥

yad'bhasa bhasyate'arkaadi
bhasyair'yatthu na bhasyate

Ch.1 What I am and what I am not

yena sarvam idam bhaathi
thath Brahme'tyavadhaarayeth (Atma Bodham 61)

The light that illumines the sun and the moon, but which cannot be illumined by their light ..and that which illumines everything ...realize that to be Brahmam.

.. स्वयमन्तर्बहिर्व्याप्य भासयन्नखिलं जगत् ।
ब्रह्म प्रकाशते वह्नि-प्रतप्तायसपिण्डवत् ॥

swayam anthar bahir vyaapya
bhaasayan akhilam jagath
brahma prakaasathe vahni
prathaptha'ayasa'pindavath. (Atma Bodham 62)

Pervading the universe in and out, Brahmam shines of itself ...like fire permeates a red-hot iron ball.

.. जगद्विलक्षणं ब्रह्म ....

Jagad'vilakshanam brahma. (Atma Bodham 63)

Brahma is other than the universe .....

(The rest confuses... *Miththya*...*yatha maru'marichika* ...unreal, like a mirage!)

Atman, the Sun of Knowledge, arises in the firmament of the heart and dispels darkness. It illumines all, and also Itself. (*Athma Bodham 67 – end*)

.. आत्मानमानन्दमखण्टबोधं यस्मिन् लयं याति पुरत्रयंचः
atmanam anandam'akhanda'bodham
yasmin layam yaathi purathrayam ca

Atma is saturated bliss and unfragmented awareness,...in which dissolve the three bodies.

.. कालत्रये यथा सर्पो रज्जौ नास्ति तथा मयि
अहंकारादि देहान्तं जगन्नास्त्यहमद्वयः

(*Atmaprabodhopanishad 29*)

> *kaala thraye yadha sarpo*
> *rajjau naasthi thatha mayi*
> *ahamkaaraadi dehaantham*
> *jagan'nasthy'aha'madvaya:*

Rope is not a snake—in the present, past or future. Similarly in me the Reality, there is no body nor the universe, nor the Jiva-bhavam.

- खटावभासको भानुर् खटनाशे न नश्यति:
  देहावभासक:साक्षी देहनाशे न नश्यति ॥

  khada'avabhaasako bhanur-
  khada naasae na nasyathi;
  deha'avabhasaka sakshi
  deha'naasae na nasyathi.

  (Atmaprabodhopanishad 18)

<u>The sun reflected in the pot does not end with the breaking of the pot. The consciousness that experiences the body, does not end with the body.</u>

- "It (Atman) should be cognized as one only"
  (*Brhadaranyaka Upanishad* IV. iv, 20)

- एकथैवानुद्रष्टव्यमेतदप्रमेयं ध्रुवम् ।
  विरज: पर: आकाशादज आत्मा महाध्रुव ॥

  As a unity only is It to be looked upon...this indemonstrable, enduring Entity— spotless, beyond space, the unborn Soul, great, enduring.

- "In Brahmam there is no diversity whatsoever"

- मनसैवानुद्रष्टव्यं नेह नानास्ति किंचन:
  मृत्या: स मृत्युमाप्नोति य इह नानेव पश्यति ॥

  (*Brhadaranyaka Upanishad* IV, iv, 19)

Ch.1 What I am and what I am not

By the mind alone is It to be perceived. ... There is no diversity. ... He gets death after death, who perceives here diversity. (I would read it as: '...who perceives diversity in Bodham' 𝒟ₙ).

•• "It (sath = reality) is One only, without another... and without names and forms.

(एकमेवाद्वितीयं सन्नामरूपविवजितं)   (Ch. Upa. vi,ii, 1)

•• एकथा बहुधा चैव दृश्यते जलचन्द्रवत्
एक एव हि भूतात्मा भूते भूते व्यवस्थित ॥
*ekatha bahudha chaiva
drsyathe jalachandravath.
eka'evahi'bhoothaathma
bhoothe bhoothe vyavasthitha*
(Brahmabindu Upa. 12)

<u>The soul in all is indeed One; it dwells in every being as its Innermost Guide. The diversity of souls is like the diversity of the reflections of the moon in the ripples.</u>

•• "It is indivisible, and yet It is, as it were, divided among beings." (*Bhagavadgita* XIII, 16)

•• Distinctions are due to the association of the Soul with upathis/ apparatus / equipments. The upathis cannot affect the non-duality and purity of the Soul. The pots, walls and caves do not partition the vast endless space.

•• सच्चिदानन्द मूर्तये...
निष्प्रपञ्चाय शान्ताय: निरालंबाय तेजसे॥
*sat-chid-ananda murthaye...
nish'prapanchaaya'shaanthaaya
niralambaya thejase*   (Niralambopanishad)

The effulgence!... embodiment of Reality-Awareness-Bliss..... ...calm...not dependent on anything (*nir-aalambam*) and devoid of the universe *(nish-prapancham)*.

•• निरालंबं समाश्रित्य सालंबं विजहाति यः
स सन्यासीच योगीच कैवल्यंपदमश्नुते ॥

*niralambam samasrthya salambam vijahaathi ya
sa sanyasi cha yogi cha kaivalyam'padam'asnute*

(*Niralambopanishad*)

One who takes refuge in the Independent ... discarding the dependent (*prapancham*) ... becomes a sanyasi (renunciate), a yogi, and attains salvation.

•• *nirmuktha'bandhana-mapaara'sukhaambu'raashim*
_{sreevallabham} *vimala bodha'khanam namaami.*

(*Vakya vrthi* by Sankaracharya)

Pure Consciousness Divine – free from all bondages – a shore-less ocean of saturated ecstacy[1].

If it is not the awareness that I talk about, then what else is it pointing to? What other extra glory is in it to point out except the supreme glory of Awareness?

Big, high-sounding names are given. (*Vedanta prabodh*: "*acche acche naam diya hei*".)

•• Seeing the Seer always; and never ever seeing the non-seer. (*Vasishtam,* Mal.) p200 (*kaanunnavane sadaapi saadho kantu, kaanaathavane orikkalum kaanaathe*)

•• The worms and insects that grow out of the dirt and scum of earth and water in the hot season and appear filthy to our sight are nevertheless endowed with pure awareness,

---

[1] 'saturated ecstacy'... I have borrowed this usage from my childhood guru Swamy Brahmasuthan.

Ch.1   What I am and what I am not

making them living beings. (*Yogavaasistham* IV.19.3) P52 of Vol.2/4.

(यो यो नाम यथा ग्रीष्मे कल्पस्वेदाद् भवेत्कृमी
यद्यऽदृश्यं शुद्धचित्खं तज्जीवो भवति स्वतः)

*(yo yo naama yatha greeshme
kalpaswedaad'bhaveth'krmi
yadyadrsyam shuddhachith-kham
thath jeevo Bhavathi swatha.)*

This should serve as a pointer of very great significance and value to the clear intellect. Don't get into the quagmire of thinking that the subject of discussion is only the "all-knowing and all-powerful" awareness. This is the confusion everybody is caught up in. The Awareness is the same in the filthy worm, in us, and in Brahma.

***   ***   ***

"A 'witness' is one who stands on the foot-path, uninvolved in the happenings on the road – say, in an accident. The Consciousness is a witness in all the life's experiences, in every living creature. In our ignorance we become so totally involved with the happenings, and get wholly committed to the joys and sorrows of our body and mind. The moment the seeker rediscovers the realm of the Self in him, he understands that, as the Self, he is ever as far removed from the pluralistic world of change and sorrow as the sunlight is from the daily drama of the world. The illuminator is always different from the illumined. 'I am the Self, the illuminator, and not the illumined". *(Swamy Chinmayananda)*.

The sun and sunlight are different from the things shown up ..revealed ..by the sunlight.

If you contemplate on the Athman, you will find that It is your Self, non-dual, without any activity or attachment. (Swamy Chinmayananda *Vivekachudamani* p.251)

Parangchi khaani / looking outward:

•• The sense organs are fitted facing outward ...and therefore we look outward, not inward within ourselves. Yet the wise, seeking immortality, introspectively behold the Soul (Athma) face to face. (*Katho.*) (*parangchi'khani....na anthara-athma*)

•• In Pancadasi X.9 it is said "that the witness reveals at one and the same time the agent, the actions, and the external things. But no knowledge is possible unless they get linked up. This is done by the witness, not by any action (for it does not act) but by its mere presence. For example 'I see' involves three factors—the 'I', the 'seeing', and the 'seen'; and to connect them 'at one and the same time' in order to produce knowledge is also the 'work' of the witness. The witness, which is knowledge and nothing but knowledge, does it by its mere presence. The witness envelops them all together as a light does its surroundings, and the knowledge 'I see' is produced." (*Pancadasi* p 429).

•• प्रकाशरूपोहमजोहमद्वयो-
सकृद्विभातोहमतीव निर्मलः
विशुद्ध विज्ञानघनो निरामयः
सम्पूर्ण आनन्दमयोहमक्रियः ॥ *(Sri Rama Gita, 43)*

prakasa rupo'ham'ajo'hamadvayo
sakrd,vibhatho'ham'athiva'nirmala
visuddha'vijnana'ghano niramaya
sampurna ananda'mayoham **'akriya'**

Ch.1 What I am and what I am not

I am self-effulgent. I am unborn. I am the One without another. I am the ever-resplendent light of consciousness. I am extremely pure, the uncontaminated mass of pure consciousness. I am holy, infinite, blissful, and **actionless**.

"This verse is specially meant for contemplation. It provides ten arrow marks indicating the direction in which the student of contemplation should hold his entire attention." (Swamy Chinmayananda)

Here follow some more arrows /pointers ..now from Acharya Sankara.

- अतः परं ब्रह्म सद्द्वितीयं विशुद्धविज्ञानघनं निरञ्जनं
  प्रशान्तमाद्यन्तविहीनमक्रियं निरन्तरानन्दरसस्वरूपम् ॥
  atah param'Brahma sat'adviteeyam
  vishudha vijnana'ghanam niranjanam
  *prasantham'adyantha'viheenam'**akriyam***
  nirantharananda'rasa'swarupam.
  (Vivekachudamani 237)

- निरस्तमायाकृतसर्वभेदं
  नित्यं सुखं निष्कलमप्रमेयं
  अरूपमव्यक्तमनाख्यमव्ययं
  ज्योतिः स्वयं किञ्चिदिदं चकास्ति ॥
  nirastha'maayaa'krtha sarva bhedam
  nityam'sukham'nishkala'maprameyam
  arupa'mavyaktha'manaakhya'mavyayam
  jyotih'swayam kinchid'idam chakaasthi.
  (Vivekachudamani 238)

In these two verses (237, 238 Vivekachudamani) Sankara gives us twenty *adjectival* phrases which *indicate* Brahmam. (The explanations to the phrases are from Swamy Chinmayananda.)

1) **Para** (transcendental) : The illumining principle (factor) behind BMI, PFT, OET, is the pure Self, the Consciousness which is one-without-another upon which the universe of names and forms is an illusory(?) projection. Hence Brahmam is indicated in Vedantic philosophy as transcendental.

2) **sath** (Real)—That which remains the same in all the three periods of time—past, present and future—is called 'real'.

3) **adwitheeyam**: (One-without-another).... The One ultimate Eternal Entity, without any other-ness to limit or condition It, is the non-dual, the One-without-another.

4) **Vishuddham** (extremely pure) – A thing is said to be pure when there is nothing other than it, in it. It is non-dual and therefore it is extremely pure, that is, it has no *vasana*-dirt in it. (Here I prefer to add 'the body and the universe' also as dirt — impurity. D_n)

5) **Vijnana-ghanam** (homogenous mass of pure Knowledge). —Knowledge of things vary according to the things. <u>This is the knowledge because of which all other knowledge is possible.</u> Object-less knowledge, Absolute Knowledge.

6) **Niranjanam** (taint-less) Vaasanas are said to be the 'taints'. The Athma, the Self is beyond all vasanas, and so 'taintless'. (Here also I prefer to add 'body and the universe' as 'taint' ....with full support from the Upanishads. D_n)

7) **Pra-saantham** (supremely peaceful) – There are no agitations in it because the mind and the intellect have been transcended. It is not a temporary cessation of thoughts as in deep-sleep or in an unconscious state. It is the realization of That which is the Witness of the very condition of peacefulness—hence supremely peaceful.

Ch.1   What I am and what I am not   91

8) **Adi-antha-viheenam** *(beginningless and endless)* – Eternal, immutable, changeless, limitless. That which is not conditioned by birth and death. No beginning, no end, no modification.

9) **Akriyam (action-less)** – Because It is all-pervading, it cannot act; there is nothing other than it, for it to serve... no field for it to function in. Also where there are no *vaasanas*, there cannot be any desires, and hence there is no activity in the All-full Brahmam.

(I want to add: *akriyam* means simply *akriyam*—inactive, actionless. No need to labour with its purports and ramifications. Don't be afraid. Look at the Upanishads...without coloured glasses....without the prejudices and notions imposed on you so far. Brahmam (Awareness) is actionless, ie inactive, "nor does it activate". All the activity is on the part of Prakrti (nature). You are the Power of Perception...that is all, and nothing else....But eternal. Be happy and peaceful, with this understanding. 𝒟ₙ)

10) **Niranthara'ananda'rasa swaroopam** — Of the nature of Eternal Bliss. It is not just happiness. Bliss is Its state, because when we are in that plane we live beyond the tossing of the mind and intellect. ... ... The man in Samadhi rises above his mind and intellect.

11) **Nirastha'maaya'krtaha sarva bhedam** — Transcending all diversities created by maya. (Think of a glass-cube with a hibiscus flower under it. Though the cube looks red, in reality there is no colour in it. The coloured look is maya. In you—the eternal Awareness, there is no body. In the space, the pot exists. 𝒟ₙ)

12) **Nithyam**: — eternal. That is eternal which is not conditioned by time. It is that which is unconditioned by the three periods of time.

13) **Sukham:** — the essence of pleasure. – Not the pleasure-emotion as such, but that which illumines all sentiments of joy and emotions of pleasure in us.

14) **Nishkalam** — without any parts... unconditioned, limitless. (Having no component parts ...not made up of parts. It is one, single, homogenous, integral whole ...cannot be dismantled into parts. $Ɖ_n$)

15) **Aprameyam** – (immeasurable) .. incomparable ....that which cannot be reached or known through any means of measure (*prama*) such as comparison or argument. How can we ever compare or measure the All-pervading Infinite Reality? With what will we measure It? With what else will we compare It?

16) **aroopam** (formless) — An unconditioned limitless eternal thing (entity $Ɖ_n$) cannot have any form.

17) **avyaktham** (unmanifest) – that which cannot be sensed by the sense-organs, cannot be felt by the mind or comprehended by the intellect.

18) **an-aakhyam** (nameless) – Since there is no form there can be no name to indicate It. Only that which has form and qualities can have a name to distinguish it from similar things.

19) **avyayam** (immutable, irreducible). That which is eternal, beginningless and endless is immutable also.

20) ***jyothi-swayam*** (self-luminous, self-effulgent) To know that no other medium, no other light, is necessary. It is the light of Consciousness by which the whole world is illumined.

There are two more indicators immediately following (in verse 240):-

21. **aheyam** (that cannot be given up): After rejecting the five sheaths, we come to a substratum which can not at all be given up – the supreme Consciousness.

Ch.1   What I am and what I am not

22. *anupaadeyam* (that cannot be taken up) : That which is not with you can be taken up by you. This great Truth is your very own Self which is already there. How can you take it up, pick it up?

Add one more (to the 22) here:— 'sarva varjitha chinmaathram.' The light of awareness purged clean of everything else.

.. ज्ञात्रृज्ञेयज्ञानशून्यमनन्तं निर्विकल्पक
केवलाखण्डचिन्मात्रं परं तत्त्वं विदुर्बुधा ॥

jnathr'jneya'jnana-shunyam'
anantham nirvikalpaka
kevalaakhanda chinmaathram
param thathwam vidhur'budha.   (239)

.. अहेयमनुपादेयं मनोवाचामगोचरं ।
अप्रमेयमनाद्यन्तं ब्रह्म पूर्णमहं महः ॥

aheyam'anupaadeyam
manovaachaamagocharam
aprameyam'anaadyantham
brahma:purnam'aham'maha: (240)

I leave these two more verses here – (239 & 240 in addition to 237 & 238) for those who want to use them …. to recite, and soak in their meaning and purport.

To sum up: Brahmam is—

(237-238): Transcendental. Real, One-without-another, extremely pure, homogenous mass of pure Object-less knowledge, taint-less, beyond all activity, beginningless and endless, <u>inactive</u>, of the nature of Eternal Bliss, transcending all diversities created by maya, eternal, the essence of pleasure, without any parts, <u>supremely peaceful</u>, immeasurable, nameless, formless, un-manifest, immutable, irreducible, self-luminous (self-revealing), self-effulgent, something that cannot be given up, something that cannot be taken up. Pure light of awareness – purged clean of everything else.

All these twenty-three terms are indicative of the Athman, the Self, which is ever-present in each one of us. ... None of them, in fact, defines the Reality. But each suggests, and all of them, in their totality, directly point out the essential Self behind the mind and its agitations. (These 23 aspects are worth meditating upon...to lead you to Reality. $Ɖ_n$)237, 238

Have a close look at one word in this (verse-237): '*prashaantham*' ..supremely peaceful, serene. In a context of 'omnipotence and omniscience' is any serenity possible?

•• Entering the superior bodies like that of Vishnu, He (the Supreme Self) became the deities; and occupying the inferior bodies like that of men He worships the deities. (*Pancadasi* X.2)

Lamp in the theatre/ witness

The lamp in the dance hall uniformly reveals the patron, the audience and the danseuse (*Pancadasi* X.11).
Similar is the role of Awareness. If a nasty scene is staged, the light does not dim down in despair, or glow ferociously in rage, or extinguish itself in protest!

***   ***   ***

Whatever exists beyond the range of time—past, present or future—is also Om ...(meaning Brahmam ...the AWARENESS). (*Mandukya Upa*.1)

•• साक्षिभूते समे स्वच्छे निर्विकल्पे चिदात्मनि
निरर्थं प्रतिबिंबन्ति जगन्ति मुकुरे यथा ॥

> *saakshibhoothe samae swacche*
> *nirvikalpe chidaathmani*
> *nirarddham prathibimbanthi*
> *jaganthi mukure yadha.* (*Vasishtam*)

In the pure Awareness. that shows up the perceptibles from the standpoint of a witness... that sticks on to nothing ...that pervades everything and everywhere equally ...in which there is no *samkalpa* (thought-creations), the universe appears as the objects in a mirror ..without any use (to the mirror). (The Awareness has no gain or loss because of the universe.)

•• 'Awarenes is not dependent on body'. (with this brilliant clarification Sri Sankaracharya clears an apparent contradiction in Bh.Gita IX.4 ...*na aham theshvavasthitha* – I am not situated in the beings).
Brhadaranyakam says: Situated in/ residing in/ located in the elements, I govern them. (situated, residing in ...but not dependent. That is the position. I reside in the house; I can stay at the foot of a tree also ...not dependent on the house. Not that if the house is not there, I am also not there.)

•• आकाशवत् कल्पविदूरगोहं
आदित्यवत् भास्यविलक्षणोहं
आहार्यवन्नित्य विनिश्चलोहं
अंभोधिवत् पारविवर्जितोहं ॥
aakaasavath kalpavidoorakohum
aadithyavath bhaasya'vilakshano'hum
aahaaryavannithya vinischalohum
ambhodhivath paaravivarjithohum.
           (*Kuntikopanishad 20, 21*)

I am expansive like the sky, which cannot be covered by a travel of a *kalpa* (kalpa=432 crore –ie, 4320 million man-years). ...I am different from the things I see, as the sun is different from all that it reveals by its light ....I am immovable like a mountain ...I am boundless like the ocean.

· · भिद्यते चेज्जडोभेद-
   श्चिदेका सर्वदा खलु ॥

bhidyathe chijjadobheda:
schidekaa sarvada khalu (Rudrahrdaya Upanishad-45)

Awareness is always One (only) ..and the division is brought about by the *jadam* / matter / bodies, seemingly.

· · खटं जलं तत्गतमर्कबिम्बं
   विहाय सर्वं विनिरीक्ष्यतेर्क:
   तटस्थ एतत् त्रितयावभासक:
   स्वयं प्रकाशो विदुषा यथा तथा ॥

khadam jalam thath'gatham'arkabimbam
vihaaya'sarvam vinireekshyatherka
thadastha ethath'thrithayaavabhaasaka
swayam'prakaaso vidushaa yadha thatha.

(Vivekachoodamani 219)

'The wise man forgets the pot, the water, and the reflected sun in it, and apprehends the real sun that reveals these three and is independent of them.' Dont confuse it here; the rays reflecting from the water are original only ...no duplicate, nothing alien ..it is the sun's own rays. Think. What is ticking, pulsating, feeling, existing, revelling in you as your awareness, is the cosmic consciousness, and not a 'bit' of it. Space is One; no divisions in it. Space cannot be divided. Awareness is undivided.

Ch.1 What I am and what I am not

.. अखण्टबोधोहमशेषसाक्षि
निरीश्वरोहं निरहं च निर्ममः (*Kuntikopanishad*)

akhanda'bodhoham'ashesha'saakshi
nireeswarohm niraham cha nirmama

Nireeswarohum = in me the Awareness, there is no God. For me the Awareness, there is no God. I am the un-fragmented *bodham* ...I see everything, witness everything. To me there is no God, no 'I', no 'mine'

***　　***　　***

* Air is one.
* Water is one.
* Space is one.
* Awareness is one ... in quality and nature, characteristics and content, in all beings.

Take a soap ...five-kilometer long. A spec of it, taken from anywhere in this length, will be the same in quality and contents. Gold is gold, taken from anywhere.

Similarly, awareness is awareness ...in the Trinity (of super gods....Brahma-Vishnu-Mahesa) ...in human beings ....down to the lowliest worms that creep in the gutters. Awareness is One ...only.

.. अत्याप्यावृतिनाशेनविभातिब्रह्मसर्गयोः
भेदस्तयोर्विकारस्यात् सर्गे न ब्रह्मणि क्वचित् ॥

athyaapyavrthi'naasena
vibhaathibrahmasargayo
bhedasthayor'vikaarasyath
sarge'na brahmani quachith (*Drg-drsya vivekam 19*)

As the veil clears, the difference between *Brahmam* and *prapancham* is seen clearly. (*Brahmam* and *prapancham* are seen to be different). In these two, the one that is in flux (changing) ...is the *prapancham*, and there is no change ever in Brahmam. (*Swami Aagamananda's elucidation*).

•• अवच्छेदः कल्पितः स्याद्यवच्छेद्यं तु वास्तवं
तस्मिन जीवत्वमारोपाद् ब्रह्मत्वम् तु स्वभावतः

avaccheda:kalpitha:
syadyavachedyamthu'vaasthavam
thasmin jivatwam'aaropaath
brahmatwam thu swabhavatha.

(*Drg-drsya vivekam 33*)

•• Divisions (limiting-s /containments) are imaginary ...the un-fragmented original is the reality. Brahmam it is, in reality ..*jivathwam* is a super-imposition.

Dr S.Radhakrishnan:

"There is no doubt that the Swetaswathara (Upanishad) admits the reality of a supreme Brahman above the changing world ...beyond space, imperturbable, free from change, becoming, and causality".

***   ***   ***

•• *Antharyami Brahmanam:* created – entered – became a creature .. and It rules the inner world of elements and their might!? (*Vakya vrthi* / Chinmaya p73) (I think this is a confusion ... has to be pondered over / investigated.)

"It is in this eternal reality—Bodham, Gargi, that the space exists like woof and weft." (*Brhadaranyakam* 3.8.11) (Q in p254 *Bhashya pradeepam*). This is in a way a figure of speech ...a way of expression. But this is a great pointer.

Ch.1   What I am and what I am not

aja'achala'mavasthutwam
vijnanam shantham advayam. (*Mandukya Karika* 4-45)

* Unborn, un-moving, non-substance   ...knowledge/consciousness, serene, non-dual.

* Clean crystallized Consciousness (*vimala bodha ghanam namaami*).

* saturated bliss awareness *(saandra'ananda-'avabodham) (Naaraayaneeyam).*

* Athman is realized as the unceasing and essential awareness of the one underlying Consciousnesss of the whole universe. (Ma.7) also Ke.1.3 etc. etc...p103 of *Sruti gita*.)

* Men of Realisation speak of that (Brahmam) (which is) Imperishable ...by negating all   possible attributes. It is neither gross nor subtle, neither short nor long, neither hard nor soft, neither visible nor invisible, neither air nor sky. It is unattached, beyond taste and odour, beyond names and forms, beyond the range of thought and word ....(p.101 *Sruti gita*)..verse 29

* Beyond light and speed (vital force), indescribable, immeasurable. ...the same internally and externally, beyond hunger and food. .. He who performs sacrifices or undergoes austerities or pursues spiritual practices, even if it be for a thousand years, if they do not culminate in realization of the Imperishable, all his efforts are wasted. He who departs from this world without realizing this Imperishable is very unfortunate   ...is to be pitied. He who departs from this world after realizing this Imperishable is to be adored   ... he is a knower of

Brahmam. This Imperishable is the unseen Seer, the unheard Hearer, the unknown Knower, the incognizable Cognizer. There is no other seer, no other hearer, no other cognizer than this Imperishable. By this Imperishable is the unmanifest ether /space pervaded. (*Br.*3.8.7-11)

* The supreme Brahmam which is realized by the wise sages is imperceptible, ungraspable, devoid of eyes and ears, hands and feet, eternal, all-pervading, omnipresent, and non-diminishing. (*Mundaka Upa.* 1.1.6)

* Brahmam is One without another; there is no experience of duality or differentiation in It. The one *athman* dwelling in different bodies appears differently, like the moon reflects differently in various water-vessels. (Bh.11. 18.32; Mu.3.1.2; Ch.6.2.1-2; Bh.Gita 2.16) (*Adhyathma Upa.* 63)

* "Prathi-bodha viditham" – that which shines in each individual intellect as the power of perception ...faculty of perception –is Brahmam. (*Kenopanishad* ..Kailas.upa-12 p.9).

* 'The eyes cannot see That; but That sees the eyes' (*Kenopanishad*)

Awareness is in the physical body (seemingly). It is in the astral body—now and after death. And beyond the astral body? Yes. Awareness is the seer of the physical body and astral body. The seer is different from the 'seen'.

In awareness the body exists; not awareness in the body. Space exists not in the pot; pot exists in space....(Firm it up).

Impersonal intelligence? Yes.

Ch.1 What I am and what I am not

· · Take a drop of water from the ocean, from a lake, pond, well, pipeline, from a glass ….all the drops are the same ..alike…, forgetting their identity with the sources. (Poojappura Gopala Swamy) *Arul Mozhikal* p.508.

* *brahmani jeevathwam*
  bhranthya pasyathi na swatha. (*Proudhanubhuthi* 59).

'Seeing jivathwam in Brahmam is an illusion …not real.' Hear it. Try to understand it. Take the case of sunlight. The earth and its objects are really not in the sunlight …not a content of the sunlight …like salt is a content of sea-water. The sunlight does not carry in it the earth and its objects.

* '*bhuthabhr'nnacha bhuthastho*' says *Bhagavath Gita*. Meaning, Awareness is not seated, situated, based, or founded on elements (ie. not founded on the things made up of elements.) And It has no affinity (*mamatha*) to the world.

* Just as liquidity in liquids, motion in wind and emptiness in space, even so is omnipresence in the Self.

  ** तदेकोवशिष्ट शिव केवलोहं

  thadekovashishta siva kevalohum

  .. the one that then remains.. ..auspious, alone .. I am that.

  ** ब्रह्मतत्वमसि भावयात्मनि

  brahma'thathwamasi bhaavayaathmani

  …in 'I am Brahmam' attitude…

  ** परब्रह्मनित्यं तदेवाहमस्मि

  parabrahma'nithyam thadevaahamasmi

.. Para'brahmam ..eternal – I am that ...itself.

** सद्वस्तु जन्मक्षयशून्यमेकं

sad'vasthu janma'kshayasunyam'ekam

.. the reality ..one only, birthless, immutable.

** सन्नामरूपविवर्जितं

san'naamaroopa'vivarjitham.

.. reality .. is nameless, formless.

** स्वप्रकाशापरोक्षत्वमयमित्युक्तितो मतं

swaprakaasha'aparokshatwam
ayamithyukthithomatham

.. self-shining, directly-experienced.

(A few above are from *Sukarahasyopanishad*).

.. य एष देवः कथितो नैष दूरेऽवतिष्ठते ।
शरीरे संस्थितो नित्यं चिन्मात्रमिति विश्रुतः ॥ 14 ॥ (3-7-2)

sa yesha deva kathitho
naisha doore avathishtate
sareere samsthitho nithyam
chinmaathramiti vishrutha

1676. This God described (as one whose knowledge gives liberation), does not live far away. He is ever present in the body and is well-known as mere Consciousness. (*Vaasishta Darsanam* - SAMATA BOOKS)

This much is more than enough to give anyone a clear idea as to — 'WHAT I AM and WHAT I AM NOT'.

2

THE PATH

* The understanding
* The impediments
* The attitude (*bhaavam*) .. sadhana.

The understanding:

…………….धनं मेरुतुल्यं-
मनश्चेन्न लग्नं गुरोरंघ्रिपद्मे
ततकिं ततकिं ततकिं ततकिं ॥

……………..... dhanam meru'thulyam
manaschenna'lagnam guroramghri'padmae
thatha'kim thatha'kim thatha'kim thatha'kim?
                                                                    (Guru-ashtakam)

Even if you have enormous wealth like Meru mountain, if your mind is not tuned towards the guru, what's the use ..what's the use …what's the use!?

- • The one and only worthy look out   ..is liberation.

- • One who has not come to grips with his reality, will have to pass through countless births and deaths—till he sees the light.

- The birth and death cycle is likely to go on endlessly ... and for this malady, proper thought alone is the right remedy (Vasistam):

    (Deerkha samsara rogasya Vicharo hi mahoushadham)

- राज्यं सुता कलत्राणि
  शरीरानि सुखानि च:
  संसक्तस्यापि नष्टानि
  तव जन्मनि जन्मनि: ॥

    rajyam suthaa kalathraani shareeraani sukhaani cha samsakthasyaapi nashtaani thava janmani janmani

    (Asht.Gita X.6)

    Kingdoms, sons, wives, bodies and pleasures have been lost to you life after life even though you were attached to them.

- दीर्खस्वप्नमिमं विद्धि दीर्खं वा चित्तविभ्रमं
  दीर्खं वाऽपि मनोराज्यं संसारं रघुनन्दन: ॥

    deerkha swapnamimam viddhi
    deerkham va chittha vibhramam
    deerkham vaapi manorajyam
    samsaaram Raghunandana. (Vasishtam)

    Rama (*Raghu nandana*), look upon this worldly existence as a long dream, or hallucination, or a day-dream.

- Liberation is not a commodity stocked by any god ..to be given out on the asking. In Bhaagavatham, when Uddhava begged for liberation, Bhagavan Krishna did not pass on liberation saying "Here you are, take it". Bhagawan was not a stockist of liberation. If he had it in stock, he would have gladly given it to his beloved, trusted, friend and bystander throughout life. Bhagawan, instead, gives him a lecture (class) on Brahma vidya ...tells him about the Reality ...knowledge about the Self ... and asks him to "go about with this Realisation".

And no Bhagawan can give you liberation; you are already ..always liberated. Only you have to understand it.

Fish story:

A Guru was tired of convincing a disciple of his Reality, and he directed him to go to Har ki Pauri (a famous ghat on the river Ganga at Rishikesh) where a fish would appear and clear his doubt. The fish appeared, and the question was presented to it: "Tell me if you know where God is".

Fish: "Give me some water ...I am thirsty, I cannot speak."

Disciple: "Why? You are in the water ...all around is water ...water above, water below. You need only to tilt a little so that water enters in you."

Fish: "That is my answer to your question also. You are what you are searching for. Only a shift in understanding is what you need."

The grip

* You are holding the rope that drags you. Release your grip, you are free ..not dragged.
* A female horse earns its death by conceiving. (jnana vasistam Mal 46) Female horse—if it becomes pregnant –dies as a consequence at delivery (?)
* One jumps into a flooded river ...and catches a blanket-like thing floating...and he finds himself in the grip of a bear!

* If the eyes fall on something good, the **mind** wants to grab it...to possess.

* "A monkey does not give any peace to a big tree. The mind does not give peace to the body". (*Yogavaasishtham*)

en-snaring of (1) the parrot (2) the monkey

1. A trap is set with an attractive food for the parrot. The parrot tries to eat... and the trap works ...the parrot hangs on a rod upside down, gripping the rod. If it releases its grip, it will be free ...but it doesn't do that. It thinks that the rod is gripping its legs. It even forgets that it has wings to fly and that there is no fear of falling even If it releases the grip.

2. A heavy coconut (or a heavy pot with foodstuff inside) with narrow mouth is kept as a trap. The monkey puts its hand inside, grabs the stuff inside, and tries to withdraw the hand, but it does not come out. He thinks the pot is holding him. ..he is caught.

In all these instances, it is you who fail to release your grip; and you think the world has you in its grip.

*** *** ***

•• *maaya thath'kaarya dehaadi mama nasthyeva sarvadaa swa'prakasaika roopohum ahamevaaham'avyaya.*

Maya, and the body and all resultant from that, are not mine at all at any time; <u>the light of self-awareness alone</u> is my form. (*Brahmajnavali maala-9*)

Nothing related to the body and mind should cause a concern to the Awareness. The distinctions .. multiplicity .. in the material field does not tarnish the Awareness.

•• रज्जुसर्पवदात्मानं जीवंज्ञात्वा भयंवहेत् ।
नाहं जीवः परात्मेति ज्ञातञ्चेन्निर्भयो भवेत् ॥

*rajju-sarpavad atmanam
jeevam jnatwa bhayam vaheth
na-aham-jiva paraatmeti
jnatamche nir-bhayo bhavet.*   (Atma Bodham 26)

The soul, regarding itself as a jiva, is overcome by fear, just like someone who regards a rope as a snake. The soul regains fearlessness by realizing that It is not a jiva but the Supreme Soul. He who thinks of God as separate from himself is overcome by fear of God. But Atman never in reality becomes a jiva; hence one's fear is groundless and due to ignorance.

•• Knowledge is the direct cause of Liberation ...just as fire is the direct cause of cooking. Light alone can dispel darkness.

(पाकस्य वह्निवत्ज्ञानं
विना मोक्षो न सिध्यति ॥)   (Atma Bodham 2)

*(paakasya vahnivat jnanam
'vinaa moksho na siddhyati).*

•• ज्ञानेनैव हि संसार- विनाशोःनैवकर्मणः
jnanenaiva hi samsaara vinaso naiva karmnaa

Samsara—recurrence of births and deaths—ends only with Knowledge (*Jnanam*); not by actions (*karma*).

•• Moon, electric bulb ...all these provide light; but for the lotus to bloom sun-light is needed.

MULLA – hanging

Mulla Naziruddin one day declared that he was going to suicide. He tied a rope to the ceiling fan and closed the door. Neighbors heard his shouts, and gathered around the room and shouted at him not to hang. His wife said: "If you want to hang, hang quick; I have to go to prepare lunch." The neighbors wondered how she could be so heartless. She asked them: "Has anybody ever died, hanging on the waist?" Mulla had the other end tied to his waist!

(If you want a result, do something that will bring about that result; and not just anything.)

•• अविरोधितया कर्म नाविद्यां विनिवर्तयेत्
विद्याविद्यां निहन्त्येव तेजस्तिमिरसङ्गवत ॥ *(Atmabodham 3)*

avirodhithaya karma na'avidyaam vinivarthayeth
vidya'avidyaam nihanthyeva tejas'thimira'sangavath

Action cannot destroy ignorance, for it is not in conflict with ignorance. Knowledge alone destroys ignorance, as light dispels darkness.

•• अज्ञानमूलोऽयमनात्मबन्धो
नैसर्गिको नादिरनन्त ईरितः
जन्माप्ययव्याधि जरादिदुःख-
प्रवाहपातं जनयत्यमुष्य ॥ *(Vivekachudamani 146)*

ajnanamooloyamanaathma'bandho
naisargiko'naadiranantha eeritha
janmaapyaya'vyaadhi'jaraadi dukkha
pravaahapaatham janayathyamushya

The bondage caused by the not-Self springs from ignorance, is self-caused and is described as beginning-less and endless. It subjects one to the long train of miseries such as birth, diseases, disabilities and death.

How sorrow is the result of the misconception that the not-Self (anathman) is the Self (Athman), is explained in this verse (v.c.146). Non-apprehension of the post creates the illusion that there is a ghost. Non-apprehension of Reality alone creates the mis-apprehension that 'I am this body'.

How and where did this misunderstanding of the *anatman* to be *atman* arise? When did the 'Absolute' become the 'relative'? Such questions in terms of time and space often arise in our minds.

'Ignorance is said to be self-caused. It is not caused by any other cause. It is the nature of the cave to have darkness. Darkness in the cave is created by the cave. If the cave was not there, there would be no darkness. Similarly when the Self is not known, there is darkness in the beginning-less and endless, ...meaning, it is essentially beyond 'time'. As long as the concept of time is there, the samsaar experiences will be there, because time is the medium in which samsaar is perceived. The moment time is transcended , samsaar also must end. 'Beginning' and 'end' are meaningful only in the medium of time.

'The sorrows of samsaar arising out of this identification with the *anathman*, unavoidably manifest as the agonies of birth, the pains of growth, the discomforts of decay, the fears of old age, the pangs of disease and the tragedies of death. The cause for all these is ignorance and the consequent identification with the not-Self.

'If all the sorrows are to be removed, the cause for them has to be removed. Ignorance can be removed only by the first-hand experience of the Infinite Reality' (Swami Chinmayananda).

* Liberation is not a product of karma.
* It is not produced by meditation either. (p.235 *Ve.pra.*)
* Stillness of mind does not bring about liberation. (p.199 *Ve.pra.*)

.. देहस्य मोक्षो नो मोक्षो न दण्डस्य न कमण्डलो:
अविद्याहृदयग्रन्थिमोक्षो मोक्षो यथस्तथ:॥

*dehasya moksho no-moksho
na dandasya na kamandalo
avidya'hrdaya'grandhi'moksho
moksho yadha'sthatha* (Vivekachudamani 559)

Giving up of the body or the staff or the water-bowl is not liberation; getting rid of the heart-knots constituted of ignorance is liberation.

Liberation is a result of Self Knowledge ... by the clarity of vision provided by Self- Knowledge. (p.235 *Ve.pra.*)

.. आदौ नित्यानित्यवस्तुविवेक: परिगण्यते ।
इहामुत्रफलभोगविरागस्तदनन्तरम् ।

*aadau nithya'anithya vasthu viveka: pariganyathe
iha'amuthra phala bhoga viraagas'thathanantharam.*

(Vivekachudamani 19)

Discrimination between the Real and the unreal is the first requisite. Aversion to enjoyment of pleasures here and hereafter, comes next.

The direct means to release is the path of knowledge (*Jnanam*). As moksha is the very nature of the Self, it is not to be brought about by actions...work-outs.

.. अहंब्रह्मेति विज्ञानात्
कल्पकोटिशतार्जितं
संचितं विलयं याति:
प्रबोधात् स्वप्नकर्मवत् ॥

*aham'brahmethi vijnaanaath
kalpakoti'shathaarjitham
sanchitham vilayam yaathi
prabodhaath swapna'karmavath.*

With the knowledge 'I am Brahmam', the karma accumulated over millions of *kalpas* (epochs) are nullified ...like the acts done in a dream are nullified on waking up.

As what stands in the way of realization is ignorance (misunderstanding), what can remove the ignorance is knowledge only.

The path of knowledge consists of --

* sravana (hearing....study)
* manana (reflection)
* nididhyasana (meditation or rather a continuance in the attitude)

The ascertainment of the true significance of the non-difference of the individual soul from the supreme Self with the aid of the *maha vakyas* such as "That Thou art" (*thath thwam asi*) is sravana.

To understand through reasonig that the meaning of this teaching has every possibility of validity is manana.

And by sravana and manana the mind has gained conviction, then it dwells constantly on the non-dual Self...and this is nididhyasana.

•• तमेवैकं जानथ आत्मानं
अन्या वाचो विमुंचथ अमृतस्यैष सेतुः *(Mundakopanishad)*
thamaivekam jaanatha aathmaanam
annya vaacho vimunchadha amrthasyaisha sethu:

"Realize the supreme One who is your own *Athman*; be absorbed in Him; giving up all other vain pursuits. This is the bridge to *moksha* or absolute Freedom".

•• एवं निरन्तराभ्यस्ता ब्रह्मैवास्मीति वासना
हरत्यविद्याविक्षेपान् रोगानिव रसायनम् ॥ *(Atma Bodham 37)*

evam niranthara'abhyastha
brahmaiva'asmi'ithi,vaasana
harathi'avidya'vikshepaan
rogaaniva rasaayanam.

The impression of "I am Brahmam" thus created by uninterrupted reflection, dispels ignorance and its distractions, just as a medicine dispels a disease.

•• When names and forms are eliminated, what remains is the imperishable Brahmam or Self, as when a pot is broken the space remains. (Pancadasi III.30)

•• यथाकाशो हृषीकेशो नानोपाधिगतो विभुः
तद्भेदाद् भिन्नवद्भाति तन्नाशे केवलो भवेत् ॥

yatha'aakaaso hrshikesho
naanopaadhi'gatho vibhu
tath'bhedaath'bhinnavath bhaathi
tan'naase kevalo bhaveth. *(Atma Bodham 9)*

The all-pervading space appears to be diverse on account of its association with various *upadhis* (limiting factors ....pot, room, cave etc) which are different from one another, and

Ch.2 The Path

becomes one on the dissolution of the upadhies. So too, the omnipresent Lord appears to be diverse on account of His association with various upadhi-s and appears one on dissolution of these upadhi-s.

* "Become conscious of consciousness ...Observe the observer" says Osho Shailendra-ji.

* "With your seemingly limited consciousness grasp the cosmic consciousness in you" says Swami Brahmasuthan. That is, the pot-space should realize itself to be the vast endless space.

* I am not a human, nor a god nor a demon.

(नाहं मनुष्यो न च देव यक्षो *(Hasthamalaka sthothram)*
na'aham manushyo na cha deva yaksho:)

.. अनित्यं सर्वमेवेदं
तापत्रितय दूषितं
असारं निन्दितं हेय-
मिति निश्चित्य शाम्यतिः॥

*anithyam sarvamevedam
thaapa'thrithaya'dushitham
asaaram ninditham heya-
mithi nischithtya shaamyathi.*   (Asht.gita IX.3)

By realising that all is verily vitiated by the three-pronged[+] misery, is transient, unsubstantial and contemptible ...and should be rejected, the wise become calm.

.. यद्वन् मृदि खटभ्रान्ति
शुक्तौ वा रजतस्थितिः

+ *aadhi bhauthikam, aadhi-atmikam, aadhi- daivikam.*

तद्वद् ब्रह्मणि जीवत्वं
भ्रान्त्या पश्यति न स्वतः ॥ *(Aparokshaanubhoothi 59)*

yadvan'mrdi khada'bhraanthi
shukthau va rajatha'sthithi
thadvad'brahmani jivathwam
bhraanthya pasyathi na swatha.

Just as we see pot in clay, silver in mussel, we see jeevathvam in Brahmam, whereas in reality there is no Jiva-hood (*Jeevathvam*) in Brahmam.

•• न नभो घटयोगेन
सुरागन्धेन लिप्यते
तथात्मोपाधियोगेन
तद्धर्मैर् नैवलिप्यते ॥ *(Vivekachoodamani 451.)*

na'nabho khata'yogena
suraa'gandhena lipyathe
thatha'athmopaadhi yogena
thattharmair'naiva lipyathe.

The space in the bottle (lit. urn) is not affected by the smell of the liquor in the bottle. So too, the athman is not affected by the properties of the *upaadhi*.

     ***   ***   ***

•• Someone to NM: "I imagine the dying process to be painful and ugly".

NM: "It need not be so. It may be beautiful and peaceful. Once you know that death happens to the body and not to you, you just watch your body falling off like a discarded garment."

•• The body that died never knew that it lived. Think.

•• वस्तुस्थित्यनुरोधतःस्त्वहमहो
कश्चित् पदार्थो न चः
पेप्येवं कोपि विभाति संसददृशी
वाङ्मानसागोचरः
निष्पापोस्म्यभयोस्म्यहं विगत-
दुःखाशंकाकलङ्कोस्म्यहं
संशान्तानुपमानशीतलमहः
प्रौढप्रकाशोस्म्यहम् ॥ *(Proudhanubhooti 14)*

vasthu'sthithy'anurodhatha:sthvaham'aho
kaschit'padartho na cha
pepyevam ko'pi vibhaathi samsadadrsi
vang'manasaagochara:
nish'paapo'smy'abhayo'smyaham vigatha-
dukkhaasankaa'kalamkosmyaham
samshaantha'anupamaana'sheethala maha:
proudha prakasosmyaham.

If the situation is analysed ...viewed properly, I am not a substance (matter / material). Yet something shines forth, always experiencing its existence ...beyond the reach of mind and words. That experiencer of existetnce is me, ...untouched by karma ...absolutely fearless ... without miseries and anxieties. I am in saturated peace ...shining with an incomparable, cool, brilliance.

Dasa purusha siddhantham – story of ten men

Ten men were travelling in a group. There was a flooded river on the way, and they swam across against a strong current. Reaching the other bank one man counted their number, to ascertain whether anyone is lost. Only nine were found. Another counted; again only nine were found. All of them counted; only nine were found. They started crying for the lost. A passer-by enquired what the matter was; and they explained. The new-comer counted; there were ten. And they were happy that no-one was lost. (Everyone counted all others, except him..and that was the loss. The Seer was not seen.)

Swakantabharanam:

आत्मा तु सततं प्राप्तो अप्यप्राप्तवदविद्यया
तन्नाशे प्राप्तवद्भाति स्वकण्ठभरणं तथा ॥

aathmaa'thu sathatham praaptho
'apyapraapthavadavidyayaa
thannaase praapthavad'bhaati
swakantaabharanam thatha. (Atma Bodham 44)

Athman is an ever-present Reality; yet, because of ignorance it is not realized. On the passing off of ignorance, Athman is revealed. The necklace is round the neck already, but people search for it all over the place ...like that. (*swa'kandtha'aabharanam*=ornament on the neck)

One night when the power went off (I was holding my torch already), I started searching for the torch—in the light of the same torch! After a moment only I realized that it was the same torch I was looking for.

Another day, while I was riding a bike, I heard a big noise—of something falling—on the road close to the bike. I thought it might be the helmet I used to hang on the handle— the helmet I did not find on the handle. Then I realized that the helmet I was actually wearing.

The glasses on the eyes—you sometimes search for. Similarly, *swa kanta'abharanam* also sometimes we search for.

You are looking out for something which is not different from you ..nothing other than you.

I want to remind you of the story of the old woman who was searching for her needle under the street light. The needle she lost in the house. But there was no light in the house; so she was searching where there was light—outside.

To find Padmanabha Swamy temple, you must look up in Thiru'ananthapuram; if you search and search in Bangalore, you are not going to find it.

Mulla's camel on the attic ?

One afternoon when a king was sleeping, he was disturbed by some footsteps on the attic. When the king asked who it was, Mulla said from the attic "I am looking for my camel, Sir."

King: "Camel on my attic ?"

Mulla : "If camel cannot be found on the attic, then you are also not going to find God in the direction you are searching."

The king got his message. And in course of time the king became a famous Sufi saint.

"Use your own *bodham* to become aware of the *Param Bodham*." (Swami Brahmasuthan—my Guru in my childhood)

*   Become aware of your Aawareness. See the seer.
*   A paradigm shift, that is all.
*   A split-second will do for that.

Someone asked Nisarga Dutta: "How long will it take, for Realisation". His answer was: "It can happen in a moment...in this moment; or it may not happen for a thousand years."

"A very fleeting second alone...is needed for the knowledge to dawn...and to remove the misconception" (*Bhagavatham*)

> (*Lolamaam kshaname ventoo jnanam ullil kadakkanum Maaliyattum Maya-yake manjupokaanum.....*) Mal.

•• Samsaar = the plane of existence where everything comes and goes. Everything appears and disappears is called 'samsaara.' (Swami Chinmayananda in *Vakyavrthi* p97)

•• "Man is subject to birth; God is unborn. Man is limited; God is unlimited. Man is a perishable being; God is imperishable. Man is mortal; God is immortal. Remove all these qualities. <u>Then what remains is Pure Consciousness.</u>

"Wise men having understood the One Essence both in Man and the God say that the essential core in God is the essential core in man. Thus hundreds of great declarations indicate and glorify the great oneness of Brahmam and Atman.

"When I look out through the body I become conscious of the objects. When I transcend the body the world of objects is eliminated. When I transcend the mind the emotions are eliminated. And when I go beyond the intellect, the thought-disturbances are also eliminated. What remains in me at that time is only Consciousness. With that consciousness when I look out—without the body, the mind and the intellect – I see in the world no objects, no emotions and no thoughts, because they were all interpretations of my BMI only. When the equipments are removed, the objects I perceive through the equipments are also removed. At that time what I see is nothing but Consciousness within and without. In this sense the scriptures say that the **Atman**, the Self in you is **Brahmam**, the Reality behind the whole universe." (Swami Chinmayananda...in his commentary to *Vivekachudamani* 249)

•• The pot-space is pot-space when viewed in relation to the pot. Otherwise it is just space.

"…..the concern ceases, and physical life becomes effortless below the level of attention. Then, even in the body you are not born. To be embodied or bodiless is the same to you. You reach a point where nothing can happen to you. Without body, you cannot be killed. Without possessions, you cannot be robbed. Without mind, you cannot be tempted. There is no point where a desire or fear can hook on. As long as no change can happen to you – (and you are eternal – $Ɖn$) - what else matters? (Nisargadatta :p469 I AM THAT)

"This reality is so concrete, so actual, so much more tangible than mind and matter, that compared to it even diamond is soft like butter. This overwhelming actuality makes the world dream-like, misty, irrelevant." (Nisargadatta Maharaj) p484 I AM THAT

Qn to NM: Well. God will look after me. I can leave everything to Him.

NM: Even faith in God is only a stage on the way. Ultimately you abandon all, for you come to something so simple that there are no words to express it.

Listened to that? Something so simple. People are interested in complicating. Swami Brahmasuthan also used to lament….that people are interested in complicating the simple!

It is simple...to be what you are. No effort is necessary. To blink the eyes, an effort is needed. To know what you are, no effort. For a king, to be a king....no effort is needed. He is king, already. Only he should not get down to the street corner with a begging bowl.

•• Qn: to NM: I am not all-pervading and eternal. I am only here and now.

NM "Go beyond 'I-am-the-body' idea, and you will find that space and time are in you, and not you in space and time. Once you have understood this, the main obstacle to realization is removed." (Nisargadutta Maharaj)

•• "Although in almost all the Upanishad-s there is a different theory of Creation expounded by the different Rsi-s, any deep student of the Upanishads can very easily detect that the ultimate anxiety of the scriptures is to lead the student to a State beyond the mind and intellect, ...to recognize and experience therein the Infinitude and Glory of the Self, pervading everywhere, Immutable, Eternal and Tranquil, in all Its Aloneness." Swami Chinmayananda, (p.181/450 *Asht.Gita*)

"To renounce or to accept there must be the still lingering shades of one's individualized ego. Where the ego has completely ended, there is none in the individual either to accept anything or to renounce anything, and that is the State of Supreme Bliss" (words of Swami Chinmayananda). Janaka says in Ashtavakra Gita: 'Therefore , giving up the ideas of renunciation and acceptance, I live in perfect peace.'

Kaivalyam: Aloneness of the Self

"The One Blissful Self envelopes all. In that state of bliss, one who has awakened to the Pure Consciousness finds that all his desires have ended, all goals have been reached, even his anxiety for liberation ceases. His mind rolls away, and all its agitations suddenly calm into an Infinite dynamic Peace, spontaneously. The body and the senses halt in their functions. Far beyond all traces of identification with the body mind and intellect, calm and serene, the seeker now comes to experience the *Kaivalya* state of the Self." Swami Chinmayananda (P239.240. *Asht.gita*)

<u>When you isolate your Awareness (from its mix-up) and experience the Pure Awareness you will know</u> that It is Absolute Existence, Awareness and Bliss – all rolled into one. $\mathcal{D}_n$

So long as you mistake yourself to be the body, you will have desires and fears ... pains and pleasures. With *Brahma'athma aikya jnanam* ...while the knowledge "Brahmam and I are not two" dawns ... with the paradigm shift in understanding, you lose 'I-am-the-body' idea. To think that the earlier status .. and the attendant fear desire pain pleasure and all will still continue is groundless. If a wealthy householder, proud of his enormous wealth, is looted completely, he grieves over it...he feels it very deeply. But when he turns into a mendicant...completely penniless, with absolutely nothing of any value in his possession, he has no fear of theft. Theft means nothing to him.

Prajapathi makes this clear to Indra in Swetaswathara Upanishad. The bodiless eternal Reality is not touched by pains and pleasures.

(अशरीरं सन्तं न प्रियाप्रिये स्पृशतः)

asareeram .... santham..na priya'apriye sprshatha

Just as a lotus leaf is not wetted by water, the knower of Brahman is not affected by the good or bad effects of actions (as he has neither ego nor does he feel any agentship) (Ch 4.14.3). This is the glory and greatness of the knower of Brahmam that he is neither proud of (lit. grows by) his good deeds nor regrets (lit. becomes little) his bad deeds. He (is established in the Athman and hence) is never affected by the good or bad effects of actions (which he apparently performs in accordance with the nature of circumstances). (Br 4.4.23).

If one realizes now (while living), he fulfils his life; otherwise great loss and damnation will be his lot. Knowing this, the wise realize the One discarding the many and thus attain immortality – they are not born again. (Ke. 2.5, Isa. 3, Tai. 2.1, 2.5, Br. 4.4.14, Bh.11.21.22

- इन्द्रियेभ्यःपरह्यर्थाः अर्थेश्च परं मनः
  मनसस्तु परं बुद्धिरः बुद्धेरात्मा महान परः॥
  indriyebhya para'hyardha
  ardhescha'param manah
  manasasthu param buddhir
  buddher'aathma mahan parah. (Kadho. III.10)

  Higher than the senses are the sense-objects,
  Higher than the objects is the mind;
  And higher than the mind is the intellect
  Higher than the intellect is the Great Self *(Athma)*.

- महतःपरमव्यक्तः मव्यक्तात्पुरुषःपरः
  पुरुषान्नपरं किञ्चित् स काष्ठा स परागतिः ॥
  mahata'param avyaktha
  avyakthath purusha para

purushanna'param kinchith
sa kaashta sa para'gati.   (Kadhopanishad III.11)

Higher than the Great (Mahat) is the Unmanifest
(avyaktha),
Higher than the avyaktha is the Purusha .
Higher than Purusha there is nothing at all.
That is the goal, that is the highest course.

.. एष सर्वेषु भूतेषुः गूठो आत्मा नः प्रकाशत
दृश्यतेत्वग्रया बुद्ध्या सूक्ष्मया सूक्ष्मदर्शिभिः॥

esha sarveshu bhootheshu
goodho'aathma'na-prakasatha
drsyathe twagraya'buddhya
sukshmayaa sukshma'darshibhi
    (Kadhopanishad III.12)

Though it is in all beings, the Soul (Athma...Self) shines forth not. It is seen only by the subtle seers with refined intellects.

.. अणोरणीयान् महतोमहीयान्
आत्मास्य जन्तोर्निहितो गुहायां
तमक्रतुः पश्यति वीतशोको..

anoraneeyaan mahaatho'maheeyaan
aathmaasya janthor nihitho guhaayaam
thamakrathu pasyathi veethashoko.
    (Kadhopanishad II.20)

Smaller than an atom and larger than the greatest is the Athma located in every creature. One without an active will (one whose will has subsided) (*a-krathu*) beholds It and becomes free from sorrow.

·· Purity is prescribed by many paths...cleanliness of the body...externally by water, and cleanliness in thoughts and actions. The exhortation of Vedantha is to wash out everything in you that is other than you....the body, mind, intellect, the whole equipment—upadhi (container / limiting adjunct).

dehatthinnu malaadikal maalinyam
deham maalinyam dehikkathupole.[+] *(Malayalam)*

Filth is a contaminant to the body;

Body is the contaminant to the soul (*bodham*).

Early morning bath, fasting and such punishments to the body ... are for kindergartens in spirituality.

(praatha snano'pavaasadi
kaaya klesaam'scha varjayeth.)

(*Yoga tatwopanishad 48*)

Bondages /impediments: (Page 483 of 112- Upanishads)

कर्तृत्वाद्यहंकारसंकल्पो बन्ध
अणिमाद्यष्टैश्वर्यासिद्धसंकल्पो बन्ध
देवमनुष्याद्युपासनाकामसंकल्पो बन्ध
यमाद्यष्टांगयोगसंकल्पो बन्ध
वर्णाश्रमधर्मकर्मसंकल्पो बन्ध
आज्ञाभयसंशयात्मगुणसंकल्पो बन्ध
यागव्रततपोदानविधिविघानज्ञानसंकल्पो बन्ध
केवलमोक्षापेक्षासंकल्पो बन्ध
संकल्पमात्रसंभवो बन्ध ॥

+ Transliteration of a verse from Bhagavatham in Malayalam.

Karthrtwadyahamkaara samkalpo bandha
Anima-dyashtaiswarya-asha-siddha samkalpo Bandha
Deva-manushya-dyupasana kaama samkalpo bandha
Yama-ady-ashtanga yoga samkalpo bandha.
Varna-asrama-dharma karma sankalpo bandha.
Aajna-bhaya-samshayatma-guna sankalpo bandha.
Yaaga-vrata-tapo-daana vidhi vidhaana jnana
sankalpo bandha.
Kevala moksha-apeksha sankalpo bandha.
Sankalpa-maatra sambhavo bandha.

(Niralambopanishad 10 to 18)

* The thought that I am a doer is a bondage.
  (Doer-ship is a bondage, whereas witness-hood is not.)
* The desire for siddhis (higher psychic powers) is a bondage.
* The thought of propitiating the gods (Devas), angels, men, etc. is a bondage.
* The thought of doing Ashtanga yoga (yama, niyama.......asana, pranayama...etc.) is a bondage.
* The thought of performing the duties of one's own caste, order of life (station in life), is a bondage.
* The thought that fear, doubt etc pertain to Atman, is a bondage.
* The thought of knowing the rules of performing sacrifices, vows, and austerity is a bondage.
* Even the desire for Moksha (emancipation) is a bondage. By the very thought, bondage is caused.
* Even the sprouting of any bit of a thought is a bondage.

(Niralambopanishad)

•• The wanting to 'become something' is a vasana that binds. (Swami Tejomayananda, in yoga vasishta samgraha p25)

The attitude (*bhaavam*)/approach/*sadhana*:

•• सोहं चिन्मात्रमेवेति
चिन्तनं ध्यानमुच्यते ॥
ध्यानस्य विस्मृतिः सम्यक्
समाधिरभिधीयते ॥

sohum chinmaathra'mevedi
chinthanam dhyaanam'uchyathe.
dhyanasya vismrthi samyak
samaadhirabhidheeyathe   (Thrisikhi)

Immersing in the thought "I am awareness alone" is meditation A state in which this meditation is also erased, is *samaadhi*.

But still,

•• तत्त्वावबोधो भगवन् सर्वाशात्रृणपावकः
प्रोक्तः समाधि शब्देन न च तुष्णीमवस्थिति ॥

thatwaavabodho bhagawan
sarvaashaa'thrna paavaka
proktha samaadhi'sabdena
na cha thushneem'avasthithi

Awareness of the Reality...that burns out all desires...is Samadhi, not a blank stillness and silence, says sage Vasishta.

•• Thrisikhi ..continues:- Acquiring Jivatma-Paramatma Bodham,—reaching the state of stability that 'I am Brahmam'—is Samadhi. In Samadhi one is devoid of all vrtthies.

.. यथा निरिन्धनो वह्नि स्वयमेव प्रशाम्यति
ग्राह्याभावे मनःप्राणो निश्चयज्ञानसंयुतः
शुद्धतत्त्वे परे लीनो जीवः सैन्धवपिण्डवत्॥

yatha nirindhano vahni swayameva prasaamyathi
(swayamevopasaamyathi – another version)
graahyaabhaave mana-praano
nischayajnaana'samyutha
shuddha thatwe pare leeno jiva saindhava'pindavath

Just as a fire subsides when the fuel runs out, in the absence of sense-objects, the mind and prana reach a state of firmed up knowledge /crystallised wisdom, and dissolve in the Pure Absolute Supreme Reality...like a piece of salt dissolves in the sea.

.. न ध्यानं ज्ञानयोगाभ्यां ब्रह्मविद्यैव स खलुः
ध्यानेनैकाग्र्यमापन्ने चित्ते विद्या स्थिरीभवेत् ॥

na dhyanam jnana'yogaabhyaam
brahmavidyaiva sa khalu
dhyanenaikaagryamaapanne
chitthe vidya sthireebhaveth   (Panchadasi XV.30)

"....As in these four types of meditation (not enumerated here) there is an admixture of knowledge and yoga, they are not mere meditations; but should be considered as (a direct means of achieving) the knowledge of Brahmam itself. The mind being concentrated by meditation, this Knowledge of Brahmam becomes steady." What I have been introducing you to ...from the very outset... is pure unadulterated Brahmavidya .. no mix-up with yoga, bhakthi, and all. All consciously, carefully, kept outside the boundary.

Nisarga Datta:

* "Perception is primary, the witness secondary."
* "Break the spell of the known, the illusion that only the perceivable is real."
* "To break the spell of the known, the knower must be brought to the forefront."
* "Don't be misled by the simplicity of the idea. Very few have the courage to trust the innocent and the simple." (P426 I AM THAT)
* "At the root of all creation lies desire. Desire and imagination foster and reinforce each other. The fourth state (thuriya) is a state of pure witnessing, detached awareness, passionless and wordless. It is like space, unaffected by whatever it contains. Bodily troubles and mental turmoil do not reach it – they are outside 'there' while the witness is always 'here'."

Witness:

•• आत्मा साक्षी विभुः पूर्ण एको मुक्तश्चिदक्रियः
असंगो निस्पृहः शान्तो भ्रमात् संसारवानिवः ॥

*athma saakshi vibhu: purna ekomuktas'chid'akriya:
asango nis-sprha: shaantho
bhramaath samsaaravaaniva.* (Asht.gita I.12)

The Self is Witness, All-pervading, perfect, non-dual, free, Consciousness, action-less, unattached, desireless and quiet. Through illusion It appears to be absorbed in the world.

•• न पृथ्वी न जलं नाग्निर्न वायुर्द्यौर् न वा भवान्
एषां साक्षिणमात्मानं चिद्रूपं विद्धि मुक्तये ॥

na prdhvi na jalam na'agnir
na vayur'dwaur na va bhavaan
eshaam saakshinamaathmaanam
chidroopam viddhi mukthaye.

You are neither earth, nor fire, nor air, nor space. In order to attain liberation, know the Self as the 'witness' of all these—the embodiment of pure consciousness. (I.3 Asht.Gita).

•• Through meditation when we withdraw our identification with our gross and subtle bodies, in the inward stillness the existing vasanas get all burnt up, uplifting the meditator to the plane of pure consciousness.

•• *Jeevo-na-aham; shivohum. (na = not).*

I am shivam ...not jeeva. ('Jiva' is so called because it upholds vitality – the *praanas* – (in a body). 'Jiva' literally means a living being, or the principle of life – the life factor.) *Shivam* = auspiciousness. *Mangalam* in almost all Indian languages.

•• चैतन्यं यदधिष्ठानं लिंगदेहश्च यः पुनः
चिच्छाया लिंगदेहस्था तत्संघो जीव उच्यते ॥

chaithanyam yad adhishtaanam
linga'dehascha ya punah
chicchaayaa lingadehastha
thad'samgho jiva ucchyathe. (Pancadasi IV.11)

The substratum ... base ..the Pure Consciousness, the subtle body, and the reflection[+] of pure consciousness on the subtle body—these three together constitute a jiva. (Pancadasi IV.11)

Even this confuses the argument-happy 'scholars'. There are arguments that *Aabhasa Chaithanyam* (Reflected Consciousness) is only a reflection ...a second-rate thing ...not original !! The sunlight coming through a dew drop is the sunlight itself; not the light of the dew drop.

Swami Swahananda (in Pancadasi p84) puts it correctly ...It is 'mixed awareness'. Explaining verse III.16 he says: "When the universe was not born (un-manifested) It (*Athman*) was shining. That is, it was in its absoluteness as pure-awareness. There was neither aught nor naught but one, unalloyed, pure-consciousness. After the manifestation of the world, whatever awareness is there is mixed or (as they call it) 'reflected' (reflected awareness), which, without being qualitatively different from it, is so haplessly unlike as not to be recognized at all as That."

· · "It (the Self) being Awareness itself, cannot be made an object of knowledge. It is in and through this that all objects are known. Objects are the content of consciousness; how can the contents contain the container?" (Pancadasi p.84)

But still, I see it this way: The Awareness knows itself, and knows everything else ...sees itself and sees everything else.

· · "To say we know the objects, and do not know the consciousness in and through which we know the objects, is self-deception. Consciousness is the basis of all acts and objects of knowledge ...it is the undeniable *sine qua non* of all knowledge." (p.84 *Pancadasi*)

+ it is not exactly reflection that is actually meant –that should be meant; it is the original itself.

- Just as a rope is misunderstood as a snake, the Self is seen as Jiva (in jeeva bhavam)
- Jiva, deluded to believe himself identified with the body, becomes subject to grief. (IV.13 *Pancadasi*)
- Brahman who is existence, consciousness and infinity is the Reality. Its being Iswara (the Omniscient Lord of the world) and Jiva (the individual soul) are (mere) superimpositions by the two illusory adjuncts (Maya and Avidya, respectively). *Pancadasi* III.37

"Is Brahmam limited by Iswara and Jiva? No, they are not transcendentally real like Brahmam which is of the nature of Reality, consciousness, infinite and eternal. Brahmam is called Iswara and Jiva according to the function it performs." (III.37 *Pancadasi*)

This same *jeeva-bhavam,* if the matter-vestures are erased, regains its original status ... pristine purity ...and shines forth, unfragmented, eternal and free. This is the Law of Bondage and Liberation. One who remembers this rule always, will find himself liberated soon. (Prof.G.B. in Prou. P64)

- Mind in agitation = is universe, prakrthi, samsar;
  Mind without agitations = is Brahmam.

This is the rule of bondage and liberation.

Amanee'bhaavam ..unmanee'bhaavam ...thoughtless stillness — not brimming with information, knowledge, contents. With thought ... information ... content = is *vyashti* (individual) + universe.

Mind without thoughts ... contents ... movements ... modifications = is Brahmam.

•• छायाशरीरे प्रतिबिंबगात्रे
यत् स्वप्नदेहे हृदिकल्पितांगे
यदात्मबुद्धिस्तव नास्तिकश्चित्
जीवच्छरीरे च तथैवमास्तु ॥

cchayaa sarire' pratibimba gaatre,
yath'swapna dehe hrdi'kalpithange
yadatma'buddhis'thava naasthi kaschith
jivaccharirecha thadhaivam'aasthu.

•• Just as you do not identify yourself with your shadow, or your reflection in the mirror, or the dream body, so too do not identify with the living body also. *(Vivekacudamani 163)*

•• कुल्यायामथ नद्यां वा शिवक्षेत्रेऽपि चत्वरे
पर्णं पतति चेत्तेन तरोः किं नु शुभाशुभं ॥

(Vivekachudamani 560)

kulyaayamadha nadyaam va
shiva'kshethrepi chathware
parnam pathathi chetthena
tharo kim'nu shubhaashubham

If a leaf falls in a stream or river, in a Siva temple, or at a cross-road, what good or evil will it bestow upon the tree?

* In front of your reality ...eternity, the reality (or unreality) of the body and the universe fade into insignificance.

* When you leave Ananthapuram for Bangalore, attachment to Ananthapuram is loosened...lost, and you get attached to Bangalore. When you get attached to your pure Self, you are no longer attached to the body.

* Atma (Bodham) is *asangam* – not attached /not connected /not related / not sticking on to (not having anything to do with) the body and the universe.

.. कार्यंहि कारणंपश्येत् पश्चात् कार्यं विसर्जयेत्
कारणत्वं ततो गच्छेत् अवशिष्टंभवेन्मुनि ॥

kaaryam hi kaaranam pasyeth
paschaath kaaryam visarjayeth
kaaranathwam tatho gaccheth
avasishtam bhaven'muni

Discard the 'effects' (*karyam*) – and see the 'cause'. (That is the emphasis, exhortation) The cause then becomes 'no-cause'. And what remains is You- ----in a transcendental silence (*muni*).

.. आत्मन्येवाखिलंदृश्यं प्रविलाप्य धिया सुधी ।
भावयेदेकमात्मानं निर्मलाकाशवत् सदा ॥ *(Atmabodham 39)*

atmanyeva' akhilam drsyam
pravilaapya dhiyaa sudhie
bhavayeth'ekam'aatmaanam
nirmala'akaasavath'sada.

The wise should intelligently merge the entire world of objects in *Athman* (the Self) itself, and constantly stabilize in the thought that the Self (Awareness) is like the clear sky.

.. रूपवर्णादिकं सर्वं विहाय परमार्थवित्
परिपूर्ण चिदानन्दस्वरूपेणावशिष्यते॥ *(Atmabodham 40)*

rupa varnaadikam sarvam
vihaaya paramardhavith
paripurna chidananda-
swarupena'avasishyate

One who knows the Reality..discards all the names and forms, and dwells as the embodiment of Infinite Consciousness and Bliss. (*vihaaya*=discarding...everything. Note it).

•• Mind at rest alone is the peep-hole through which the seeker rediscovers his real nature... declares *Mahopanishad*. (IV.100) Q. Chinmaya, Asht.gita – big p206

•• The eye is our instrument of cognition... that cognizes (the light of) the sun, fire etc. The eye's eye is the mind. 'I' am the one that lends reality to the mind. When you come to grips with this fact, you will realize that 'I am the one that lends reality to the whole universe'. The experiencing of this reality is the ultimate aim of Vedantha. (prof. GB in *Proudhanubhoothi* p.8)

•• *jeeveswarau maayikau vijnaaya*
sarvavisesham nethi-nethi'thi vihaaya
yad'avasishyathe thath adwayam Brahma.

Realising that Godhood and Jeeva-bhavam is a duality that does not really exist (Maya)... discard everything by the 'not-this not-this' process, ...and what then remains is the non-dual Brahmam. (*Adwaya taarakopanishad*. Upa-112 p155) Ah! Look at this. This supports my view of Vedantha. And the Upanishad calls it 'adwaya'. If this is the 'non-duality' I give a big hug to this Upanishad....all my burden is relieved.

Yet another verse that supports the same view:

•• निरालंबं समाश्रित्य
सालंबं विजहाति य:
स सन्यासी च योगी च:
कैवल्यमनुपश्यते ॥

> *niraalambam samaasrthya*
> *saalambam vijahaathi ya*
> *sanyaasi cha yogi cha*
> *kaivalyamanupasyathe.*

Depend on the Independent, discarding the dependent... and you attain *kaivalyam*.

> .. घटे नष्टे यथा व्योम व्योमैव भवति स्फुटम्
> तथैवोपाधिविलये ब्रह्मैव ब्रह्मवित्स्वयम् ॥
>
> *khade nashte yatha vyoma*
> *vyomaiva bhavathi sphutam*
> *thathaiva upathi vilaye*
> *brahmaiva braqhmavid swayam*
>
> *(Vivekachudamani 566)*

When a pot is broken the pot-space becomes the limitless single space; so too, when the conditionings are gone the knower of Brahmam becomes Brahmam Itself.

When the body mind and intellect are transcended the knower of Brahman becomes Brahman, ie, what was till now an intellectual understanding becomes a direct subjective experience (*Brahmavid Brahmaiva bhavathi*).

Upaathi-vilayam (dissolution) is possible only in mind; how else is it possible to dissolve the universe and your own body? So this *upaathi vilayam* has Aacharya's approval.

> .. क्व माया क्व च संसारः क्व प्रीतिर्विरतिः क्व वा ।
> क्व जीव क्व च तद्ब्रह्म सर्वदा विमलस्य मे ॥
>
> *qua maaya qua'cha samsaara*
> *qua preethir'virathi qua va*
> *qua jiva qua'cha thad'brahma*
> *sarvada vimalasya mae*

•• Where is illusion and where is the world of change? Where is attachment and where is detachment? Where is jiva and what is Brahmam for me, who is ever Pure?*(Asht.G.XX.11)*

•• Where is the knower, or the means of knowledge; where is the object of knowledge or where is the knowledge itself? Where is anything, or where is nothing ... for me who is Ever Pure? *(Asht.gita XX.8)*

•• *proudhananda chideka sanmaya vapuh:*
shuddho'smyakhando'smyaham. (Proudhanubhoothi)

I am of the form of pure, Mature, Awareness-Reality-Bliss, trananscending all distinctions.

•• *sattha'chid'sukha rupam'asthi sathatham*
(Proudhanubhoothi p172)

Reality Awareness Bliss – this form exists eternally.

•• *na saastha na saashram na shishyo na siksha*
na cha twam na cha'aham nachayam prapancha
swaroopa'avabodho' vikalpaasahishnu
sthathekovasishta shiva kevaloham. (Dasasloki 7)

This verse was discussed in Chapter-1. The word '*vikalpa'asahishnu*' needs further probing:

I am single, independent ...that allows / tolerates no duality in It. **Vikalpa'asahishnu** = intolerant of vikalpa (vikalpa=conjured-up distinctions/divisions). Mark it. Intolerant of distinctions. The eye is intolerant of foreign bodies ....it repels, it does not hold on to any foreign body and enjoy it, like a magnet attracts and holds on. A donkey carries load; many other animals don't tolerate a load. Awareness does not tolerate any load on it ....intolerant. It is pure, it wants to continue to be pure. Please note here that

Ch.2   The Path

this goes counter to the common belief and teaching that the universe is the body of Brahmam—the Awareness. Think.

* * na jagran'namae swapnakova'sushupthir-
 na viswo'na va taijasa: praajna ko va
 avidyaathmakathwath trayaanaam turiya-
 sthat'ekovasishta siva kevaloham.

I don't have any waking, dream or deep sleep states, and therefore I am not *viswan, taijasan* or *prajna*n. These three states are seen in me due to ignorance; and I am in the fourth state (*thuriyam*) beyond these three. I am the then-remaining Auspicious (*sivam*) Absolute Single Reality (awareness).

* * Neither void nor non-void—because of non-duality.

(*na sunyam nacha'asunyam advaitakathwath*)   (*Dasasloki 10*)

* * अस्ति-भाति-प्रियं नाम-रूपं चेत्यंश पञ्चकं
 आद्य त्रयं ब्रह्मरूपं जगद्रूपं ततोद्वयं *(Drg-drsya vivekam 20)*
 asthi bhaathi priyam
 naama'roopam chethyamsha'panchakam
 aadya'thrayam brahma'roopam
 jagad'roopam thatho'dwayam

Reality (existence), Awareness, Bliss; and Names and Forms — Five such components. The first three constitute Brahmam; the other two forms the Jagath (the universe).

* * उपेक्ष्ये नामरूपे द्वे सच्चिदानन्दतत्परः
 समाधिं सर्वदा कुर्याद् हृदये वाधवा बहिः
 upekshye naama-roope dwe
 satchidaananda thathpara
 samaadhim sarvada kuryad'
 hrdaye va'adhava bahi: *(Drg-drsya vivekam 22)*

Discard the names and forms, and get solidified in Reality-Awareness-Bliss, doing Samadhi in the heart or outside.

•• हरो यद्युपदेष्टा ते हरि: कमलजोऽपि वा
तथापि न तव स्वास्थ्यं सर्वविस्मरणादृते ॥

Haro yadyupadeshta tae
Hari Kamalajo'pi va
thadha'pi na tava swasthyam
sarva vismaranaadrte. (Asht.Gita XVI.11)

Even if Siva, Vishnu or Brahma be your instructor, yet, unless you forget all, you cannot achieve abidance in peace.

Dhyanam: what it is:

•• ब्रह्मैवास्मीति सद् वृत्या निरालंबतया स्थिति
ध्यानशब्देन विख्याता परमानन्द दायिनी ॥

(Aparokshanubhuti-123)

brahmaivaahamithi sad'vrthyaa
niraalambathayaa sthithi
dhyana sabdena vikhyaathaa
paramaananda'daayini.

If the mind abides in 'I am the Brahmam' attitude ...without depending on anything else ...that is *dhyanam* (meditation) that leads to eternal peace.

Samadhi

•• *samaadhi: sa thu vijneya*
sarva vrtthi vivarjitha: (*Trisikhibrahmanopanishad* 161).

In Samadhi there is no *mano-vrtthi*—no modifications of mind...no pulsation of mind .....mind at rest.

Ch.2   The Path   139

- निर्विकारतया वृत्या ब्रह्माकारतयः पुनः
  वृत्ति विस्मरणं सम्यक् समाधिर् ज्ञानसञ्जितः

  nirvikaarathayaa vrthyaa
  brahmaakaarathaya punah
  vrtthi'vismaranam samyak
  samaadhir jnanasamjnitha. (Aparokshanubhuti -124)

Without fluctuations .. modifications .. vibrations .. the mind acquiring the form of Brahmam ...and thereafter reaching a state in which that too is forgotten ...is samaadhi.

- नाहं देहो न च प्राणो नेन्द्रियाणि मनो नहि
  सदासाक्षिस्वरूपत्वाच्छिव एवास्मि केवलः
  इति धीर्या मुनिश्रेष्ठ सा समाधिरिहोच्यते ॥

  (Jabaladarsanopanishad X.5   p463 Upa-108)

  naaham deho na cha praano nendriyaani mano nahi
  sadaa saakshi'swarupatwath'siva evaasmi kevala
  ithi dheeryaa'munishreshta sa samaadhirihochyathe

I am not the body, nor the mind, nor the praana; <u>I am the Consciousness that witnesses everything</u>. Always abiding in this firmed up conviction ...is samaadhi.

- ततःसाधननिर्मुक्त
  सिद्धोभवति योगिराट् ॥

  thatha: saadhana'nirmuktha
  sadyo bhavathi yogiraat.   (Aparokshanubhuti 126)

Reaching this state, casting away all the usual spiritual practices and workouts, the supreme-yogi abides with the satisfaction of having reached the ultimate destination (siddha).

***   ***   ***

•• त्वय्यनन्तमहाम्भोधौ विश्ववीचिः स्वभावतः
उदेतु वास्तमायातु न ते वृद्धिर्न वा क्षतिः॥
*thwayyanantha mahaambhodhau
viswa veechi swabhaavatha:
udethu'va'asthamayathu
na thae vrddhir'na va kshathi.*

(Asht.Gita XV.11)

In you the infinite ocean (of consciousness) the waves of the universes rise and fall according to their own nature. That doesn't mean any gain or loss to you. (This is yet another great pointer. Read it closely. Read it a hundred times. Read the lines, between the lines, above the lines, below the lines. Try to understand fully what it purports.)

•• नाहं देहो न मे देहो जीवो नाहमहंहिचित् :
*na'aham deho na mae deho..
jivo naaham aham hi chit.* (Asht.gita II.22)

I am not the body ...for me there is no body. I am not a Jiva (ie, individual ....individuated entity); I am Awareness.

•• There are compositions of Sankaracharya and portions in upanishads where the verses end with profound slogans such as below ....which could be gainfully utilized for fast progress:-

* *chidanandaroopa shivohum shivohum* (*Nirvana shadkam*)
  (Awareness-Bliss is my form; I am auspicious; I am auspicious).

* *Brahma thathwam asi bhavayathmani* (*Viveka chudamani*) (Hold fast to 'I-am-Brahmam' attitude.)

* *Tadekovashishta siva kevaloham* (*Dasa sloki*)
  (The one that then remains, I am that.)

* *param Brahma nithyam tadevaha'masmi* (The supreme... Brahmam...eternal—I am nothing but That.)
* *Ahamevaha'mavyayah (Brahmajnanavalijmala)* (I am That.. immutable, irreducible.)
* *proudha prakasosmyaham (Proudhaanubhoothi)* (I am that Light... grandiose.)
* *sivosmyaham* (I am this auspicious entity)

          ***   ***   ***

Don't be enamored about manthras.

Have a look at what TEJO-BINDU UPANISHAD has to say in the matter of mantras:

"Aham Brahma'asmi is the only manthra ...the ultimate" ...and the Upanishad repeats it 30 times, to assert.

"One should cognize one's own Atman alone. One should always practise the manthra of his Atman alone. The manthra 'Aham Brahmaasmi' (I am Brahmam) removes all sins of sight, <u>destroys all other mantras</u>, destroys all the sins of body and birth, disables the noose of yama, shuts out the pains of duality, the thought of difference, the pains of thought, the defects of buddhi, the bondage of chittha, puts out the passions and grief instantaneously". ... (more details of the text in Appendix)

          ***   ***   ***

- The sun in the mirror ...looks exactly like the original ... looks real.
- The night, morning, evening .. are real to us; but the sun actually does not rise or set.

These are experiential realities …not absolute realities. What is really not there, also we see.

But can we relegate the reality of the universe to this category? If we relegate, are we justified?

If you start digging up for answers to questions about the universe, you will end up with questions and further questions. In my view, you don't have to solve the question of universe first, to turn towards Reality. Straight away you can turn to your Reality; and let the universe remain or dissolve in the process.

•• *aho vikalpitham viswam, ajnanal mayi bhaasathe*

The universe is seen in me through ignorance.

As the *nididhyasanam* progresses — when you think along the proper line, you will feel that this statement (above) is true. This does not connote that the universe is unreal. To me it means only that I as the Awareness do not carry the load of the body and the universe. I remain free, even while seemingly mixed-up. The light in the dance hall does not carry the dance hall.

•• To get convinced that Brahmam (Awareness) is Real, it is not conditional that you must get convinced that the universe is unreal. Let the universe be real or unreal, it is a fact that we all experience it.

***   ***   ***

•• 'I-ness' is the *bheda'chintha* ... separate-ness .... separation+ (*Radha sathyam*-Mal.)

+ Very many schools/ teachers explain this bheda-chintha thus: "all are the sons of God. All are alike. One should not find any difference among people. There are no high caste, low caste. One should not look at the rich and the poor differently. ALL ARE ALIKE. Here ends their understanding of 'duality'/bheda-bhavana.

'I, the wave, is different from the ocean'—This is *bheda bhavana* (assumption of difference).. duality, separate-ness.

- • 'I' as a person/individual entity —should be effaced.
- • "You as a person never existed" ...(Swami Vivekananda)

      ***   ***   ***

"To come into relationship (to possess and to be possessed) is common to all embodied beings; but the yogis are for ever vigilant, and that vigilance is the worship of the self. Adopting this inner attitude, and with a mind utterly devoid of any attachment, I roam in the dreadful forest of samsaara (world appearance). If you do so you will not suffer" (Vasishtam)

My identiy is with pure Brahmam. Not with *prakrti* (nature)+Easwaran. Power and all such, are related to this combination ...not to pure Self.

* Thath twam asi
* Ayam Atma Brahma
* Prajnanam Brahma
* Aham Brahma asmi

So say the maha-vakyas; and not Aham Iswara (God) asmi.

Omnicient

When you advance spiritually, ..when you know what Brahmam is ...when you start knowing that 'I am Brahmam', then if you don't find yourself all-knowing and all-powerful, don't be concerned about it. Don't worry about it. Don't be upset about it. Don't think about it. It is so. It is a wrong reading, ..wrong teaching that you should be all-knowing and all-powerful. (Swami Chinmayananda also has written some strong reassuring words in this direction – ref. lost). Your identity is with Brahmam; not with the Prakrthi+ Brahmam mix-up, with its seemingly transposed power of Prakrthi.

- - अहं ब्रह्मेति विज्ञानात् कल्पकोटिशतार्जितं
  संचितं विलयं याति प्रबोधे स्वप्नकर्मवत् ॥

  (Vivekachudamani 448)

  aham Brahmethi vijnanaath
  kalpa'koti shatharjitham
  sanchitham vilayam yaathi
  prabodhe swapna'karmavath.

Through the realization of one's identity with Brahmam, all the accumulated *karma* (actions) of a hundred crores of cycles come to naught, like the actions of the dream on waking up.

- - अज्ञानकलुषंजीवं ज्ञानाभ्यासाद्विनिर्मलं
  कृत्वा ज्ञानं स्वयं नश्येज्जलं कतकरेणुवत् ॥

  (Atmabodham 5)

  ajnana kalusham jivam
  jnanaabhyasath vinirmalam
  krthva jnanam swayam nasyeth
  jalam kathaka'renuvath.

Through repeated practice, Knowledge purifies the soul, stained by ignorance, and then it vanishes, just as the *kataka*-nut-powder disappears after cleansing muddy water.

- - नेतिप्रमाणेन निराकृताखिलो
  हृदा समास्वादित चिद्सुखनामृतंः

त्यजेदशेषं जगदात्तसद्रसम्
पीत्वा यथाम्भः प्रजहाति तत्फलम् ॥ *(Rama Gita 34)*
*netipramaanena nirakrtakhilo
hrda samasvadita chid ghanamrtam:
tyajedasesham jagadattasadrasam
pitva yathambha prajahati tathphalam.*

Rejecting all the apparatus/equipment/upadhi using the scriptural statement "not this, not this", and experiencing the immortal, changeless mass of pure Consciousness in his heart ... having enjoyed the ever-existent blissful Self, the wise man should discard the entire world, just as one throws away the empty shell of a coconut after drinking the sweet water.

•• स्वात्मानमात्मस्थमुपाधिवर्जितं
swaathmaanam athmastham upadhi'varjitham

With your Self, abide in the Self, ..casting off all upathis.

•• त्यजेदशेषं ज़डमात्मगोचरं
tyajeth ashesham jadam atmagocharam.
(Rama Gita 42)

Discard the inert matter-vestures found on the Atman / Self – in its entirety.[1]

---

[1] 'That which words cannot express, but which is the very substratum of our personality, is experienced by the seeker in his own heart. That pure Self is experienced as devoid of all entrapments such as the gross, the subtle or the causal bodies. When once this experience has descended upon the contemplator, let him thereafter totally stop entertaining the gross, inert world of objects, emotions and thoughts.' (Swami Chinmayananda)

Don't worry about the things discarded:

* whether they exist (real or unreal)
* what is their purpose
* why, how, etc.

If you start digging for answers, you can end up digging ...and digging, with no result. There are various theories explaining why and how. Some are very plausible; but at a closer look, useless.

•• Just as a rope is misunderstood as a snake, the Self is seen as Jiva (jeeva bhavam).

•• *Jeevo-na-aham; shiovohum.* I am shivam ..not a jiva.

This same jeeva-bhavam, if the matter-vestures are erased, regains its original status / pristine purity and shines, eternal and free, transcending all distinctions. This is the Law of Bondage and Liberation. One who remembers this Rule always, will find himself liberated soon. (Prof.G.B. in Prou. P64)

•• *aananda buddhi purnasya*
mama dukkham katham bhaveth?

In me the fullness of consciousness and saturated bliss, how can there be any misery? (*Atmaprabodhopanishad*)

Purnasya = to that which is complete. A thing that is complete ...does not need anything to be complete. Treat similarly ..*aananda*..saturated

•• *aathmaanam anjasaa vedmi*
kapyajnanam palayinam?

Now I know my Self (athman) clearly, effortlessly; which way did *ajnanam* run away?

·· *karthrtwam adyame nashtam*
karthavyam va'api na kvacit.

*   Doership I lost long ago; I have no vestiges of duties remaining. (p 395 U-108) Atmaprabodhopanishad II.21
*   *Soka-naasam* (end of miseries) .. alone is not enough. (*Arul mozhikal*; Poojappura Gopalaswamy)
*   Let the mind die out (dissolve) with all its desires and activities.
*   Abiding in the Self always, the yogi's mind dissolves.
    (swatmanyeva sada sthitthva
    mano'nasyathi yoginah)
*   Forget everything, without ever remembering again. That alone is definitely desirable. (forget the world).
    (apuna smaranam manye
    sadho vismaranam varam) (*Vasishtam*)
*   Just as you see the moon through the tip of a leaf, always see the motionless awareness in the midst of all movements. $\mathcal{D}_n$

·· With a bright intellect, dissolve all '*drsya*' (all that is seen...all the sense objects) in the Self ..in the Awareness. (Atma bodham) (*atmanyevakhilam drsyam pravilaapya...*)

·· Remaining wide awake, abide in a deep sleep state. (*jagrathil sushupthiyay*) *Mal.*

·· "I am shouting at the top of my voice with raised hands... but nobody listens. A mind without thought vibrations does the ultimate good; why don't people understand this?"
(*Vasishtam*)

·· "*Brahma'vishraanthi paryantho*
vicharosthu thavanagha."

Until you find your repose in Brahmam, keep up the thought process *(mananam)*, my worthy son.

Look at the simplicity and tranquility of the word! '*vishraanthi*'—repose, relaxation –no activity, no impulse. Where there is omnipotence no *vishranthi* is possible. Agitation alone is possible.

- दृष्टि स्थिरा यस्य विना स दृश्यं.. *(Nadabindu Upa. 56)*
  drshti sthira yasya vina sa drsyam

  "Vision stabilized, with the absence of visuals ….."

***   ***   ***

- Look at the precision, superiority, incisiveness of the Vedic /Upanishadic path …where they lead one through *vanaprastham*, and then to *sanyasam*…. A mendicant is supposed to change his name every five years. This way the system ensures that it is close to impossibility to trace a person …after he has assumed *sanyasa*. If one has relinquished the world, the world should not run after him …the world should not chase him.

***   ***   ***

- "Without craving and without rejecting, that which is effortlessly and naturally obtained may be enjoyed. One should not get excited or depressed when faced with insignificant or significant objects, just as the space is not affected by the existence of objects in it." Siva to Vasista.

- अकिञ्चनभवं स्वास्थ्यं   कौपीनत्वेऽपि दुर्लभं ॥
  akinchana bhavam swasthyam
  kaupeenathve'pi durlabham.   *(Asht.Gita XIII.1)*

Without possessions, one is completely free. Even the possession of a loin cloth brings about that much bondage.

Ch.2 The Path

Look at what a sage thinks about the pomp and splendor of a king's court…..(in Kalidasa's *Shaakunthalam*): The king asks, and the sage answers: "I look upon your splendor …

- as one who is fresh and clean after a good bath looks upon one who is unclean and waiting for a bath.
- as one who is awake looks upon one who is sleeping.
- as one who is free to move about, looks upon one whose legs are chained"

> (*supthane uthprabuddhan……
> baddhangane swahithagaami'yum'orkumaare
> chitthathil ingu sukha'sakhthare orthidunnen.*)
>
> *Shakunthalam in Malayalam*

- A king is not tempted to run after a beggar with a begging bowl.
- One who sits on Everest, is not tempted by the height of any other peak in the world.
- A female deer does not raise the heart-beat of a jungle tree by rubbing against it.

In saturated ecstasy …what else can penetrate? What else is wanting?

- सन्तु विकाराः प्रकृतेर्दशधा शतधा सहस्रधा वापि ।
  किं मेऽसङ्गचित्तस्तैर्न घनः क्वचिदम्बरं स्पृशति ॥

  (*Vivekachudamani 512*)

  > *santhu vikaaraa prakrthe dasatha
  > shathatha sahasradha vaapi
  > kim mae'asanga chithasthair
  > na khana kvachidambaram sprshathi.*

•• 'Let there be tens, hundreds, thousands of modifications in Prakrthi; what have I to do with it? I am unattached, Knowledge Absolute. The sky is not disturbed by the clouds'

***   ***   ***

•• नाहंदेहो जन्ममृत्यु कुतोमे
नाहं प्राणः क्षुत् पिपासो कुतोमे
नाहं कर्ता बन्धमोक्षो कुतो मे ॥

(Sarvasaropanishad 21)

na'aham deho, janma mrthyu kutho mae
na'aham praana: kshuth pipaaso kutho mae
na'aham karthaa: bandha-moksho kutho mae

* I am not the body: how can there be birth and death to me?
* I am not *praana* : how can there be hunger and thirst to me?
* I don't do anything: how can there be bondage and liberation to me?

•• *Thrigunas* are not in me. (निस्त्रैगुण्य पदोहं) (*Atmabodhopanishad*) In my state ... in my situation ...there are no *thrigunas*. Meaning, these *gunas* are not in me. Like the mirror saying 'These objects you see in me are not in me'. Think.

•• स्वशरीरे स्वयंज्योतिःस्वरूपं सर्वसाक्षिणम्
क्षीणदोषाः प्रपश्यन्ति नेतरे माययावृताः॥

(Rudrahrdayopanishad 49)

swa shareere swayam'jyothi-
swaroopam sarva'saakshinam

*khseena'doäsha prapasyanthi
nethare maayaya'avrtha.*

One with purified mind sees in his own person this all-witnessing self-shining form; not seen by others engrossed in the world.

A mirror is of no use to the blind. One who is tied up with wife, children, relatives, house, property etc. ... cannot see the light of spirituality. A resplendent sun is a non-entity to the blind.

∙∙ अयमेवाहमित्यस्मिन संकोचे विलयंगते
समस्त भुवनव्यापी विस्तारं उपजायते

*ayameva'aha'mithyasmin samkoche vilayam'gathe
samastha bhuvana'vyaapi visthaaram upajaayathe.*

When your shrinking — confining — into the body – vanishes, (when the belief that I am the body, is gone) ...when you let go the limiting of your awareness into the body, you assume the expansiveness of the universe. The pot space becomes the limitless, entire vast space.

∙∙ आकाशमेकं सम्पूर्णं कुत्रचिन्नैव गच्छति
तद्वत् स्वात्मपरिज्ञानी कुत्रचिन्नैव गच्छति ॥

(Rudrahrdayopanishad 51)

*aakaasam'ekam'sampurnam
kuthra'chin'naiva gacchthi
thad'wath swathma'parijnaani
kuthrachinnaiva gacchathi.*

The space is one....a totality: it cannot move anywhere. So too, Athma-jnani also does not move about.

∙∙ अयमेवशिवं परमार्थैव
अभिवादनमत्र करोमि कथं

ayameva'sivam paramaartha'iva
abhivaadanam'athra karomi kadham?

I am the auspicious single Reality—one only. How do I greet, how do I bow? (to whom?) (*Bhikshu gita*)

- आत्मानमात्मनि सुमित्र कथंनमामि (*Avadhootha gita*)
  aathmaanam'athmani sumithr katham namaami?

  Tell me dear friend, how do I bow to myself?

- आधारमानन्दमखण्डबोधं
  यस्मिन लयंयाति पुरत्रयं च ॥
  aadhaaram'aanandam'akhanda-bodham
  yasmin layam yaathi pura-thrayam'cha

  The base and substratum is the blissful un-fragmented Awareness ...in that dissolves the three bodies.

- ब्रह्मप्रकाशते वह्नि (*Brahma prakaasathe vahni*)

  Brahmam shows up the fire.(If you entertain any doubt that Brahman is awareness, .. have one more close look at these words:. "*Brahma prakaasathe vahni*".

- चित्वदर्शनं तत्वदर्शनं
  chitthwa darsanam tattwa darsanam

  Viewing the awareness in you—coming to grips with the awareness in you—that is the real theory...the theory of Reality. ...the vision of reality.

- ईशदर्शनं स्वात्मरूपतः
  Isa-darshanam swaathma'rupatha

  See the God as your own awareness. (Ramana Maharshi)

- आत्मसंस्थिति स्वात्मदर्शनं ॥
  (*athma'samsthithi swathma'darsanam*)

Seeing the Self, ..viewing the Self..is the Abidance in the Self.

•• तया व्याप्तमिदं विश्वं त्वयि प्रोतं यथार्थतः ..
शुद्धबुद्धस्वरूपस्त्वं मागम क्षुद्रचित्तताम् ॥

(Asht.gita. I.16)

twaya vyaptham'idam'viswam
twayi protham yadhardhatha
shuddha Buddha swsarupas'twam
maa gama kshudra'chithathaam:

You pervade the universe; in fact the universe is in you ... woven in you ...like woof and weft. (Where else will the universe stand except in the awareness that knows the existence of the universe?). You are Pure Consciousness by nature; do not belittle yourself. (Don't think you are something insignificant).

•• दृश्यं आश्रयसीदंचेत् तत् सचित्तोसि बद्धवान् ।
दृश्यं संत्यज सिदंचेत तदा अचित्तोसि मोक्षवान् ।

drsyam ashraya seedam'cheth
thath sachithosi baddhavaan
drsyam sam'thyaja seedam'cheth
thadha'achithosi mokshavaan.

When you identify with the body, <u>you acquire the related mind</u>...and get entangled with it. (It en-snares you). If you forsake the identity with the body, you lose the mind ... you are free ...liberated.

•• त्वं शुद्धबोधोसि हि सर्वदेहिनां
आत्मास्यधीशोसि निराकृति स्वयं   (ref.lost)

twam shuddha bodhosi hi sarva'dehinaam
aathmaa'thyadheesho'si niraakrthi'swayam

Being formless yourself, you rule over the bodies of beings as their awareness.

.. सर्ववेदान्त सारं यद् ब्रह्मात्मैकत्वलक्षणं
वस्तवद्वितीयं तन्निष्टं कैवल्यैक प्रयोजनं ॥ *(Bh. 12.13.12)*

*sarva'vedantha saaram yad
brahma'athmaikathwa'lakshanam
vasthu'adwitheeyam thannishtam
kaivalyaika prayojanam.*

Hai. Look at that. It does not insist that universe is non-existent. It does not confuse these two things – Braham and universe. This verse limits its discussion to Brahnam alone. And it declares – The quintessence of Vedantha is the oneness of Brahma and Athma (brahma' athma' ekathvam). There is no duality as Athma and Brahma. The end result is Liberation (kaivalyam – one-ness, alone-ness).

.. मुखाभासको दर्पणे दृश्यमानो
मुखत्वात् पृथक्त्वेन नैवास्ति वस्तुः
चिदाभासको धीषु जीवोपि तद्वत्
स नित्योपलब्धिस्वरूपोहमात्मा ॥ *(Hasthamalakam 5)*

*mukha'abhasako darpane drsyamaano
mukhathwaath prthaktwena naiva'asthi vasthu
chidaabhaasako dheeshu jivopi thad'vath
sa nithyopalabdhi swaroopohamaathma.*

The image of a face in the mirror has no real exisence apart from the face. Similarly, jiva (the individual Self) is also a reflection of Consciousness in the intellect. I am of the nature of that ever existing Athma.

•• यथा दर्पणाभाव आभासहानौ
मुखं विद्यते कल्पनाहीनमेकं
तथा धीवियोगे निराभासको यः
स नित्योपलब्धिस्वरूपोहमात्मा ॥ *(Hasthamalakam 9)*

yatha darpanaabhaava aabhaasahaanau
mukham vidtathe kalpanaaheenam'ekam
thatha dhee'viyoge niraabhaasakoya
sa nithyopalabdhi swarupoham athma.

When the mirror is removed, the image vanishes ...and only the original face remains without reflection. In the same way, dissociated from the intellect ...dis-identifying with the intellect ..pure awareness alone remains without any reflection. I am of the nature of that ever existing Athma.

•• वदन्तु शास्त्राणि यजन्तु देवान्
कुर्वन्तु कर्माणि भजन्तुदेवताः
आत्मैक्यबोधेनविना विमुक्तिर्
न सिद्ध्यति ब्रह्मशतान्तरेपिः॥ *(Vivekachudamani 6)*

vadanthu shasthraani yajanthu'devaan
kurvanthu karmaani bhajanthu devatha
aathmaikya'bodhena'vinaa vimukthir
na siddhyathi brahma'shathaantharepi.

Recite all the scriptures, invoke the gods through sacrifices, perform elaborate rituals ....yet without experiencing one's identity with the Self there shall be no liberation even in the life-time of a hundred Brahmas.

•• न गच्छति विना पानं
व्याधिरौषधशब्दतः

विनाऽपरोक्षानुभवं
ब्रह्मशब्दैर् न मुच्यते ॥ *(Vivekachoodamani 62)*

na gacchathi vinaa paanam
vyaadhir'aushadha'shabdatha
vina'aparoksha'anubhavam
brahma'shabdair'na muchyathe.

Without taking the medicine, by simply chanting the name of the medicine a disease cannot be cured. Without direct realisation, liberation is not possible by chanting the word 'Brahmam'.

•• अकृत्वा दृश्यविलयं अज्ञात्वा तत्वमात्मनः
ब्रह्मशब्दैः कुतो मुक्ति-रुक्तिमात्र फलैर् नृणां ॥ *(V.chu.63)*

akrthva drsya'vilayam
ajnatva thathwam'athmana
brahma'shabdai kutho mukthi-
rukthi'maathra phalair nrnaam.

Without dissolving all that is seen, and without realising the real nature of the Self, a mere repetition of the word 'Brahmam' surely will be a useless vocal exercise.

•• जाग्रस्वप्नसुषुप्तिषु स्फुटतरं
योसौसमुज्जृम्भ्यते .....
नित्यानन्दचिदात्मना स्फुरति तं-
विद्धि स्वमेतं हृदि ॥ *(Vivekachoodamani 217)*

jagrad-swapna-sushupthishu sphuta'tharam
yo'sau'samujjrmbhyathe
nithyaananda'chidaathmanaa sphurathi tham-viddhi
swametham hrdi.

That which clearly manifests with all intensity in the waking, dream and sleep as your ego (the individual entity – the 'I-ness') ...is your Self; understand that clearly. The subject illumines the objects outside. The subject can be recognised inside, in the deeper recesses of the personality, as the ever-expressing 'I, I, I', the individuality. The 'I' (aham) is the factor by whose grace our experiences within and without are made possible. The one Reality illumining the various types of experiences at the various personality levels, and ever expressing Itself as I, I, I, — shining as Existence-Knowledge-Bliss Absolute deep within, is your real nature to be realised.

•• सद् भाव वासना दार्ठ्यात्
तत् त्रयं लयमश्नुते ॥ *(Vivekachoodamani 316)*

sad'bhaava vaasanaa'daardhyaath
thath'thrayam layam'asnuthe.

Through the strengthening ..solidifying .. of the proper attitude (I am the Reality) these three (thoughts, actions and vasanas) are purged.

•• .....मलमांसमयं वपुः
त्यक्त्वा चण्डालवत् दूरं
ब्रह्मीभूयः कृती भव ॥ *(Vivekachoodamani 287)*

.....mala'maamsa'mayam vapu:
tyakthva chandaalavath'dooram
brahmee'bhooya: krthee bhava.

Shun the body away at a distance—like an outcast; it is made up of flesh and all other impurities. Be thou Brahmam and realize the consummation of thy life.

The Approach

• • विषं दृष्ट्वाऽमृतंदृष्ट्वा विषं त्यजति बुद्धिमान्
आत्मानमपि दृष्ट्वाऽमनात्मानं त्यजाम्यहं ॥

visham drshtwa amrtham drshtwa
visham tyajati buddhiman
atmanamapi drshtwa ham'
anatmaanam tyajamiaham.

Out of the poison and *amrtham* (ambrosia/nectar – that keeps death away) seen in front, a sensible person keeps away from poison, and chooses amrtham. Cognizing the *Atman* (Self), I discard the *an-Atman* (not-self).

(Atmaprabodha Upa. II.17)

The Attitude:

• • निष्क्रियोस्म्यविकारोस्मि
निष्कलोस्मि निराकृतिः
निर्विकल्पोस्मि नित्योस्मि
निरालंबोस्मि निर्द्वयः

nish'kriyosmyavikaarosmi nishkalosmi niraakrthi
nirvikalposmi nithyosmi niraalambosmi nirdwaya.

I am action-less, immutable, un-partitioned, formless. I am transcendent, eternal, not founded on anything, and non-dual.

• • Where the sense organs are not utilized to engage with their respective objects ... in the absence of utilization of sense organs ... senses retire.

(...स्वस्वविषयसम्प्रयोगाभावे)   (*Yogasutra*-54 P68)
(*swa-swa vishaya samprayoga'abhaave*)

- *neti-neti pramanena niraakrtho'khilam jagath
hrda samaaswaaditha chid'khanamrtham*

(Drg-drsya vivekam is underneath this).

Eliminating the universe – including your body – by the 'neti-neti'-process (I am not this, not this), remain enjoying with your heart the immortality and glory of your Awareness, in saturated ecstasy eternal ..'*chid'khana'amrtham*'.

- मनसैवेदमाप्तव्यं नेह नानास्ति किञ्चन
मृत्यो स मृत्युं गच्छति य इह नानेव पश्यति ॥
*manasaiveda-maapthavyam
neha nana'asthi kinchana.
mrthyo sa mrthyum gacchathi
ya iha naneva pasyathi.*

"By the mind, indeed, is this (Realisation) to be attained. Multiplicity is not here at all. He who sees anything other than Himself (his Self) / Brahmam – passes from death to death."

I prefer to take it with an amendment: 'Multiplicity is not in me, the awareness'. Whatever there is, is in the field that I witness ...that does not affect me. Like the lamp in the house. I am the 'eye of the universe' ...the awareness.

Mulla story – train

Mulla travels in the train, fully drunk always. One day he got off the train in a down-and-out condition—vomiting, sweating, feverish. A friend enquired as to what went wrong.

Mulla: "You know I always like to sit facing the engine end of the train, not the tail end. Otherwise I am in trouble"

Friend: "You could have exchanged seats with the person on your opposite seat?

Mulla: "Am I a muff? I thought of that; but there was no-one on the opposite seat!"

People spend the whole life senseless....and still think they are very wise.

— The universe remains non-reconciled. ..Yes. But if you know –when you know – that you are eternal, peaceful, unchallenged by anything – any super authority either....that is a very great glorious state – enough to rejoice ..to be peaceful absolutely. Let the universe remain (separately though) you have nothing to do with it. It cannot in any way affect you—whether it rotates, revolves, expands, contracts and then explodes – it does not matter to you at all in the least. So don't worry on that score ....the universe cannot even scratch your surface.

But if you insist on a dissolution of the universe – an absorption of the universe in you – is it going to be possible? How will anyone obliterate this vast universe?

It stays in your Awareness; it stays outside also. It stays inside as a mirror image; the object is definitely outside— definitely not inside the mirror. How can we negate – refute – simply cast away and forget the universe and the working of its laws of physics and chemistry and our irrefutable experience? If someone argues that the universe is all atoms— molecules—electron-proton-neutron – quarks – and ultimately only energy-pulsation, does that relieve you of your physical body, its pains and pangs, the perils of the world faced by you and your near and dear ones and all others around—and all the fireworks going on in this universe?

Awareness envelops the universe.....the universe revels in Awareness ... universe revolves in awareness ...the universe exists in awareness (so to say) ...the Awareness holds the universe in it. The existence or non-existence of the universe in you the Awareness, does not matter a bit to you the Awareness. The waves that rise and subside in the ocean, do not cause any addition or diminution to the ocean ...no gain or loss to the ocean. Ocean is unaffected by the rise and fall of the waves. Awareness is unaffected by the universe ...by the existence or non-existence of the universe.

I.	PURE Awareness ... one Universe ... another $1+1 = 2$ This is COMMOM SENSE equation
II.	INTEGRAL WHOLE nothing else (kevalam) $1+1 = 1$ (Awareness is; universe is not. Therefore One.)

To me this (II) seems to be what the Maya theory says.

Suppose we try to understand as—

    Awareness holds everything in it
    'Everything is born of me
    Everything stays in me
    Everything dissolves in me'
    ...is it tenable? —valid?   true?

Mirror or camera captures the scene; but the scene is outside. Situations are outside; but their impact / scintillation/ prick / effect is inside.

Thadaathmyam ...identifying with it ... superimposition ... taking on the situation inside—is the reason. Know that you are Pure—and still deal with the situation. (*thena thyakthena bhunjitha*)

A glass cube to look red, there should be something red outside.

***   ***   ***

•• The mind that subsides by control of breath ...comes alive on breathing. ... A caged bird flies off, the moment the door opens. (Ramana Maharshi: *vaayu rodhanath leeyathe mana: ....jaala pakshi vath...*)

•• Advaita Jnanam (knowledge of non-duality) is also a state of mind (*mano vrtthi*). (*Vedanta prabodh*)

•• "Experiencing the bliss of existence—is Samadhi." Osho Shailendra-ji

"You are you, because of the Infinite functioning through the total *vasanas.* When you remove your equipments[1], there is neither a world for you, nor a concept of God. Then alone will you come to understand that *Jeeva* and *Iswara* are one and the same. In order to realize that You are Brahmam, the Reality, .. the intellect must be prepared by the study of the scriptures, as well as by independent thinking and reflection.

"By an intellect which has been so prepared for this great flight, you must negate the body, the mind and the intellect and come to apprehend the Truth.

"In the profound declaration "That Thou Art", the implied meaning has to be ascertained and appreciated by an intellect which has already been prepared by the study of the scriptures. The word meaning, in itself, certainly sounds

---

[1] Body, mind and intellect.

absurd. One should try to understand the implied meaning of the sacred words of the great Rishis which burst forth from them in the white-hot moments of their Experience-divine.

"If you dandle the words, they convey no meaning. They talk directly of an impossibility. Therefore you have to go deeper, analyse ruthlessly, and understand the secret sacred meaning behind them, in order to get into the very experience of the Oneness—the experience of the common denominator in you and God—the Infinite Eternal Truth." (the awareness – $\mathcal{D}_n$) (Swami Chinmayananda in his commentary on *Vivekachudamani* 247)

- • Let the physical, material universe exist with all its fireworks—explosions and turmoil; but the lasting, more lasting, ever-lasting Eternal Factor, Entity remains unaffected.
- • When you see the entire space, the pot-space vanishes (even while it exists).

"The body and the mind are limited and, therefore, vulnerable. They need protection, which gives rise to fear. As long as you identify yourself with them you are bound to suffer. Realise your independence and remain happy. I tell you this is the secret of happiness.

"To believe that you depend on things and people for happiness is due to ignorance of your true nature. To know that you need nothing to be happy, except Self Knowledge, is wisdom. The ultimate security is found only in Self Knowledge." (*words of Nisarga Dutta Maharaj*)

Nisarga Dutta also said a few words when he was asked: 'Do you pray?'.

"Whom do I pray? And what for? ...and some more. You may look up 'I AM THAT'.

anantham **vibhum** *nirvikalpam nireeham*
sivam sanga-heenam yad'omkara-gamyam
niraakaara-mathyujjwalam mrthyu-heenam
param Brahma-nithyam tadeva'ham'asmi. (1)*

aksharam paramam Brahmam
jyothi'roopam sanathanam
gunaateetham niraakaaram
swecchamayam *ananthakam*   (2)*

I was looking out for pure, unmixed, verses for use in my meditation. These two verses (above*) came very close to my expectation; but I found that like a pebble among pearls the word 'vibhum' (in the 1st verse), and 'sweccha-mayam' (in the 2nd verse) contaminated them. **Vibhu** = that forms into many. I don't think this fits well with Awareness. **Sweccha-mayam** = self-willed (will) / with desire. Almost all teachers teach this—in the midst of pure stuff. I was weighed down by these. I used to find it incongruous ...in the way of clear thinking. At long last, Swami Vivekananda's words, spoken with undaunted courage and conviction, came to my help. I was relieved, happy. A stone that weighed me down, rolled away.

Swami Vivekananda:- "True Being is undifferentiated+ and **eternal.** How does the Perfect Being become mixed up with will, mind, thought—all defective things? It never has become mixed. You are the Real You. You never were will, you never have changed, you as a person never existed. It is illusion." (SV Vol.6, p.45)

•• अवस्तात्रयभावाभावसाक्षी

स्वयं भावरहितं   (*Sarvasaropanishad-4*)

+ Partless, component-less, not divided, single, whole, without anything else other than Itself.

avasthaa'thraya bhaava'abhaava'saakshi
swayam bhaava'rahitham

Witness of the three states... witness of existence and non-existence of things and attitudes ....and itself devoid of any attitude!

Setting aside all this Upanishadic teaching, how do people assert that It is self-willed?

•• नरिच्छो वर्तते कार्ये स जीवन्मुक्त उच्यते ॥
(Mahopanishad 51) U-112/II-p222

nirichcho varthathe kaarye
sa jivan-muktha uchchyathe

He is jivan-muktha who gets along without even a semblance of desire or will.

Even for jivanmuktha '*nir-iccha*' is a required qualification. Then how is 'iccha' (will/desire) thrust on Brahmam? (sweccha-mayam....)? Gaudapaada also asks a pertinent question: How is it that the 'desireless' becomes desireous?" (*aaptha'kaamasya ka sprha*).

•• (*bhogartham ... annye, ... kreedarthamithi'chaapare ...*) Some say that the world is created for *bhogam* (for the *jivas*/ souls to enjoy and suffer (the consequences of actions/ karma) .. some others say it is created for fun (to get rid of boredom). Gaudapaada looks at this with disapproval ...and he says, there is no possibility of a creation in Brahmam (bodham) ...and so nothing is created ...if you see anything, it is illusion. Here the confusion is further confounded ....to my understanding. How can anyone swallow this theory of illusion?

Conceiving something ...conjuring up something ...is the faculty of the mind. They bring in the Universal Mind here –

Hiranyagarbha. But a mind ...macro or micro –is a black mark on the pure consciousness. If a mind is added on to it, it then becomes impure. Copper-added gold cannot be said to be pure gold.

•• स्थावरं जंगमं व्याप्तं
यत् किञ्चित्सचराचरं । *(Guru sthothram)*
*sthaavarm jangamam vyaaptham
yath'kinchit'sacharaacharam.*

"It pervades the movables and immovables; but It does not have these in It." This is yet another beacon light thrown on your path...a clean pointer.

To me, it says that sense objects are not in Awareness; awareness is all-pervasive. Sense objects are not a product of awareness. ...Awareness is not a producer of sense objects. It only shows up if something exists.

Power? .... Swami Ram Tirth points out that 'The power that grows the trees, ...that grows the hair' ... is your Reality/ Brahmam. But I tend to believe that it is the power that **'knows'** that the hair is growing ...the tree is growing.

     ***   ***   ***

•• तथा जगदभावेन सदात्मैवावशिष्यते ॥ *(Advaitanubhoothi 69)*
thadha jagad'abhaavena sadaathmaivavasishyathe.

Likewise, in the absence of the world, Athman alone remains always.

•• यथेश्वरादिनाशेन ताम्रनाशो न विद्यते
तथेश्वरादिनाशेन नाशोनैवात्मनःसदा ॥
(Advaitanubhoothi 67)
*yadheswaraadi naashena thaamra'naso na vidyathe
thatheswaraadi naasena naso'naivaathmana sadah.*

The figure of a god embossed on a copper plate fades out, and even then the plate remains. Similarly, with the dissolution of the gods and all, your Self remains...eternally.

What is grahyam (fit to be taken)?

•• देशकालवस्तुपरिच्छेदरहित चिन्मात्रस्वरूपं ग्राह्यं
desa-kaala-vasthu-pariccheda'rahitha
chinmaathra'swarupam grahyam.

Only that Reality of Absolute Consciousness which is not conditioned by space, time or substance *(Niralamba Upanishad 37)*

Who is vidwan (the learned)?

One who has cognized the true form (reality) of his own consciousness that is present in all. *(Niralamba Upanishad-32)*

(सर्वान्तरस्थ स्वसंविद्रूपविद्धिद्वान्)
(sarvantharastha swasamvid'rupa viddhi'vidvan)

***　　　***　　　***

•• "You **knew** that you did not understand. Understand the one who **knew;** that will do." (Swami Bodhananda in the course of a discussion)

•• आत्मज्ञानमयः पुण्यो देहो मांसमयोऽशुचिः
तयोरैक्यं प्रपश्यन्ति किमज्ञानमतःपरं ॥

(Aparokshanubhuthi-19)

athma jnana'mayo punya
deho maamsa'mayo-asuchi
thayor'aikyam pra'pasyanthi
kim ajnaanam'atha'param?

Athma is Awareness clean...and body is flesh unclean. We think we are a combination of these... integral. What ignorance can be there greater than this?

••
    aatmanam araneem krtwa
    pranavam chotharaaranim
    jnana nirmadhana'abhyasath
    paapam dahati pandita.

Using Athma as the base-*arani,* and *Pranavam* (or for that matter **shivohum)** as the upper *arani* ...by constant churning of knowledge the learned burn up their *paapam* (get rid of the bondage of karma).

••
    त्यागप्रपञ्चरूपस्य चिदात्मत्वावलोकनात्
    त्यागोहि महतांपूज्यः सद्योमोक्षमयोयतः

(Aparokshanubhoothi 106)

    tyaga prapancha rupasya
    chidathmathwa'avalokanath
    tyago hi mahathaam pujya
    sadyo'moksha'mayoyatha:

Seeing your Awareness —cognizing the Awareness (chid-Athma) ...having a clear grasp of your awareness, ...(firming up that you are the object-less eternal Awareness), discard the *prapancham* (sense objects..the world). This is the greatest ..noblest.. thing to do.... that brings about instant liberation.

••
    दृढधियः तुष्णीं शिलावत् स्थित : *(Proudhanubhoothi 13)*
    drdha dhiya: thushnim shilavath sthitha

Those who are firmly rooted in the Reality will only sit quiet like a stone...(not engaging in arguments).

•• यथा निरिन्धनो वह्नि
स्वयमेव प्रशाम्यति
yadha nirindhano vahni
swayameva prasaamyathi

As the fire subsides when the fuel runs out——

•• बहुनात्रकिमुक्तेन
संक्षेपादिदमुच्यते
सङ्कल्पनं परोबन्ध:
स्तदभावो विमुक्त ॥

bahuna'thra'kim'ukthena
samkshepa'didam'uchyathe
samkalpanam paro'bandha:
sthath'abhavo vimukthatha. (Vasishtam)

Why discuss at length? To put it in a nut-shell, conjuring up of objects-emotions-and-thoughts (OET) (mental modifications) is the Bondage; and its absence is Liberation.

•• Some people use the word 'superconsciousness' to denote Turiyam (fourth state) … Samadhi. What does this word mean? Sitting with a mind filled with a massive collection of thoughts and knowledge of all the minds? A thoughtless state is Samadhi …a transcendent consciousness.

•• निमिषार्थं न तिष्ठन्ति बुद्धिं ब्रह्ममयिंविना
यथा तिष्ठन्ति ब्रह्माद्य सनकाद्या शुकादय: (Vasishtam)

nimishartham na thishtanthi
budhim Brahma-mayim vinaa
yatha tishtanthi Brahmadya
Sanakadya Sukadaya.

Even for a split-second, don't shift from the Brahmam-attitude (Brahma bhavam). Brahma-Vishnu-Mahesa, and Deva Rshis such as Sanaka and human Maha Rshis such as Suka.. are all in this *bhavam* always. Always be in this awareness ... I AM REALITY-AWARENESS-BLISS ABSOLUTE

* like a woman who tasted conjugal pleasure for the first time always remembers it, and even while engaged in household work, always looks out for her lover. (This is from an Upanishad)
* like a mother who has a baby sleeping in the next room, and she is working in the kitchen ...more than on her work, her main attention is centred on the baby.
* like someone who kept milk on fire to boil.
* like a mother with her baby in hand moves along as a pillion rider (whatever she does – looking at the scenes around, watching the road etc. her main attention is riveted on the hold on the baby).
* like a danceuse with a water-pot on her head. While stepping in tune with the music and presenting a wonderful performance her main anxiety is to see that the water-pot sits safe on her head.

(sangeetha'thala'laya'nrttha'vasangathaangi maulistha kumbhha parirakshana vyagratha...)

(*Vivekachudamani*)

•• "When you realize your Athma-hood, you know all as the one Athma. No distinction is felt nor can it be recognized as separate. It is not possible to distinguish the different 'essences' collected by the different bees from various flowers which commingled to form the one unified honey'.

(Ch. 6.9.1-2)

•• When you are aware of your identity with the Athman, you are free from all the distinctions entailed by name and form—like a river loses its identity and individuality when it merges into the ocean. (Mu.3.2.8, Br.2.4.12, 4.5.14, Tai.2.1, 2.6, Ch.6.2.1. 7.24.1)

•• When you have directly realized that 'I am that Brahmam', where is the need for you to follow the instincts and temptations of the body and mind and suffer with them? (Br.4.4.12)

•• He who considers the pleasures of the senses as the all-in-all of life, gets rebirth into such conditions in which pleasures are in plenty. But others whose desires are extinguished, will not have to be born again—all will be over in the present life itself (Mu.3.2.2)

•• *So'hum-bhavo namaskara*: (*Athmapuja-Upanishad*) In Athmapuja. the attitude 'I am That' is the *namaskaram* (salute to deity).

•• Athma should be realized with the Athma (awareness) itself. (*Kathopanishad*)

•• A stage where even the seasoned stabilised intellect[+] ceases functioning ...is the ultimate state. ..*paraa gati*. (Katho. p39 Kailas.) God Death does not say here that in the ultimate state you will be all-knowing and all-powerful. Note it, closely, please.

'This much is the essence of Vedanta. *Vishuddham, amrtham, shuddham* – pure, eternal, clean'. ..says God Death. (Katho. p40 Kailas) Listen to it. He does not point out that It is all-powerful. No insistence ...no mention even. It is so. Don't think otherwise. Don't get into a jungle.

•• Your own awareness is nothing distant to you; It is your closest and most intimate experience (*swaprakasam, aparoksham*) ...it is not hidden ...it is apparent ...like daylight

---
+ Seasoned in Brahma-jnanam, stabilized in Brahma-bhavam.

...not to be searched with a microscope or telescope. Only a shift in understanding is required .. that is all. Fish should not be thirsty in the water *(paani mae meenu pyaasi)*. To blink the eyes a little effort is required; even that much effort is not required for realizing what you already are.

•• The idea of meditation is a declaration of one's own sense of imperfection—an unforgivable sin against the Perfect Self. (Swami Chinmayananda)

•• श्रवणादिभिरुद्दीप्त ज्ञानाग्निपरितापितः
जीवस्सर्वमलान्मुक्त स्वर्णवद्द्योतते स्वयं ॥ *(Atmabodham 66)*
*sravanaadibhir-uddeepta jnanagni paaritaapita
jeeva sarva malaan mukta swarnavat dyotate swayam.*

Burnt in the fire of 'sravanam–mananam-etc' the impurities of jiva are removed, and it shines like burnished gold.

•• "Thinking along these lines ... the mind of the practitioner becomes more and more quiet, the bliss of his own nature overwhelms him and his mind attains a total stillness. There is a complete cessation of all objects . ... In *nirvikalpa* Samadhi one experiences an infinitude free from all limitations and consequent desires. The mind remains ever so calm and Self-absorbed. In such a dynamic calmness, there is no boredom and thus no need for entertainment". (Swami Tejomayananda in his commentary on *Drg Drsya Viveka p89*)

•• Abidance in your own form ...abandoning the conditioned form ...is liberation.

•• The soul / Self abides in its own nature ...pure, alone, emancipated ...even beyond the sat-chit-ananda bhavana ..beyond the reach of words.

•• It is untouched by the pathos of the world. (*na lipyathe loka-dukkhena*) like sunlight. (P35 Katho... Kailas) ...even in the midst of the greatest of calamities.

•• I simply leave these four (4) Sanskrt verses here for those who know a bit of Sanskrt can have at least a glimpse of their profundity:-

(1) द्वे पदे बन्धमोक्षाय निर्ममेति ममेति च ।
ममेति बन्धते जन्तुर्निर्ममेति विमुच्यते ॥

(Mahopanishad 72)

(2) चित्ताकाशं चिदाकाशमाकाशं च तुरीयकं ।
द्वाभ्यां शून्यतरं विद्धि चिदाकाशं महामुने ॥

(IV 58 Mahopanishad)

(3) उपेक्ष्ये नामरूपेद्वे सच्चिदानन्दतत्परः discussed before
समाधिं सर्वदा कुर्याद् हृदये वाऽथवा बहिः

(Drg-drsya vivekam-22)

(4) पौरुषेण प्रयत्नेन यस्मिन्नेव पदे मनः
योज्यते तत्पदं प्राप्य निर्विकल्पो भवानघ ॥

(Mahopanishad IV.102)

The actor casts off his costumes[1] and the related role ...and remains what he really is: ...the Awareness ..the Eye of the World, **"Prajna Nethro Loka"**.

---

[1] When the actor casts off his costumes — as Prof. Balakrishnan Nair usually puts it.

3

JIVANMUKTHI — THE GOAL

Here is a passage from TURIYATITA-UPANISHAD — a question-answer session between Brahma and Bhagawan Narayana where the state of jivanmuktha is exhaustively explained:-

"He does research with his own soul; and having known the mystery of all illusions, he throws his *kamandalu, langoti, kaupina*[1], garments (all the things normally carried by a sanyasi) into water. He becomes fully naked. He abandons also the deer-hide, chanting of hymns, shaving, bathing, *tripundra* on forehead, gives up all worldly and *vedic* rites and even abandons the feelings of good and bad as also the ignorance. He endures the pains of weather (heat and cold) the vicissitudes, honour and insult etc. He burns into ashes the trio-passions of his body, the feeling of criticism, praise, ego, vanity, malice, desire, envy, anger, greed, affection, gaiety, sorrow. He even does not care about self-protection[2] and self-endurance. He looks upon his body as a corpse. Profit and loss are alike for him; he is contented (in his own self). He sleeps under the trees. Hands are his begging bowl.

---

1 The minimal, narrow piece of cloth with which male genitals are wrapped.
2 He does not carry any sort of a device for self-defence / protection.

"He keeps himself free from greed, the learning and pedantry. He keeps the divine mysteries duly accumulated within his heart and outwardly looks like an idiot. He neither grieves in sorrow nor feels elated on gaiety. Affection has no place in his heart; and good or bad happenings do not impact him. All his senses are cooled down. He becomes reluctant and distanced from all his preceding *asrama*, learning, religion and influences of his past; and abandons the etiquettes prescribed by *varnasrama*. Day and night are alike for him. His body is something that he needs casting off. The water-sources he meets on the way (ponds, wells) are his water-pot. He is unconcerned with everything. Outwardly, he moves like an intoxicated person, or a child. He is alone always. He doesn't talk to anyone. He is engrossed in his Genuine Form." (TURIYATITA-UPANISHAD)

He lives contented with whatever is met for food, like a cow ...sumptuous, frugal, scanty, bitter, sweet, tasty, not tasty ... whatever comes his way, he is satisfied with it. (*mrshta, shushka, kad'vamla kashaya*..etc. Upanishad. Ref lost.).

•• After churning the butter out of butter-milk, even if the butter is left in the buttermilk it does not dissolve back. Similarly, once you see the Reality, then there is no sliding back.

•• Jeevan-muktha sees the world—
- * as a picture (without a hard-and-fast reality)
- * as a snake-skin (with no snake in it)
- * The world for him is a burnt rope. (it looks like a carbon-fibre rope, but it cannot tie anything. Blow air at it, it flies off as ashes.)

He walks the world as a "walking dead-body" (no thoughts, no feelings, no fear of death either). (*Nada-yaadiya pinam - / Tamil*)

* He walks through the world as you walk through a market in which things not required by you are stored.
* He does not run after anything; nor run away from anything.
* Vagaries of nature do not worry him.

•• *dharmartha kama moksheshu*
jeevithe marane thadha
kasyapyudaara chithasya
heyopadeyatha nahi.   (Asht.Gita XVII.6)

He has neither attraction nor aversion to piety, worldly prosperity, desire-fulfillment. Liberation doesn't mean anything to him; even life and death doesn't make any difference to him.

•• 'Free from the impulses of the mischievous mind, released from the jarring broils of the world, ….the body is in repose in its highest and perfect felicity…at death'. (IV.15.23 Yogavaasistham) Similar is the situation with the *jivanmukthan* also.

Strong swimmer on a flimsy bridge:

Imagine a strong swimmer walking on a flimsy bridge across a harmless river. He is not so much concerned about the bridge staying or giving way. Even if the bridge gives way, nothing serious is going to happen to him. A splash down into the water, a little swim to the shore, and the botheration of managing the wet clothes – nothing serious.

Ch.3 Jivanmukthi — The goal

<u>Similarly death is not a great concern for one who knows that he is deathless.</u>

- - *drsya'darshana nirmuktha*
  kevalaamala rupavaan
  nithyoditho niraabhaasa
  drshta saakshee chidaathmaka
  chaithanya nirmuktha chidroopam
  poorna'jyothi'swaroopakam

  (Mahopanishad VI.80 p. 675, Upa.108 related p.265 in Upa.112)

This verse is in Ch.I p25. I want to repeat ..I would like you to repeat it here also. (please go back and re-read).

Mahopanishad continues:-

- - *samshantha sarva samvedyam*
  samvin'maatrhram'aham'mahath.
  samshaantha sarva'samkalpa
  prashaantha sakaleishana
  nir'vikalpa'padam gathva
  swastho'bhava muneeshwara.

With all the sense perceptions abated ...with a mind void of worldly issues   ...bereft of all mental modifications ...with all desires faded out ....remaining as the power of Perception (*samvid*)   ....reach the '*nir-vikalpa*' state and settle down in silence.

- - अत्यन्त कामुकस्यापि
  वृत्तिकुण्ठति मातरिः
  तथैव ब्रह्मणिज्ञाते
  पूर्णानन्दे मनीषिणः ॥   (*Vivekachudamani 445*)

> *athyantha kaamukasyaapi*
> *vrtthi kundhathi maathari*
> *thadhaiva brahmani'jnaathe*
> *poornaanande maneeshina.*

Even an extremely uncontrollable super-sensitive libertine will not indulge in sensuality in the presence of his mother. So too, worldly propensities will not raise their hood in one who has realised the knowledge of Brahmam, and abides in bliss Absolute.

•• सानुरागं स्त्रियां दृष्ट्वा
मृत्युवा समुपस्थितं
अविह्वल मनाः स्वस्थो
मुक्त एव महाशयः ॥   *(Asht.Gita XVII.14)*

saanuragam sthriyaam drshtwa
mrthyuva samupasthitham
avihwala mana swastho
muktha eva mahaasaya

He is not perturbed by the sight of an amorous woman ... as well as approaching death.

•• He is undisturbed by the *prana* and the mind.

(अप्राणोह्यमनो स्वस्थः
मुक्तएव महाशयः॥
aprano'hyamano swastha
muktha eva mahasaya).

•• The absolute and single[+] eternal blissful 'Reality ...Awareness' .. is his god. *(Advaitha sadanando devata).* (*Nirvana-Upanishad*) (p126 Upa-112/II)

+ Non-dual, one only, no-two.

•• घटे नष्टे यथा व्योम व्योमैव भवति स्फुटं
तथैवोपाधिविलये ब्रह्मैव ब्रह्मविद्स्वयं ॥

(Vivekachudamani 566)

khade nashte yatha vyoma
vyomaiva bhavathi sphutam
thathaivopaadhivilaye
brahmaiva brahmavid'swayam

Pot-space becomes the endless space. Awareness knows its stature. (explained in Chapter II)

•• निर्धनोपि सदा तृप्तोऽप्यसहायो महाबलः
नित्यतृप्तोऽप्यभुञ्जानाऽप्यसमःसमदर्शनः ॥

(Vivekachudamani 544)

nirdhanopi sadah trptho'pyasahaayo mahaabala:
nithyathrptho'pyabhunjaanah'pyasama:samadarsana.

Though without wealth, he is ever-satisfied. Though without help, he is very powerful. Though he does not enjoy sense objects, he is eternally contented. Though without any equal, his vision is equalized.

•• "When you go deeper, you lose yourself in the abysmal depths, then the Reality which is the Athma that was behind you all the while, takes hold of you. It is an incessant flash of I-consciousness –you can be aware of it, feel it, hear it, sense it, so to say. This is what I call *AHAM SPHOORTHI*" (self fulfillment). *(ref. lost. Words of Nisarga Dutta, I think.)*

"De-hypnotised from the enchantments of the sense-objects, he lives deriving his satisfaction and fulfillment from the self, and therefore any object-of-experience that reaches him accidentally – be it good or bad – can cause in him neither a great pleasure nor a terrible pain. No object-of-the-world gained can add to his Absolute Bliss, nor can the loss of any object reduce his Infinite Bliss.

"The mind of the *jivanmuktha* has discovered a complete sense of fulfillment in the experience of the Infinite Self, and therefore there is no question of his mind roaming away into the world of sense-pleasures, of its own initiative. He remains at peace with himself and with the world around.

"Never does he lose sight of his own inner kingdom of the experience of the self. He lives in a state of unbroken *samaadhi* even while he lives and acts as a member of the community.

"His senses have become inoperative. The perfected man sees, hears, smells, tastes and touches; his senses function, but none of them bring their share of storms into the bosom of the sage, since his mind has already merged in the Universal Consciousness. In his world the devastating storms of thoughts have ceased. "In him the ocean of the world has dried up". (*ksheena samsaara saagare*) (XVII.9 Asht.Gita)

"He is so firmly established at the substratum, that there can be no attachment or aversion towards the world of objects, beings, and happenings.

"One who has awakened to the Pure Consciousness finds that the One Blissful envelopes all. In that blissful state he finds that all his desires have ended, all goals have been reached, even his anxiety for liberation ceases. His mind rolls away, and all its agitations suddenly calm themselves into an infinite dynamic Peace – all by themselves, spontaneously. The body and the senses halt in their functions. Far beyond all traces of identifications with the body, mind and intellect – calm and serene – the seeker now comes to experience the Kaivalya-state of the Self – all-pervading and

Ch.3 Jivanmukthi — The goal 181

immutable." (*words of Swami Chinmayananda commenting on Ashtavakra Gita Ch.XVII*).

- आत्मन्येवाखिलंदृश्यं प्रविलाप्य धिया सुधी
  भावयेदेकमात्मानं निर्मवाकाशवत्सदा । *(Atma Bodham 39)*

  atmanyeva'akhilam drsyam
  pravilaapya dhiyaa sudhee
  bhaavayet'ekam'aathmaanam
  nirmalaakaasavath sadaa

The wise should intelligently merge the entire world of objects in Atman alone, and constantly think of that Atman like the pure space. (*nirmalaakasavath*).

- रूपवर्णादिकं सर्वं विहाय परमार्थवित्
  परिपूर्ण चिदानन्द-स्वरूपेणावतिष्ठते ॥ *(Atma Bodham 40)*

  roopa'varnaadikam sarvam
  vihaaya paramartha'vith
  paripurna chidananada
  swarupena'avathishtate

He who has attained the Supreme Goal discards all names and forms, and dwells as the embodiment of Infinite Consciousness and Bliss.

- येन विश्वमिदं दृष्टं स नास्तीति करोतु वै
  निर्वासनः किं कुरुते पश्यन्नपि न पश्यति॥

  (Asht.Gita XVIII.15)

  yena viswamidam drshtam sa naasti'ti karotu vai
  nir'vaasana kim kurute pasyan'api'na pasyati.

He who sees the universe, may have a necessity to discard it. What has the desireless to do? He sees not, even though he sees.

•• अहो विकल्पितं विश्वं अज्ञानान्मयि भासते
रूप्यं शुक्तौ फणी रज्जौ वारि सूर्यकरे यथा   *(Asht. Gita II.9)*

aho vikalpitham viswam
ajnanaal mayi bhasate
roopyam shuktau bhani rajjau
vaari surya'karae yadha.

'The universe appears in me ….by a delusion …like silver in mussel, snake in a rope, water in sunbeam. (mirage is meant here). These are the classic examples commonly cited to explain *adhyasam* …what looks real, but does not exist'.

I suggest you forget this normal approach …and simply try to see that IN YOU THE UNIVERSE DOES NOT EXIST …IN YOU THE AWARENESS THE UNIVERSE DOES NOT EXIST …YOU ARE CLEAN, PURE … NO MIX. But universe exists …outside. And seemingly the awareness is mixed up with the universe. <u>Your awareness seems mixed up with body and mind.</u> Remember the drama stage lamp, here; the scene, and the light. And also the glass cube + hibiscus flower.

•• तरङ्गस्थं द्रवं सिन्धुर्न वाञ्छति यथा तथा ।
विषयानन्दवाञ्छा मे मा भूदानन्दरूपतः ।
दारिद्र्याशा यथा नास्ति संपन्नस्य तथा मम ॥

tarangastham jalam sindhur'
na'vanchathi yatha thatha
vishayaananda vaancha mae
maabhoothananda'rupatha.
daaridryaasa yatha nasthi
sampannasya thatha mama.

(Atmabodhopanishad II.15 &16)

Ch.3 Jivanmukthi — The goal

The ocean has no eye on the waters of the waves. In a wealthy person the desire for poverty does not arise. Similarly in me – steeped in Brahmic Bliss – the desire for sensual pleasures cannot arise.

·· तीर्त्वा मोहार्णवं हत्वा रागद्वेषादि राक्षसान्
योगीशान्तिसमायुक्त आत्मारामो विराजते ।

*theerthva mohaarnavam,
hathwa raga-dweshaadi raakshasaan
yogi shanthi samaayuktha
atma'aramo virajatae.   (Atma Bodham 50)*

Crossing the ocean of delusion, killing the monsters of passion and aversion, a jivankuktha becomes united with Peace and dwells in the Bliss derived from the realisation of the Self.

·· बाह्यानित्य सुखासक्तिं
हित्यात्मसुखनिर्वृतः
घटस्थदीपवत्स्वस्थः
स्वान्तरेव प्रकाशते ॥   (Atma Bodham 51)

*bahyaanithya sukhaasakthim
hitwatmasukha nirvrtha
khadastha'deepavat swastha
swanthareva prakaasathe.*

Relinquishing attachment to illusory external happiness, the Self-abiding jivanmuktha, satisfied with the Bliss derived from Atman, shines inwardly …undisturbed …like a lamp placed inside a jar.

·· हर्षामर्ष भयक्रोध कामकार्पण्यदृष्टिभि
न परामृश्यतेयोऽन्तः स जीवन्मुक्त उच्यते ॥

> harsha'marsha bhaya krodha
> kaama kaarpanya drshti bhi
> na paraamrsyatheyo'ntha
> sa jivanmuktha uchyathe
>
> *(Vaasista sudha p.246, verse 116)*

The mind of one who has seen his Reality is shut ...door-closed ...to all feelings. Elation, resentment, fear, anger, desire, *kaarpanya drshthi* (the feeling that 'I am in a pitiable condition – needing the help of others) all such feelings-emotions-and-thoughts have no entry into the heart of one who has seen his Reality. The mind becomes defunct ...for ever ...as in deep sleep; and he lives on.

•• उपाधिस्थोऽपि तद्धमैरलिप्तो व्योमवन्मुनिः
सर्वविन्मूढवत्तिष्टेदसक्तो वायुवच्चरेत् ॥ *(Atma Bodham 52)*

> upadhistho'pi thath'dharmair'
> aliptho vyomavan'muni
> sarvavin'mudhavath'thishte'
> dasaktho vayuvad'chareth.

Though associated with upadhis (body, mind etc.), the contemplative one is undefiled by their traits – like the sky – and he remains unruffled under all conditions, as if he is a dud. He moves about like the wind, not tied up to anything.

•• यो वै भूमा तत् सुखं न अल्पे सुखमस्ति
(Chandogya Upanishad 7.23)

> yo vai bhuma thath sukham na alpe sukham asthi

Peace is in the totality, fullness ...not in the limited forms.

•• यत्र नान्यत्पश्यति नान्यच्छृणोति नान्यद्विजानाति स भूमा
(Chandogya Upanishad 7.24.1)

Ch.3   Jivanmukthi — The goal

yathra nanyath'pasyathi naanyachrnothi
naanyadwijaanaathi sa bhuma.

Where one sees nothing else, hears nothing else, knows nothing else, that is fullness….complete…totality. (There is no occasion for fear in this situation.)   The concern of the upanishad is that '*bhooma*' has no death, and no threat from any quarters; whereas '*alpam*' (limited) has threats all over and it dies. Viewed from this point also, …for Awareness –a deathless, endless, eternal totality (*bhooma*) — having, viewing, seeing (as the eye of the world) and seemingly interacting with the world …is no reason for fear! …Think!

.. अर्थानर्थौ न मे स्तित्या गत्या वा शयनेन वा
तिष्ठन् गच्छन् स्वपन् तस्मादहमासे यथासुखम् ॥

ardha'nardhau na mae sthithya
gathya va shayane na va
tishtan gacchan swapan ..tasmath
aham aase yatha sukham. (Asht.Gita XIII.5)

By staying, going or sleeping..I don't gain anything or lose anything. Whether I stay, go, or sleep …I live in happiness.

.. गच्छन् तिष्ठन्नुपविशन्
शयनो वाऽन्यथापि वा ।
यथेच्छया वसेद् विद्वान्
आत्माराम सदा मुनिः ॥ *(Kuntikopanishad 32)*

gacchan'thishtan'nupavisan
sayano'vanyathaapiva
yadhecchayaa vasedvidwan
aathmaaraama sadah muni.

Walking, staying, sitting, lying or doing whatever he likes, one who knows his reality abides always in the bliss of his Self.

•• "Theirs is an unalloyed bliss, independent of material conditionings". (ref. missed)

•• One who has reached this silence gets absorbed in the totality – like water in water, space in space, light in light.

(जले जलं वियद्व्योम्नि
तेजस्तेजसि वा यथा ॥) *(Atma Bodham 53)*

*(jale Jalam viyad vyomni
tejas tejasiva yatha)*

•• No duality when the mind subsides. (from *Gowdapaada darsanam* p.28)

(amanee'bhaave dvaitham naivopalabhyate)

•• Avadhuthan does not have any destination for himself. Like a dry leaf in the wind, he lets his body drift wherever the situations take it. A *sanyasi* started walking eastwards. A strong wind blew westward. He turned round and walked westward...with the wind.

•• "He is in harmony with everything as they are around him, under all circumstances. Externally when the world lashes on him, he receives them—but he never reacts to them. Inwardly, in his supreme happiness he lives – seeing, hearing, touching, smelling, eating; in short, he never runs away from the world. Nor has he any aversion towards the world. Assimilating sense-experiences he spends his days peacefully, eating in the world through all his mouths! It is not external behavior, but the state of his inner consciousness that distinguishes a Man-of-knowledge from an ordinary worldly-sensuous-being. Since the wise man lives in the same world, externally he must behave as any other human-being. In his inner Wisdom alone he is a Superman, not in anything else. *(Swami Chinmayananda; Asht.Gita* commentary p250).

•• लोकानुवर्तनं त्यक्त्वा
त्यक्त्वा देहानुवर्तनं
शास्त्रानुवर्तनं त्यक्त्वा
स्वाध्यासापनयं कुरु ॥

*lokaanu'varthanam thyaktva
thyaktva deha'anuvarthanam
sasthra'anuvarthanam tyakthva
swaadhyasa-apanayam kuru.*

Don't go by the dictates of the world, don't follow the dictates of the body, don't follow the dictates of *sastras* (codes of conduct) ...free yourself from all that is imposed on you ...and ultimately from the superimposed body also.

•• दृश्यं ह्यदृश्यतां नीत्वा ब्रह्माकारेण चिन्तयेत्
विद्वान्नित्यसुखेतिष्ठेद्धिया चिद्रसपूर्णया ॥

(Aparokshanubhuthi 142)

*drsyamhyadrsyathaam neethwa
brahmaakaarena chinthayeth
vidwaan'nithya'sukhe thishted–
dhiyaa chidrasapurnayah*

Casting off all the objects (the BMI, the universe, everything that forms the visual world) – away from sight / not ever remembering it, the knower, with his intellect immersed in the bliss of Eternal Awareness (*Brahmaakaara vrtthi*), abides in eternal Peace.

•• दृश्यं नास्तीति बोधेन मनसो दृश्यमार्जनं
सम्पन्नंचेत् तदुत्पन्ना परा निर्वाण निर्वृति ॥

drsyam naasthi'ithi bodhena ...meanig, with the conviction that there are no sense objects (keep this aside for a while..till we can assimilate it...till we get convinced ...if we get convinced) ...

> ....*manaso drsya maarjanam*
> *sampannam cheth'thathuthpanna*
> *paraa nirvaana nirvrthi.* (Vasishtam)

If we take it that there are <u>no *drsyam*</u> (sense objects) <u>in me the Awareness</u>, that is sensible; any child can understand it. With this understanding ....that in Me the Awareness there are no sense objects, shake off all objects from you ...free yourself from the sense objects, mentally, and from that will emerge the supreme *nirvana nirvrthi* ...ecstatic contentment of nirvana.

- - अधिष्ठानं समस्तस्य जगतः सत्यचिद्घनं
  अहमस्मीति निश्चित्य वीतशोक भवेन्मुनिः ॥

  adhishtaanam samasthasya
  jagatha sathya'chid'khanam
  aham'asmithi'nischithya
  veethashoka bhavenmuni

The foundation on which the universe stands ...is the crystallised Awareness-Reality, and that is me. With this solidified conviction one becomes free from grief.

- - "This firmed up conviction itself is Liberation."

- - यस्य सर्वत्र भूतानि एकत्वमनुपश्यतः
  तस्य का मोहः का शोकः एकत्वमनुपश्यतिः

  yasya sarvathra bhuthaani ekatwamanu'pasyatha
  thasya kaa moha kaa soka ekatwamanupasyathi

Ch.3 Jivanmukthi — The goal

One who sees the one single Awareness in all the beings, has no delusion, no grief. He sees the One (forgetting the *upathis*.. containments, the beings).

.. देहस्तिष्ठतु कल्पान्तं गच्छत्वचैव वा पुनः
क्व वृद्धिः क्व च वा हानि- स्तव चिन्मात्ररूपिणः॥

(Asht.Gita XV.10)

*deha'sthishtathu kalpaantham
gacchathyadyaivava'punah
kwa vrddhi kwa cha va haani's-
thava chinmaathrarupinah*

Let the body last till the end of eternity (lit. end of *kalpa*, the cycle of time), or fall off right at this moment; that doesn't make any difference to you, the pure Awareness (lit. You wont grow, you wont shrink). (Body is not your form; you are formless.)

.. प्रकृतिविकृतिशून्यं भावनातीतभावं॥

(Vivekachudamani 410)
prakrthi'vikrthi'sunyam bhaavanaatheetha bhaavam

Beyond the Nature and its mischiefs ..(*prakrti vikrti shunyam*= not having the Nature and its mischiefs in it – devoid of the Nature and its mischiefs); and in a state (attitude) beyond all imagination.

.. अचरममरमस्ताभास वस्तुस्वरूपं
स्तिमित सलिलराशि प्रख्यमाख्याविहीनं
शमितगुणविकारं शाश्वतं शान्तमेकं
हृदि कलयति विद्वान् ब्रह्मपूर्णं समाधौ ॥

*achara'mamara'masthaabhaasa vasthu'swarupam
sthimitha salilaraasi prakhyamaakhyaaviheenam*

> *shamitha gunavikaaram shaaswatham*
> *shaantham'ekam*
> *hrdi kalayathi vidwaan brahmapurnam samaadhau.*
> *(Vivekachudamani 411)*

The wise man …in samadhi …realizes in his heart the nameless deathless infinite eternal Brahmam …as the positive Entity that cannot be negated ….like a placid ocean of peace, with all its waves (*guna, vikara*) subsided. He lives vitally the experience of Reality (*vasthu* = the stuff that is). (*Vivekachudamani* 411)

•• प्रपञ्चो विस्मृतप्रायः (*Vivekachudamani* 429)
prapancho vismrtha'praayah

With the phenomenal world almost forgotten (in the state of jivan-muktha)

•• स्वबोधमात्रं परिशुद्ध तत्वं
विज्ञायसंखे नृपवच्चसैन्ये
तदाश्रयःस्वात्मनि सर्वदास्तितो
विलापयःब्रह्मणि विश्वजातं ॥ (*Vivekachudamani* 265)

swabodhamaathram parishuddha thathwam
vijnaaya samkhe nrpavathcha sainye
thathaashraya swaathmani sarvadah sthitho
vilaapaya brahmani viswajaatham.

As you recognize a king in an army, discern the pure objectless-Awareness from the midst of all sense objects, and abide always in it, merging the univese into Brahmam.

•• It is a bliss one can sink into without the participation of the body, even while the body exists; in absolute Peace-Happiness-Tranquillity-Bliss all rolled into one.

•• "By thus contemplating upon that which is ever-present everywhere, which is the essence in every form, the seeker's entire attention gets lifted from the world of plurality, and gets settled upon the Self within. The mental agitations then cease. Thoughts end. Mind halts. The ego disappears into the vision of the Supreme – in a most direct and subjective experience-divine." (*Swamy Chinmayananda* commenting on *Vakyavrthi*-34 p72)

•• When this idea gets solidified and sits squarely ...fits squarely in the intellect (without any room for anything else) ...then the situation is something special ...something pleasant, something grand, unusual, elevating ....free, fearless and glorious. 𝔇ₙ

Saturated ecstasy

The moment you get a glimpse of your reality ..the moment the stature of your awareness dawns on you in a flash ..there onwards you will be in limitless happiness, saturated ecstasy.

* Imagine the happiness of a blind man gaining sight suddenly.
* Imagine the happiness of one who is sentenced to death gets a release order the day before his hanging.
* Imagine the happiness of a mother whose son was lost a few years back, suddenly gets information that the son is alive and is in a happy situation and that he is coming home soon.

The ecstasies of these mundane situations are like candle-lights in front of the mid-day sunlight of the ecstasy of Brahma-jnanam.

***   ***   ***

•• "Don't call me a tyagi. I am enjoying my bliss of Existence—the Supreme Bliss. I am the greatest bhogi. You are tasting something lesser—so you are the tyagi." (Santh Yukteshwar)

•• In truth, the *muktha* has no body; ... and there are no grades of *mukthi*. (*Pancadasi* p.xix)

•• *The bodiless eternal Reality is not touched by pains and pleasures.*

(अशरीरं सन्तं न प्रियाप्रिये स्पृशतः)

asareeram .... santham ..na priya'apriye sprshatha.

•• अजातस्य कुतो नाश (ajaathasya kutoh nasah)
How can the unborn die? (*Vivekachudamani* 462)

•• Athma-jnani's death never happens!
How can the eternal awareness die?

•• "Death also dies ...in front of your Shiva-swaroopam. –in front of your auspicious Absolute eternal Existence" (words of Rthambhara Saadhvi)

•• Even the sense of contentment of the mind and the state of desirelessness of the intellect can have no meaning for the liberated-in-life (*jivanmuktha*) as he has transcended both his mind and intellect. (*Swamy Chinmayanandda commenting on Ashta.gita* XX.2)

•• This state is not for our intellectual appreciation, it is to be 'realised'. And it can be realized only when the seeker accomplishes what these verses are screaming. The knowledge of the Self lies not in the texts of even the Vedas. It awaits your direct experiencing in your own SELF. (*Swamy Chinmayananda*)

Ch.3 Jivanmukthi — The goal

'The world becomes non-existent, even while it exists'. (*Poojappura Gopalaswamy* in Arul Mozhikal p.508). By his grace, he makes it clear ...'even while it exists'. He does not assert that the world is 'non-existent' as do many others. It only means that the world exists, but it becomes meaningless to the man of realization ...it has no impact on him.

•• "Soaking in the ecstasy of the Self, I reach a transcendental state".

> (swananda'manubhunjaano
> nirvikalpo bhavamyahum) (Kuntikopanishad 31)

Tejobindu Upanishad (p510 Upa.112) throws some light on the state of a *jivanmuktha*.

> yasya dehadikam naasthi yasya Brahmeti nischaya:
> paramaananda poornoya sa jivanmukta uchyate
> sarvatra purnaroopathma sarvatraatmaavaseshaka,
> aananda rati ravyakta paripurna chidatmaka
> shuddha chaitanya roopaatma
> sarva sanga vivarjitha,
> nithyaananda prasannatma hyanyachintha vivarjitha
> na mae chittham na mae buddhir
> na ahamkaro na chendriya
> na mae deha kadachidva
> na mae praanaadaya kvachid
> ...... na mae daivam ......
> na mae jaagran'namae swapnam
> na mae kaarana'manvapi
> na mae tirtham na mae seva
> na mae jnaanam na mae padam.
> na mae bandho na mae janma
> na mae vakyam na mae ravi,
> na mae punyam na mae paapam

na mae karyam na mae shubham.
na mae jiva na mae swatma
na mae kinchid'jagad'trayam
na mae moksho na mae dwaitham,
na mae vedo na mae vidhi.
aparichinna roopathma anu-sthoolaadivarjithae
turya-turya paranando vaidehi mukta eva cha.
na mae kaalo na mae deso
na mae vasthu na mae mathi;
na mae snanam na mae sandhya
na mae daivam na mae sthalam.
na mae dhyatha na mae dhyeyam
na mae dhyanam na mae manu;
na mae sheetham na mae'chooshnam
na mae trshna namae kshudha;
na mae mithram na mae shathrur'
na mae moho na mae jaya;
na mae poorvam na mae paschan'
na maechordhwam na mae disa:
na mae vakthavyam'alpam va,
na mae shrothavyam'anvapi;
na mae ganthavyameeshad-va
na mae dhyatavyam'anvapi.
na mae bhokthavyam'eeshad-va,
na mae smartharthavyam'anvapi;
na mae bhogo na mae rogo
na mae yogo na mae laya.

(Tejobindu upanishad has still more ...not reproduced here.)

Meaning of the portion quoted above:-

'The Kumara asked the geat Lord: "please explain to me the nature of *Jivanmukti* (embodied salvation) and *videhamukti* (disembodied salvation)."

Ch.3 Jivanmukthi — The goal

The great Siva replied: "I am chidatma, I am Para-Atma. I am nirguna. Greater than the great". One who holds on to this attitude and simply stays in Atman, is called a jivanmuktha. He who realizes "I am beyond the three bodies, I am the pure consciousness and I am Brahman" is said to be jivanmuktha. He is said to be jivanmuktha who realizes: "I am of the nature of the blissful and of the supreme bliss and I have neither body nor anything else except the certitude 'I am Brahmam' only. Jivanmuktha has not at all got the 'I' in himself, but stays in absolute consciousness alone (*chinmatra*), whose interior is consciousness alone, who is all-full of pure consciousness, who has given up all affinities for objects, whose bliss is unconditioned, whose Atman is tranquil, who has got no other thought than Itself,[1] and who is devoid of the thought of the existence of anything. Jivanmuktha is one who realizes : 'I have no mind, no buddhi, no ahamkara, no senses, no body at any time, no prana, no Maya, no passion and no anger'.

"I am something supreme. I have none of these objects of this world, I have no sin, no characteristics, no eye, no mind, no ear, no nose, no tongue no hand, no waking, no dreaming or causal state in the least, or the fourth state. I have no time, no space, no objects, no thought, no *snana* (bathing), no sandhyas (junction-period ceremonies), no deity[2], no sacred places, no worship, no thought of spirituality, no sitting postures, no relatives, no birth, no speech, no wealth, no virtue, no vice, no duty, no auspiciousness, no jiva, not even the three worlds, no salvation, no duality, no Vedas, no mandatory rules, no proximity, no distance, no

---

[1] Itself? Yes, no he no she...it is It now; genderless.

[2] 'Deivam' is the word in original (Sanskrt). It is God ...nothing less, nothing different that is meant. 𝔇n

knowledge, no secrecy, no guru, no disciple, no diminution no excess, no Brahma no Vishnu no Rudra, no moon, no earth-water-vayu-akasa-agni, no clan, no aim, no mundane existence, no meditator nor any object of meditation, no heat or cold, no hunger no thirst, no friend no foe, no illusion, no victory, no past present future, no east-west-north-south, nothing to be said or heard in the least, nothing to be attained, nothing to be contemplated enjoyed or remembered, no desire, no yoga no absorption, no quietude, no bondage, no love, no joy, no hugeness no smallness, no increase no decrease, no *adhyaropa* (illusory attribution), nor *apavada* (withdrawal of the conception), no oneness no manyness, no blindness no dullness , no skull, no flesh, no blood, no lymph, no skin no bone no marrow, no whiteness, redness, blueness, there is nothing important to me nor non-important, no delusion, no perseverance, no mystery, nothing to be abandoned or received, nothing to be laughed at, no policy, no religious vow, no fault no bewailment, no happiness or unhappiness, no knower, knowledge or knowable, no Self, no you no I, no old age no youth nor manhood; ... I am Brahmam for certain, I am Chith, I am Chith". He is said to be jivanmuktha who cognizes: 'I am Brahmam alone; I am Chith alone, I am Awareness alone and I am supreme'. No doubt need be entertained about this. 'I am Hamsa, I see myself through myself. I reign happy in the kingdom of Atman and enjoy in myself the bliss of my own Self'. Jivanmukta is himself the lord and rests in his own Self. (*112 Upanishads* p511)

Ashtavakra pours forth a few verses worth inclusion in this context ...and they proceed like a torrent:-

•• He whose work has ceased with the dawn of Knowledge, does not find an opportunity to do anything or say anything,

Ch.3 Jivanmukthi — The goal

even though in the eyes of ordinary people, he is working. (*Asht.Gita* XVIII.77)

•• The wise one neither abhors birth and rebirth nor wishes to perceive the Self. Free from joy and sorrow, he is neither dead nor alive. (*Asht.Gita* XVIII.83)

•• Glorious is the life of the wise, free from expectations, free from attachment for children, wife and others, free from desire for the objects of the senses, and free from the care of even his own body. (*Asht.Gita* XVIII.84)

•• Reposing on the foundation of his own being, completely transcending death and birth, the great soul <u>does not care whether his body stays or dies.</u> (*Asht.Gita* XVIII.86)

•• Blessed is the wise who stands alone, who is attached to nothing, who is without any possessions, who moves freely and at pleasure, who is free from the pairs of opposites, and whose doubts have been rent asunder. (*Asht.Gita* XVIII.87)

•• There is no heaven, and there is no hell; there is not even liberation-in-life. In short, nothing exists in yogic consciousness. (*Ash.Gita* XVIII.80)

There is neither death nor birth, neither a bound nor a struggling soul, neither a seeker after liberation nor a liberated one—this is the ultimate Truth. *(na mumukshur na vai muktha, ithyesha paramarthatha)* (*Mandukya Kaarikka* 2.32)

•• From a mind that gets absorbed in Brahma-bhaavam, the universe fades out ...like **a flower drops off from a sleeping hand** (*'suptha hasthasya pushpavath'*).

•• Imagine a canoe ...with no occupant in it ...and no route map, drifting down the river. Similar is the state of a jivanmuktha. Just floating in the river of life ...flowing with the river.

JADA BHARATHAN

A very fine example of a jivan-muktha you will find in Jada Bharathan (a story in Bhagavatham). In his consummate knowledge and wisdom, Jada Bharathan used to live on like a walking dead body. The villagers used him for all sorts of menial jobs ...wood-cutting, fetching water from a distance, and so on ...which he accepted, and he used to get food in return. In the ox-drawn oil mill, if an ox fell ill, Bharathan was used to fill that gap ...and he used to get oil-cake to eat in return. He never resented, never complained, never spoke a word against the ill-treatment meted out to him. One day a scare-crow broke and fell down. The crop in the field was ripe and so for the time it took to reinstall another scarecrow Bharathan was asked to stand on the pedestal of the scarecrow. After some time, some tribesmen came running along. Someone they kept in captivity for a human sacrifice to Goddess Kaali, escaped. As they came near the scarecrow, one of them said 'Hey it is a man. Let us get him'. And they pounced upon him and carried him to the Kaali temple. He did not resist, did not protest, did not even ask what for he was being taken. He certainly sensed that he was to be sacrificed.

In the midst of ritual dance, drum-beat and all ...a huge weapon was raised above the chopping block. Before it fell on his neck, there was a thunder and lightning ...and goddess Kaali appeared, snatched away the weapon and sacrificed all those who were there except Bharathan. Seeing the goddess smile at him, a glimmer of a smile appeared on his lips. He did not even say 'thank you, Devi'. Death was not an event to him ....life or death ... everything was okay. Devi disappeared.

4

CONFUSIONS & CONFLICTS

There is more confusion than clarity in the matter of spirituality. There is confusion enough and more as to what God is, His role, what He does, what He does not. Also there is great confusion in understanding the Self. There are confusions in plenty as to the paths to be followed. A very big avenue of confusion is thrown open by the theory of Maaya. In the Indian scriptures ...in Upanishads and all ...super-brilliant ideas fill me up like a balloon and lift up to great heights, and at the end – like a pin-prick to the balloon – they say nothing really exists except the Awareness. I am suddenly dropped down to abysmal depths of confusion, from the heights to which I was lifted.

"Neither you nor I, nor this nor these exist. There is in It no mind to think 'I am the supreme Brahmam'. This world is Brahmam only. Thou and I are Brahmam only. I am *cinmathra* simply, and there is no *un-Athman*. Rest assured of it. This universe is not (really at all). It was nowhere produced and stays nowhere. Some say that chittha is the universe. Not at all. It exists not. Neither the universe nor chittha nor ahamkara nor jiva exists (really). Neither the creation of *Maya* nor *Maya* itself exists. Fear does not exist. Actor, action, hearing, thinking ...none of these exist anywhere." (*Tejobindu Upanishad*)

Half of this is good, acceptable, brilliant; but the talk about non-existence is confusing.

"When the blueness of the sky is real, then the universe is real. When the silver in the mussel can be used for making ornaments, when a man is bitten by a rope appearing as snake, when milky food is obtained in the (barren) Vindhya forest, when cooking becomes possible with plantain pith (as the firewood), when curd resumes the state of milk, when the milk (milked) goes back through the teats of a cow ...then will the universe really be. When the dust of the earth shall arise from the ocean, when a mad elephant is tied by means of a tortoise hair, when Meru mountain is pulled away with a lotus thread, when the fire flames downward, when a flame shall become cold, when a lion is killed by a gnat, when the objects seen in a dream come in the waking state, when the lions shall be conquered by the bravery of dogs, when a good crop can be raised sowing burnt seeds, when the delivery of a barren woman becomes fruitful, when the heart of a *jnani* is known by the fools, when the sky falls on earth, when a reflection arises from a plain glass-plate (without silver coating) ...then the world really is." (This again is from Tejobindu Upanishad.) This much elaborately it is emphasized that the WORLD IS NOT. But how are we to take it? How can anyone with common sense understand this?

This is the sample of talk by which Maya is described all over the scriptures.

Dream lion

The appearance of a lion in front of you wakes you up from a dream. The nightmare ends ... you are relieved. If the waking life (*jagrat*) is also made of the same stuff as the dream+, is there a shortcut for a sudden end to this dream? In a bad ...sad ...situation is there a waking up possible? All the drama and horror and pathos continue unabated. You can try to detach yourself from the situation mentally ...intellectually ...emotionally; even if that be possible are you absolved of the responsibilities cast upon you by that situation? If your only child is in the grip of a terminal illness – and the child looks into your eyes helplessly..hopelessly – can you sit back saying that it is a dream that will soon pass off? Swami Chinmayananda says: "You have a responsibility towards your dream-wife and children also".

A fire that has caught hold of you in a dream, is totally out the moment you wake up. In hopeless situations in *jagrath* is there such a waking up possible, shaking off the nightmarish realities?

Certainly dream and waking states are of different stuff. Waking life *(jagrath)* is a solid reality. It forms the basis for dream. Dream fades off totally, leaving no trace. But waking state leaves indelible marks. It is a continuum...passing through days into years ...generation after generation ...millenniums after millenniums.

In many places it is said that Maya is eternal. But in some places it is said that Maya has an end. ("Maya is beginningless, but it has an end...when you get enlightened.") Even when you get enlightened where will the world go? You know that you are an eternal reality, and there is no body or universe in you, ...but the universe exists AS-IT-IS. Only it may not bother you....You get a bit distanced/ detached from the scene ...sometimes almost totally. You may be able to

---

+ This is the widely prevalent argument.

live on like a drop of water on a lotus leaf. You will still be acting on in this word, as the circumstances demand...but still unruffled, untainted, untouched. This much is possible. But to say that the world is unreal...non-existent is — to me — unswallowable. Some western critic has called it an 'audacious outrageous lie'. Until I am convinced otherwise, my conclusion is —

The world/ **universe is a reality, and you are a far greater reality than the universe;** and in front of your reality...eternity..., the reality of the universe dwindles into insignificance.

This theory of Maya—that nothing really exists....I could not so far understand however much I tried.

Not only it is Sankaracharya who said to his disciple: "I don't exist, you don't exist, ...nor does the whole visible universe exist",

(.. नाहं नचत्वं मृषा
नेदं वापि जगद् प्रदृष्टमखिलं
नास्तीति जानीहिभो ॥
*naaham nacha twam mrsha
nedam vaapi jagath pradrshtam akhilam
naasthi ithi jaaneehi bho)*

sage Vasishta also said the same thing..in the same words...to his disciple Sri Rama. (*Yoga Vaasishtam*)

It is explicitly said : "non-existent" (*naasthi=na asthi*). At some other places it is called 'mitthya' (unreal). And some scholars explain that 'unreal' does not mean 'non-existent'.

And there are theories of various realities:-

- ➤ Relative reality (*praathibhasika sathyam*)
- ➤ Experiential reality (*vyaavaharika sathyam*)
- ➤ Absolute reality (*paaramarthika sathyam*)

'Anvaya-Vyathireka yukthi'

This theory says: 'If awareness is there, everything is there. If awareness is not there, everything is not there. So everything is awareness. And it is clear even to a child'. Maybe they are trying to drive home some deep idea, but the terminology used does not convey that explicitly, unequivocally. *Anvaya-vyathirekam* – Lord Brahma explained to Devarshi Naarada! Let us forget it for a while …and try to see things straight. Some people hire modern science to assist. They say 'the world—as we see it—does not exist. It is made up of molecules—atoms—electron-proton-nutron—quarks—and finally reduced to energy!'

Is this an answer? In solid form or as energy, it exists; it is not non-existent.

Analysing a human body chemically, suppose someone declares that it contains …. so many grams of calcium, so much phosphorus, so much potassium,… so much water, iron enough to make two nails, …and so on…..is it the impression that you get when you look at a face that launched a thousand ships?

And energy stems from Awareness? Awareness gets condensed into energy? I have a doubt here ….Awareness gets condensed into non-awareness? …Because the condensed stuff …prakrti, ..matter ..material …substance doesn't show any faculty of awareness; it is inert …*jadam.*

And does that provide any solace? The world — the nature — red in tooth and claw .... the raging planet...the grim planet (as the Discovery channel calls it) masquerades with all its horrors.

Gas...hydrogen, helium—gravity—condensation—heat build-up—formation of stars—dissolution of stars—birth of supernovae....black holes..BIG BANG. The scientific conclusions go in this direction. It sounds rational. Black holes are formed by the laws of physics. If all these are created by a creator, why should a black hole be created? In a river why is a whirlpool created? To drown some humans? Like Sankaracharya said in the context of the universe— *'dukkhaaya tava ugraaya; na sukhaaya kadaachana'* (for limitless pain to you, with not a bit of pleasure in it).

•• God is nirguna; God is saguna also. This is the idea preached by very many. It is like saying "I don't know how to swim; and I also know how to swim." Push one of them down to water; if he swims, then the first statement is wrong. Truth can be only one; not both. When you say '*saguna*', the '*nirguna-tvam*' is erased automatically ...it doesn't stand.

•• 'Self is the substance of the universe' . (like gold is the substance of an ornament). This is the generally-upheld theory.

I wonder whether those who explain away like this actually know what they are saying. I cannot make out the head or tail of it. A pot is made of silver, with the figures of elephants, horses and camels embossed on it. The figures have to be nothing other than silver; they cannot be of iron or copper. Out of Brahmam which is sath-chith-anandam, how can a universe be born which has none of these qualities – which is totally a-sath, a-chith, an-anandam?

How can the pure awareness become a substance? Sankaracharya supports my view: "*kaschith padaartho na ca*" says he in *proudhanubhuthi*. 'Not a *padartham*' (substance). If at all you think that 'Self is the substance of the universe' ...have a look at the substance ...what a dirty look it has:

•• Take an opinion poll of all the people all over the world, close to death at ripe old age or close to premature death with diseases, disasters, calamities—with oozing wounds in bodies and minds. What will be their assessment of life? And how many will be there to say something good about this God's Creation?

•• *Jivo'jivasya'jivanam.* One eats another.

"Eat, and get eaten up"...is the general law The Upanishads also have come to grips with this grim reality. '*jeevo jeevasya jeevanam*' Peace and co-existence—where do we find in the animal world?

•• How do the lions die in old age, in this world so beautifully created by the God? Lions are eaten by hyenas—alive!

•• The sea-lion. Within minutes of birth, the baby sea-lion is eaten up by wolf. Is it born only to become a meal in a few minutes?

•• A centipede catches a geko (house lizard) and eats up its brain and discards the rest! (Taking a life just for the sake of its brain? Some alternative stuff could have been provided to it easily?) And after this drama a toad appears on the scene, and swallows this centipede with its brain-eating brain.

•• When a buffalo sees plentiful fresh blades of grass, it can Praise the Lord. But when a lion pounces on it, can any buffalo Praise the Lord?

•• Why a millipede is graciously, generously created – so loathsome, and without eyes?+

•• The hunters have their eyes fitted in front to see to a great distance. The hunted have their eyes on their sides. Also fitted with the instinct of fear and flight. Created not with great dignity. Why the hunters at all? One spiritual leader .. teacher ... a towering personalty ....asked me "Who are we to question the God's design?" But that is not an answer.

Kindergartens in spirituality

"*Me're Pitah* (my father) is just like me. A powerful light. Shining in the centre of the forehead, I, the Atma is a point of light...star-like. …..Crossing the sun, the moon and the stars I go to the land of silence and purity—the abode of *Paramatman, me're Param Pitah (*the Supreme Self, my Ultimate Father). You are the children of that Ocean of Bliss ...And I come back—as a point of light, back to my forehead, and to my field of activity."

This is the peak of spirituality for some people. (It gives me the creeps......) From 8000 centres all over the world

---

+ Supporters of karma theory will jump up and tell me that millipede is created for human beings to suffer in that yoni (cast, mould) ..to suffer in that body. Some other sect will tell me that "Paramaathma has revealed to us that human soul will not pass through other yonis;" we are made humans, and will continue through millenniums ..into eternity as humans. Dr. Michael Newton's research also supports this view. The age-old Indian belief is challenged. 84 lakhs of yonis (8.4 million life-forms) ...to work out karmas!) Some close look, and research is needed here. ...Two men who sat to my right and left at Osho Centre for a 'regression into past lives' ...one happened to be a horse last life, and the other a goat! Not a thing to be brushed aside lighly.

they yell ..again and again. "The light at the centre of eyebrows is the Atma" Spiritual nonsense! And they are happy with the 'small point' status.

•• Some other people who entertain some similar line of thought, say that if one gets a proper Realisation, he/she will not last long. How will a 25-watt bulb withstand the power of a million-watt current?!

•• "Any way, the candle is burning. It has to burn out. Why not burn from both ends …and celebrate – the double-end burning and its intense light?" This is another spirituality!

•• Watch out every moment, intensively, day and night, and ward off the master's strike with his sword. ….This also is spirituality! Concentration!

•• Sit waiting around a cauldron in which tea is boiling ..and enjoy the smell of tea (meditate upon the smell); then hold the cup with both hands ..feeling the rotundity of its shape (meditate) …feel the warmth of the pot when the tea is poured in it (meditate) …and finally drink the tea and meditate on it. This is another sample of spirituality.

•• Do a hundred *kapalabhathi* …stop it suddenly …and watch the stillness. This is also said to be spirituality.

•• Laugh a lot – collectively. Then suddenly stop, ..and enjoy the silence. This is another sample.

Where do we reach with these spiritualities?

Spiritual nonsenses, more:

<u>Prayers</u>: God-s come to help when we pray.(?) God must know when someone needs help. A mother gives food to her children without asking. If He doesn't condescend to help, will He help if we put it down in black-and-white—as a

petition (as a prayer)—with some minor bribe promised? How many percentage of prayers are answered? A statistics is needed.

* Prayers, even third-party prayers (people hired for praying), and for Christians in Kerala there are prayer towers for effective reach!

*** *** ***

* Some very big TV channel teachers explain that 'Om is everywhere ..you look at the eye-brows, they are in the form of Om (written with Devanagri script[+]). You look at the lower end of your rib-cage, it is formed like Om, open someone's mouth and look inside...with the glotis hanging, you will find Om at the throat...and so on .. wherever there is a semblance of two adjacent curves.' It is in these that they find the presence of Brahmam!!!

In a land where 'Thath-Twam-Asi' was born, now (alas!) out of that *Parama Jnanam* such teachers have made *Paamara Jnanam*[1]. It stinks; my head sinks in shame.

[[1]*parama jnanam* = ultimate knowledge;
paamara jnanam = layman's knowledge]

Various & varying theories/ beliefs:

•• In heaven, luxuries are in plenty—outwardly. Inwardly not all in peace.

•• *Sat-karma and dush-karma* (right and wrong doings) – both are not that good, ultimately. Both cause bondage.

[+] That is not a script of any language exactly – it is a pictorial representation.

•• And according to some people, there are different compartments in heaven for occupants with varying grades/levels of *punya*. So there is disparity in heaven also?

•• The *Devas* also yearn for human body—to do sadhana and progress. In heaven, no *sadhana*—only *bhoga-sadthyatha* is there (possibilities of enjoyment) endless.

If the heaven is there to exhaust *punya*, and hell is there to exhaust *paapam* (sins), then where is the reason for a rebirth in difficult situations? Dr Michael Newton, after extensive interactions with his subjects in regression, concludes: "There is no hell for souls, except perhaps on Earth. (Destiny of Souls p3).

Bhogaartham...annye ....kreedaartham'ithi'cha'apare

To face the effects of karma....is one aim of creation, it is said. That looks relevant once karma is set in motion. But how did the original karma originate? ..and the first body? That is done by the Supreme power for fun? (*kreedartham*). Human beings....all the beings... are cheap playthings for the Super Power?

In the spirit world exposed by Dr Michael Newton also rebirths are planned to work out karma. And also new souls are produced.....for no valid reason apparently. So do we have to conclude that the souls are created for somebody's fun? Vedantha finds an escape route by saying that nothing really exists. Simply by saying that nothing exits, will anything cease to exist?

It is said that this duality is brought about by Avidya (Maya). In the ocean of Saturated Bliss, the wind of Maya(Avidya/ignorance) creates this wave of universe (your body inclusive). But wherefrom / how did this wind arise to whip up this wave? Any answer? 'Somehow' is not an answer. In pure Awareness where is the scope for Avidya? What is its locus? How can darkness exist in midday sun-light? Dream appears real while you experience it. Things produced by a magician in a magic show appear real; you can eat the apple produced by him. These are experiential realities... with no absolute reality. Vedantha holds the view that the waking state also has no absolute reality; that too is like a dream or a magicians show.

In the theory of Maya, the explanations offered are:-

— like **Swapnam** = like dream.... (but that needs a mind as its locus!)

— **Anirvachaniyam** = that cannot be defined

— **Akaaranam** = unreasoned, without any valid reason.

— **Inexplicable** = with no explanation possible.

— **yukthi-heenam** = illogical. (*yukthi-heena prakasasya sabjna Mayethi kathyathe*: says Sureswara Acharya).

Look at this solid foundation on which Maya stands! I withhold my comments.

•• Among the many theories, there is one called— Drshti-srshti vaadam[+], a limitless absurdity! It says that the things that you see are created by the eyes instantly, and the things vanish when you don't look. Again when you look, things are newly created!.

Vaadam-s there are many. And so *vaada-kolahalam*. ..the din and bustle of arguments ... belief systems. "*Shabda*

[+] Vaadam= belief system, argument, angle of view.

jaalam maharanyam...buddhi bhramana kaaranam" (I think it is Sankara Acharya who said it.) A wilderness of theories, ..that cause the head to reel.

•• Conscious *karma* binds; unconscious karma does not cause any karmic binding! Animal predators are thus exempted! Their killing is labeled 'instinct'-ive. But still ...is it not done consciously? Every killing is planned and executed with the utmost caution and ingenuity ..isn't it?!

Someone told me that a reading of '*manthra sasthra*' (the science of manthtra) will throw more light on the fact of illusion of the world. I don't want anything that proves the existent as non-existent. It should be something negative, spurious. Nor do I need any proof for the existence of my body and mind and the world around. I am not committed to uphold anything or decry anything; I have no compulsion to negate the world.

Hard nuts

•• न च त्वं न चाहं नचायंप्रपञ्चः *(Dasasloki 7)*
   na ca tvam na ca hum na cha ayam prapancha:
   Neither you exist, nor I; nor even this universe.

•• न किञ्चिज्जायते जीव सम्भवोऽस्य न विद्यते
   एतत्तदुत्तमं सत्यं यत्र किञ्चिन्न जायते ॥
   (Mandukya Kaarika III.48)
   na kinchith'jjaayathe jiva
   sambhavosya na vidyathe
   ethath'thadutthamam sathyam
   yathra kinchinna'jaayathe.

'No jiva is ever born. No cause is found to exist which can produce it. This is the highest Truth that nothing is ever born'.

मनो दृश्यमिदं द्वैतं यत् किञ्चित्सचराचरं
मनसोह्यमनीभावे द्वैतं नैवोपलभ्यते ॥

(Mandukya Kaarika III. 31. p72 Thuriyam).

*mano'drsyamidam dwaitham
yath'kinchith'sacharaacharam
manaso'hyamaneebhave
dwaitham naivopalabhyathe*

'All these objects, comprising everything that is movable and immovable, perceived by the mind ..are mind alone. For duality is never perceived when the mind ceases to act.' When the mind ceases to act, duality is not seen. True. So what? The universe sinks? shrinks? vanishes?

(For further confusions see Acharya Sankara's commentary on these two *kaarikas* : III.31 & III.48)

•• How can unreal body have a *prarabdha karma*?

(प्रारब्ध मसतःकुतः) *(Vivekachudamani 462)*
(praarabdha'masatha'kutah)

•• It is a mis-interpretation that if the awareness were not there nothing will exist.

•• From the Awareness (Brahmam) emerged prana and mind!? Some people explain that the awareness itself gets condensed into energy ...and ultimately into universe. In the same breath the Upanishads say that It is changeless, immutable. How can change and changelessness go hand in hand?

•• "*Prajnathma* (prajna+athma) is the cause of everything." (*Mandukya Upa.*). p80 Kailas. Upa-12.

•• It rules, governs. It is the lord. Such statements need investigation.

Ch.4   Confusions & Conflicts

•• As the waves, foam and bubbles are not different from the ocean, so the universe, streaming forth from the self, is not different from the self. (*viswam aathma'vinirgatham*) (II.4 Asht.Gita). To me, this doesn't answer the question – the phenomenon of the universe. Does it stream forth from awareness?

Why awareness streams forth as snakes, scorpions, venomous spiders...tarantulas, black-widows, centipedes, millipedes, worms, lions, elephants, fire-ants , wasps, electric eels, jelly fishes assassin bugs, parasites, vampire bats..all devils of nature as the Discovery channel prefers to call them? ...all not so comfortable for human-beings!

Whether it is awareness or God that creates – if there is a faculty for creation – what is the great use of rats on this earth ...and that too so many types—big and small? To eat away one-tenth of human food production? (You know the statistics better). And their urine and feces pass on horrible diseases to humans.

What is the big role of mosquitoes in the eco system ...except contributing to the woes of other beings? Mosquitoes bite others and die in the attempt.

Why the dogs have to open the mouth and put the tongue out? You try that—is it normal, comfortable?

Why men have so much of beard ...a high botheration! ... and also hair at other places where we don't find it so much welcome.

What is the rationale behind filling the earth with so much of oceans and undrinkable water?

The earth, with so much of turmoil – molten core and a thin solidified crust, and typhoons, tsunamis and all ....certainly not an ideal home created benevolently for man.

Why 'jivo-jivasya-jivanam'? Why eat one another? It could have been created differently. Why not create a lion that loves, kisses and caresses a deer, instead of pouncing on it as a prey? ..as one-time meal?

Creatures could have lived like vegetation ...living on sun-light and earth and water. Humans have created mighty machines ...that don't eat anyone, and still live and work hard!

One-time meal?

If one is meant to be eaten by another (*jivo-jivasya-jeevanam*) why is it not made like a bun? Like a banana? Like a mango? These are expressly/apparently meant to be eaten; not for anything else. They don't run; they don't get terrified. When a tiger catches a man to appease its hunger, why does the living flesh not co-operate willingly ...why does this food-stuff struggle for life? Why should it feel pain? Why is it not made that way? Even if a small thorn pricks, we feel pain. Why the process (of provision of food to all the beings) is not made painless? The all-mighty – if It so willed – could have managed the show that way—peacefully? Or is It not that mighty? Things are out of Its control? Or does the Creator want to derive a malicious pleasure from this infliction of colossal suffering? When a tiger eats a human it is a tragedy for us. When it eats an animal, it is a spectacle for humans. What is it for the God, the creator of this order? Dance Divine?

Seeing the beauty of some creatures (particularly newly hatched-out) many sing the glory of the creator. Where is the great sanctity in the creation of a piece of beauty if it is to be devoured by a monster any moment unceremoniously ... if it is meant to end up within hours of birth as one-time meal to some other creature? Out of a thousand tortoises that hatch out of the eggs, nearly one-half is eaten up before they cover a short distance to reach the sea. Only two in a thousand get a chance to live a full life-span.

A zebra. If a thorn pricks its flesh, it suffers pain. If a bone breaks, it suffers terrible pain. At the sight of death a shudder of terror goes down its spine. When a lion pounces on it, does the God expect it to feel happy? .. It is one-time meal to the lion ... and the God also considers it so.

The crocodile, with its formidable fortification, is crushed in the grip of anaconda. What is the big use of this fortification?

Child birth ...is painful, in any species. Even African elephants suffer—an elephantine suffering. Nowhere it looks to be pleasurable as a conjugal mating. Many female horses die in child birth (?) (says yogavasishtam). The hen's eggs often have blood streaks on them. It seems they rip through muscles and blood vessels. Only polar bear seems to be an exception; it delivers in sleep! That seems to be a better design. Why the human being is not made after this design?

Even in mating danger lurks in many species. Black widow (a female spider) eats its mate after mating ...also tarantula does the same. Whales. Some half-a-dozen mammoth males fight to death in the competition to mate a female.

•• *Jeevo jeevasya jeevanam* ...the creatures live eating one another. It must be a heartless entity that created this horrible order. Even small children (3-4 years) have started asking "Who ordained it this way"? The Hindu scriptures have come to grips with this reality of the 'Nature red in tooth and claw' ...with creatures eating one another; but I haven't come across any explanation/justification to this.

••   'ahasthaani sahasthaanim
apadaani chathushpadam
......jivo jivasya jivanam' (*Bhagavatham* 1.13.46;
Bhagavaatha Hrdayam:p.39)

'One that has hands eats one that has no hands; one that has four legs eats one that has no legs. Creatures live eating one another'.

•• Brain has no pain cells (?) Why is it not true with the whole body...of eatables? ...Then there would be nothing much wrong (painful) when one eats another?! Eating can go on ...painlessly. ...And why live at all ...to eat?

•• "It is believed that God creates this world for a purpose and runs it according to a plan. The purpose is good and the plan is wise." NM.   May be. But I don't like very much the plan that I see around. *Dn*

              ***   ***   ***

••   अध्यस्तो रज्जुसर्पोयं सत्यवद् रज्जु सत्तया
तथा जगदिदं भाति सत्यवद् स्वात्मसत्तया ॥
(*Advaitanubhoothi-68*)

adhyastho rajju'sarpoyam
sathyavath'rajjusatthayah
thathaa jagadidam bhaathi
sathyavath swaathma'satthayah.

'You see a snake superimposed on the rope because of the rope. So too, the world appears real because of the Awareness'. "Appears real" ...the connotation is the usual line of thinking of Vedantha that 'it is unreal'. Forget the question of 'the real' or 'unreal' and read it this way: The

Ch.4 Confusions & Conflicts

world appers because of Awareness. The Awareness reveals ...throws light on ...the world. Clean. <u>Not that a non-existent world gets projected because of Awareness.</u>

   ***   ***   ***

•• A big guru appearing in TV channel[+] says: *'hum paramatma ka putr hai'* ...I am the son of the great Reality/ We are the children of the Reality. He and his followers are happy with the status of 'children'.

Whereas, Vedanta points to a situation where there is no 'thripudi' (triad)...[(i) the seer, (ii) the things seen and (iii) the act of seeing] ....where the seer alone remains, without the other two components of thripudi ..and therefore no fear.

••   ... महानहं विश्वमहं विचित्रं..
  (mahaanaham viswamaham vichithram)
  'I am great, I am the univere .... strange!'

••   ... हिरण्मयोहं (*hiranmayohum*)
  'I have all the resources in me'.

••   ... अपाणिपादोहमचिन्त्यशक्ति
    (*Kaivalyopanishad p.421 Upa-108*)
  apaani'paadohum'achinthyashakthi

I have no hands, no legs, but I have unimaginable power. (Does it have the power to foresee and prevent natural calamities? I doubt. There are planets in the universe that have gone dry. Many are frozen.)

•• The snake in a rope .. and water (mirage) in the desert are presented in Vedanta as examples to drive home the

---
[+] Not one, hundreds all over.

ultimate in the theory that Brahmam (the Reality) ...being nondual ... there is really no creation or dissolution. (*Proudhanubhoothi* p.181) Prof. G.Balakrishnan Nair.

'This is the Reality. If you see anything other than the Bodham..all that you see is unreal...Maya..non-existent.' ….. Saying this Vedanta leaves the stage. Then where do we bury the world that we have so solidly in front of us? Can anyone get rid of the world by calling it Maya?—by sticking a label 'non-existent' on it? If you stick on a wall a label that "this wall doesn't exist", can anyone walk through that wall?

What I say is: Let the world be there as what it is..as a hard reality..not as Maya. It doesn't do any harm to you, the Awareness...it cannot pose a threat to you, it cannot affect you in the least in any way.

.. मय्यखण्डसुघांभोधौ बहुधा विश्ववीचयः
उल्पद्यन्ते विलीयन्ते मायामारुतविभ्रमात् ॥

mayyakhanda'sukhaambhodhou
bahudhaa viswa'veechaya
uthpadyanthe vileeyanthe
maayaa'maarutha vibhramaath.

In me the infinite ocean of Peace and tranquillity the universes (many) rise and fall like waves... because of the wind of Maya. Ashtavakra Gita and Yoga Vasishtam also repeat the same thing, in different words.

'No Brahma-Vishnu- Maheswara...no Iswara...no jagath in Bodham (awareness)...; ie, no trinity. no single god, no universe. These are in Maya; not in reality'. p.832 Upa-108

"God is a phenomenon that reflects in prakrthi (nature)....*(maayayil prathibimbithan Iswaran)*" ... I have heard it in Malayalam; but it is not 'reflection' ...it is 'interaction', a mix-up with *Prakrthi*.

Awareness mingling with the prakrthi .... the power that is in the prakrthi gets transposed on to Awareness (seemingly, not actually) and you get an entity called God. ...that is omnipotent, omnicient and all that ....perhaps. (I say 'perhaps', because I doubt whether 'all is well and wisely put', and whether this God is all-powerful – powerful to put things properly.)

•• "The world-experience is a conjured-up feeling... hallucination. Hallucination is not real. Vedantha does not say that there is a world different from Brahmam, and that world is unreal." I don't get any meaning from this...can you?

Let the universe ...and your body...be an un-reality—misperception—incomplete vision....or let it be a hard, solid reality; let it be what it is; but *you* are a solid reality... greater reality... than the BMI and the universe. This is a good-enough stand.

•• Aham Brahma Asmi. Some so-called scriptural scholars get indigestion with this. I am Brahmam? *Hum Iswar hai*? No, *Iswar ka puthr hai*...they add water to it to digest (We are the children of God) ... As if they found some great truth, they declare: "You cannot be your own father!".

•• With the *parama jnanam* of Upanishads, the Puranas made *paamara jnanam* .. .. the platform on which these scholars stand.

•• "Things conjured up by imagination, which itself is a product of delusion, can never be accepted as 'facts'." (Viveka Chudamani... 194) But where did this imagination arise, how, and why? Is any such agitation possible in nischala-Brahmam? Don't dump this responsibility on Maya ...she is non-existent. The world is existent.

•• 'Power ...Muscle-man and his muscle-power. *Shakthi* is in *shakthan*.' Power is not powerful by itself? Anyway, AWARENESS is not like the muscle-man. Awareness is not powerful that way. Awareness does not need any power.

* Iccha shakthi
* Kriya shakthi
* Jnana shakthi   ..... powers of Maya?

I find some confusion here. 'jnana shakthi'....is anyway not nature's. Think.

•• '*Manaso'hyamaneebhaave dwaitham naivopa'labhyate*'!! When the mind is absent, duality is not seen. (*Man. Kaarika*) Is it not like saying 'when I close the eyes I don't see anything'? So the *advaitham* (non-duality) of Vedantha is not an absolute non-duality; only a 'refusal to see the world' – shutting out the world. The one in mindless state (*amanee'bhaavam*) sits up there ...with a real body with hunger and thirst, ... sits in a world that is really real! This is really a duality! Why call it 'non-duality'?.

Perfect samples of confusing:-

(i) '*Sad-asad*', '*sad-asad-vihinam*': 'real and unreal ..yet without reality or unreality.'

(ii) न सन्नासन्न सदसद् भिन्नाभिन्नं नचोभयं
न सभागं न निर्भागं नचाभ्युभयरूपकं

na sannaasanna sadasad'
bhinnaabhinnam na chobhayam
na sabhaagam na nirbhaagam
nachaabhyubhaya'roopakam

'Not real nor unreal ..nor both put together – different from real, different from unreal ...and still not that way too.'

Ch.4 Confusions & Conflicts 221

Why not straight away accept the reality of the world? Why find escape routes ...so laboriously, and still without any success?

These (iii) are further samples of arguments :-

i) *kva gatham kena'vaa neetham adhunaiva mayaa drshtam!*

Where did it go? ...who moved it (the world)?; I have been seeing it just now!

ii) *abhootha'bhinivesosthi*
dvayam thathra na vidyathe

... nirnimitho na jaayathe. (IV.75 Mandukya Karika)

(abhinivesham = desire/ yearning/ longing)

Only a desire exists (in awareness!?) for what is not yet happened! No duality is seen; and no reason ..no room ..no possibility is seen for it to happen/ to exist!

And a desire ...a longing ..for this nasty world!? We all desire only pleasant things ...we don't have a longing for diseases, disasters, accidents, calamities and death!?

(iii) *Aadaavanthe cha yannaasthi*
Varthamaane pi thath thatha.

(Q. in *Radha sathyam* p285)

What is non-existent in the beginning and end (past and future) ...should be non-existent in the present also.

Unreal: So much is said so emphatically about the non-existence of creation (by Goddess Saraswathi also in Leelopakhyanam in Vasishtam) that creation itself will start doubting about its own existence!

•• No creation without a creator. But the creation doesn't present a picture of a very benevolent creator. When the lovers of the creator sing the glory of creation ...my mind grapples with the ghastly sight of a deer in piercing pain in the stranglehold of a lion.

•• 'If the universe were true it would have been perceived even in deep sleep. Since it is not at all perceived, it must be false and unreal like a dream.' (*Vivekachudamani* 234) *(Yadi sathyam bhaveth viswam.....*) This is one argument put forth to establish the unreality of the world! What is the big proof in it? Is this an argument? Childish....and less than that.

If in deep sleep you fall from your cot, hitting the nose, nose will bleed, no doubt ....because the world is there, real. The one that keeps awake next to you don't find you evaporated ...vanished in thin air, in deep sleep? You exist in deep sleep, and the world co-exists. The world does not evaporate, .. only you down the shutters of your sense organs; ....you hibernate, and the world rolls on.

Those who want to ponder over the further 'proofs' for the unreality of the world may see Vivekachudamani-232 (*sathyam yadi...*)

•• 'God created us and the world; sends us to this world, looks after us. And calls us back. We are always under His will, His supervision, protection. So why worry about death, and life?' This is the common belief. Some channel Guru-s repeat this every day.

Is everything running as smooth as that? God created the dinosaurs...and a meteor (hit on earth) wiped them out?

One, more serious doubt. Can this (that the God created us, we are under his surveillance) match the 'absolute fearlessness' to which the Upanishads lead? ... Under the nose of an extra-cosmic deity conceived as a whimsical despot, any fearlessness is possible?

God created the world and everything in it ...for humans; that is the common belief all over. (And human being is the ultimate in creation.) If you build a house for you, will you necessarily, naturally, happily accommodate in the house a few rhinos, hippos, elephants, tigers, deadly scorpions, king cobras, tarantulas, centipedes, millipedes, cockroaches?

Waking life *(jagrath)* is also a dream?

I heard one big guru – on a TV channel – saying that *'jagrath'* (waking life) is made of the same stuff as the dream. Then is there an 'Emergency Exit' available from the nightmarish life situations? In a nightmare, the intensity of agony wakes us up. Any such wake-up is possible in life in an emergency?

There stands a tree; there lies its shadow. Shadow has no content and reality ....so tree also has no content and reality. Is this logic?

Had there been a dream ...the same dream every night...with a definite progression of events in time as in waking life....we would have started doubting which is real.

Spirit is matter?

Theosophic society: speaks about identity of spirit and matter ....spirit is *potential* matter, and matter simply crystallized Spirit (as ice is solidified steam) — visible and solid matter is simply the periodical manifestation of the spirit.

Awareness gets condensed into non-awareness?! In this situation, when the universe is there, the awareness cannot be there; and if the awareness is there then the universe should not be there!. Or one-half gets crystallized and the other half remains awake, conscious, and watching? –as in the *'artha kukkuda'-nyayam* (theory) of Sankaracharya?

(Acharya asked: 'Can you cook one half of a hen and leave the other half to lay eggs?' He used this logic to assert that no universe comes out of Bodham/ Brahmam.) I want to ask the same question to those who preach that Brahmam is *nirgunam* and at the same time *sagunam* also.

Why are people so adamantly, vehemently interested in refusing an independent status to the universe?

Mind creates?

Yes. But where is the mind?

On a morning walk through an unfamiliar road in dim light I saw something jutting out from a roadside compound wall. The mind presented a well-defined picture of a rock first. Then when I moved still closer it looked like a cow. When I came very close, it was a stump of a tree with its jumbled roots sticking out.

So the mind projects clear pictures ...with something meager provided to it for a base. But where is the locus for this mind? Awareness disowns the mind and body ...You cannot upload any such thing on awareness ...don't superimpose. It is a sin to do so. Where does the mind stand? Does the mind not need a body as its base? Then where does the body stand? So, the universe. Everything is loaded on to Awareness, again !! No, the Awareness does not accept this charge levelled against it. Now what is really the locus for mind, and body?

Dream is a creation of the mind? Agreed ..with the locus of mind in the body.

But how can we place the waking and the dream states on the same pedestal? For the wakeful mind – if the universe and in that the body are not there, where does it stand and create? (Everybody swears that the mind creates all this). And if at all there is a mind capable of standing nowhere and creating, why should the mind invite suffering? Diseases, disasters, calamities, death – all these are created by the mind? To inflict suffering on itself? Why not create only things that are pleasant?

•• 'With the constitution of a drop, the constitution of the ocean should be known. With the constitution of the dream, the *jagrath* should be known.' This is the general thinking. Just because a shadow is unreal .. one should not argue that the object that caused the shadow is also unreal.

•• "O Rama, the unreal jiva perceives the unreal world on account of the unreal influence of the unreality. In all this, what can be considered as real and what as unreal? An imaginary object is imaginatively described by someone, and one understands in one's own imagination and imagines that he understands it." *The Supreme Yoga,* Vol.II p.43 (Swami Venkatesananda) Is this talk of any use to anybody?

•• If a pot has not come into being, how does the pot-space arise? How did the one single whole space get delimited?

•• "When great sorrow (like the loss of wealth and relatives) befalls you, enquire into the nature of truth; you will not be affected by joy or sorrow. ... They do not belong to you, you do not belong to them. Such is the unreal nature of the world." (!?) ..."Dear Rama, you are pure consciousness which is not affected by the illusory perception of the diversity of creation."

What I have to emphasize is ...Consciousness is not affected whatever be the reality or unreality of the situation. For this, the world does not have to be unreal. Even in the midst of a hard and fast reality of the world, consciousness is not affected. Only you have to learn to see it that way. Consciousness is really aloof ...and we mix it up. "If you see this, how will notions of the desirable and undesirable arise in you? Realising this, O Rama, remain established in the turiya (transcendental) state of consciousness."

•• "It is formless, though it appears in all forms. The world-appearance is but the flesh in which the truth, which is pure consciousness, is clothed."

"When you wake up to the reality of your awareness, ..the universe must fade out. Like darkness when the light comes." (*radha sathyam* p284) A literal vanishing is ever seen? But in a sense ...figuratively ...the universe fades out ....fades into insignificance ...even while it remains.

"It is that self or cosmic consciousness alone which is indicated by expression 'this world'. What a mysterious wonder it is that the self which is pure consciousness or intelligence 'somehow' seems to forget its own nature and comes to regard itself as the jiva (the individual). In fact in that cosmic being which is the reality in everything, there is not even the division into worshipper, worship and the worshipped. It is impossible to describe that cosmic being which supports the entire universe without division, it is impossible to teach another concerning it. And we do not consider them worthy of being taught by us, who consider that god is limited by time and space." (words of Lord Siva to sage Vasishta ...*Yoga Vasishtam: Supreme Yoga* p395)

'If one enquires into the nature of the self and at the same time refrain from actions that promote avidya or ignorance, the darkness of ignorance vanishes. However it is only the self that becomes aware of the self. Do not look upon this diversity as the self. Do not entertain the feeling that self-knowledge is the result of the teaching of a

Ch.4 Confusions & Conflicts

preceptor. The self is not revealed either by the scriptures or by the instructions of a guru, and the self is not revealed without the instructions of a guru and without the help of the scripture either. It is revealed only when all these come together. It is only when the scriptural knowledge, instructions of a preceptor and true discipleship come together that self-knowledge is attained.

"That which remains after all the senses have ceased to function and all notions of pain and pleasure have vanished, is the self or Siva (sivam) – which is also indicated by expressions like 'that', 'truth', 'reality'. However that which is when all these cease to be, exists even when all these are present ...like the limitless space. In the scriptures they have used words like 'bodham' (consciousness), 'Brahmam', 'sivam', 'self', 'Lord'. 'supreme self' (*paramaathma*) etc. The truth indicated by these words is indeed pure consciousness.

"That pure consciousness appears to be a knowable object and gives rise to the concept of intelligence, though it is not an object of knowledge, being the innermost self. On account of a momentary conceptualization, this pure consciousness gives rise to the ego-sense ('I know').

"The ego-sense then gives rise to the notions of time and space. Endowed with the energy of the vital air (*praana*) it then becomes jiva ...the individual. The jiva thenceforward follows the dictates of the notions and slips into dense ignorance of its reality. Thus is the mind born in conjunction with the egosense and the different forms of psychological energy. All these together are known as the '*aathivaahika body*', the subtle body that moves from one plane to another. ('*aathivaahika*' means that which carries).

"After this the substances (objects of the world) corresponding to the subtle energies of the '*aathivaahika*' body were conceived of and thus were the various senses (sight, hearing, etc.), their corresponding objects and their connecting experiences brought into being. These together are known as the *puryashtaka* and in their subtle state they are also known as the *aathivaahika* body.

"Thus were all these substances created; BUT NOTHING WAS CREATED IN FACT.(!!?) All these are but apparent modifications in the one infinite consciousness. Even as dream-objects are within the dreamer himself, all these are non-different from the infinite consciousness. Even as when you dream those objects, they seem to become the objects of your perception, all these too appear to be objective realities.

"When the truth concerning them is realized, all these shine as the Lord. However, even that is untrue, for all these have never become material substances or objects. On account of your own notions of their being substances which you experience, they appear to have a substantiality. Thus conjuring up a substantiality, the consciousness sees the substantiality.

"Conditioned by such notions, it seems to suffer. Conditioning is sorrow. But conditioning is based on thoughts and notions (sensuous and psychological experiences). But the truth is beyond such experience, and the world is an appearance like a mirage.!" *(Vasishtam/ Supreme Yoga* p.397)

The world is—

* not born
* not created
* not modified
* not transformed   ....It is simply not there! (?!!)

What a jungle of words! Anybody understood anything?

Some brilliant thoughts –(I have underlined some) .. thoughts that lead us to the highway (from jungles) – very intelligible; but ultimately everything gets deflected to useless conclusions. If this is Vedantha, — with its whole effort focused on saying that the world is 'appearance', 'illusion' — I fail to understand it ...my mind repulses it ..revolts.

<u>8 kilometre, 4 people</u>: Four people get down to an unfamiliar road. From the milestone they calculate that the distance they have to cover is 8 km. One of them says: "8 kilometre and four people ...so one has only 2km to walk". Sounds logical. Sounds arithmetical. But in front of common sense, where does it stand? To me, all the 'vivartha vaadam' and 'maaya vaadam' boil down to this ...this arithmetic.

Spiritual nonsenses ...still more:

•• Heard in a TV channel...from someone. ''On auspicious occasions we break coconut. We spend crores of Rupees and make a film. The inauguration of its screening is done by breaking a coconut. Why a mango is not thrown, why not an apple, or a banana? Brahma, Vishnu and Shiva are supposed to be residing in coconut....it has three eyes".

I have a question to ask him here: So you throw the three super-gods along with the coconut and break them...smash them...to bring auspiciousness? There are people speaking any nonsense in front of millions watching the TV channels ...and thousands sitting in front of them, with their intellects in their pockets.

•• Bhagawan says in *Gita*: 'I, as the *vaiswanara* fire, occupy the bodies of living beings..and digest the food in four ways." "*Ahum vaiswanaro bhutwa*...." What a great injustice –

damage – has the Bhagawan done!! The creatures feel hungry because of this act of God.

When a lion chases a zebra, if the zebra gets the idea that it is being chased because of this incongruous act of God, it would like to kick Him with its hind legs before it succumbs.

Ahum never becomes *vaiswanara* ..ahum never becomes anything. Since *Bhagavad Gita* is a part of *Maha Bharatham* which is a *purana*, all these happen. A dilution to the Upanishadic brilliance.

People spend the whole life senseless. ...and still think they are very wise.

•• "I myself is this tree; I myself is my neighbor. If you are everything, what are you afraid of?" asks a TV-channel Guru. Is this the way to achieve 'fearlessness'?. Is a 'fearlessness' possible in this fashion?

'*dwaithath vai bhayam bhavathi*' is the brilliant upanishadic teaching. Where there is more than one, there is fear from 'the other'. These enlightened 'teachers' have pulled this down to the gutters ...*parama jnanam* is converted into *paamara jnanam.*

The awareness has no threat from anything; the existence of the world or even the dissolution of the world poses no threat to awareness. These two are not in conflict.

At the sight of these, my mind revolts – head sinks in shame. How can men (and women) the descendants of the Upanishadic Rsis – the torch-bearers (supposed to be) of the Upanishadic brilliance, stoop so low – even below the bottom!!

The eyes that got used to the light of fireflies, refuse to open in front of the sun!

Ch.4 Confusions & Conflicts

•• A blind man was treated with a sumptuous repast in a household. The guest liked the *payasam* (kheer) very much; and asked the guest how this was prepared. He said the basic material was milk. 'What is milk' was the next doubt. He was told that it is a liquid, white in colour. White colour? What is that? It is white like the crane (bird). What is a crane? The host formed the shape of a crane with his arm; and the blind man felt the shape by running his hand over it, and understood that the milk is of this shape.

This is the way people understand things ..and teach others ...far from truth, ...far from what is intended.

•• "*Praana* is one ...that extends into all beings" (p.318 *Bhagavatha Hrdayam*). This is the version of *Bhagavatham*! Then when one being dies, all others must die! (This is an example of the *parama jnanam* of Upanishads reduced to *pamara jnanam* in puranas.) Sankaracharya yells: *na cha prana sabjno, na vai pancha vaayu.* (Not what is denoted by the word *prana*; nor the five *vayu-s*) ...Awareness is one ..that extends into all beings.

•• One line of thinking is that God (or Brahmam; not knowing the hairline border between these two, there is a confusion also) became the world. The world is the body of God. Then how can one organ eat another organ? How will a lion eat a deer? If you feel hungry, will your mouth venture at a big bite on your biceps? The direction from the brain will be – "better starve to death ...don't bite".

The God will admonish the lion when it springs upon a prey: "you are doing harm to me; don't do that. Eat grass; the elephant also eats grass. And the grass does not run."

Manasa puja?

'Imaginary puja' is an approved practice in Bhakthi.

"*Vilva phalam* (a fruit), in diamond studded pot. Payasam (a sweet in liquid form) ...all created in my imagination ……..You take it my God." This is the method! It is a mockery…..what else? Can any god tolerate this mockery? Astral beings (devas and all) get satisfied with the sight and smell of offerings. They cannot take these things in physically, though, ...being astral. When you don't even show them to have a look, how will they please?

Arguments:

"The source is not the doer at all" Heard from somewhere. Then how can it be the source?

I am pure Awareness / chaithanyam/ bodham. From that manifests the world. And my body is a spec of it. (Then don't call it 'pure').

Brahmam desired to manifest into the Prapancham (universe)! How can there be a desire in the desire-less?

You get an itch; then you scratch, and get some pleasure (*sukham*) out of it. But an itch-less scratch-less situation is better still, .. isn't it? Why desire at all? An itch-less scratch-less situation …..is it not the stillness of the stone? Yes, and much more.

•• With or without anything in its path to show up, the sunlight is always sunlight – and holds in it the light and heat to show up things that come on its way, and to warn up, and also activate. The world comes alive with sunlight. Why not think that the efficiency to come alive – and to put forth plants and trees and all living organisms – is in the earth itself? (Like a seed). It is the efficiency of Nature that sprouts forth in the presence of Awareness.

We grow sugar-cane and bitter-gourd in the same field. One grows sweet, the other bitter. It is the efficiency of the plant that manifests, not the efficiency of the soil. The soil is the same, the water provided to both is the same, the sunlight is the same, the manure is the same …. but one grows sweet, and the other bitter.

•• To support this view there are very many statements in the scriptures that It is Saakshi Chaithanyam (witness). In its presence things happen. Seeing that many people say that 'It does' *(..kaaka-thaaleeya nyayam)*. Whereas the doer is someone else/ something else. (kaaka-thaaleeya nyayam: *kaaka* = crow. *thaali* = palmyrah tree. A crow lands on a palmyrah tree, and a palm-fruit falls. Both happen simultaneously …a simple coincidence. The fruit was over-ripe ..ready to fall any time. But the crow is considered responsible.)

Why not consider that Prakrti (Nature) holds the efficiency—like a built-up computer (minus the electricity)? All capabilities are built-in, and all these capabilities come alive in the presence of electricity?

•• Prakrti — everything formed of five elements (the earth, the universe, your body) – is simply matter/material, perhaps dormant with some efficiency ingrained in it. But Purusha / the Self / the Awareness – is alive .. always .. knowing it's existence and the existence of whatever that exist .. ..the light of lights – *Jyothishaam Jyothi*.

'God has two aspects, they say: 1. Brahmam – with the powers, not showing up—latent. 2. God, with all the powers manifest. *Iccha shakthi* — will to become multifarious.

234 The Eye of the Universe

In seed form, nothing is complete and clear. In a cotton seed, you won't see cotton stacked up microscopically. But all the qualities of the plant manifests only from that seed. So it stems from Brahmam...'. The dirty diabolic universe ..its creatures eating one another...riddled with diseases, disasters, calamities and death—its inmates tearing at one another to sustain life — the universe red in tooth and claw — is a blossoming of Brahmam? Absurd.

Those who say this, also feel that all is not well – the way it looks.

So it is labelled "Maya". And that Maya does not exist; it is inexplicable, ie. un-explainable. Maya has two powers: *aavaranam* and *vivartham*[1]. It has three gunas: satwa, rajas, thamas ...it has the capacity to put together anything that cannot be put together[2], show up anything that does not really exist ... and still it itself is non existent !!! A Maya that does not exist, creates this universe! This is the birth certificate of the universe: "IT DOES NOT EXIST".

"A God that is not born (meaning, non-existent) creates, preserves and destroys—through Maya." (*Bhagavatham* 1.8.16) And that Maya is itself non-existent! So the fate of the universe is sealed: 'THE UNIVERSE IS NON-EXISTENT'.

> *sattha'chid'sukha rupam'asthi sathatham*
> *na'aham na cha twam mrsha;*
> *nedamvaapi jagat pradrshtam akhilam*
> *naastheethi jaaneehi bho*
> *yath'proktham karunaa'vasaath'twayi mayaa*
> *thath sathyam ethath'sphudam*

---

[1] Veiling the reality, and projecting what is not.
[2] *Akhaditha khadana padiyasi maya.*

*sraddha'swanakha shuddhabhddhir'athichen-
maathraasthu tae samsaya*
(*Proudhanubhuthi*-16 Mal. Prof GB p.172)

'Sath-chid-ananda swaroopam (reality-awareness-bliss in its own form) alone exists always ...Neither you nor me nor this universe seen through the senses exist. I tell you this out of compassion to you; with a clear head, ...if your mind is oriented towards the truth, think over and understand it to be true, without any vestige of doubt'.

This is the aspect of Vedanta that confuses ... This whole book is aimed at clearing this confusion.

Look at a verse (of Gaudapada) that crowns this line of thought:

मृगतृष्णांभसिस्नात
खपुष्पकृतशेखरः
एषवन्ध्यासुतोयाति
शशशृंगधनुर्धर

*mrga'thrshna'ambhasi'snatha
kha'pushpa'krtha'sekhara
aesha'vandhya'sutho'yaathi
shasha'srnga dhanur'dhara.*

"There goes the son of a barren woman, bathed in mirage waters, wearing a crown of sky-flowers, and a bow of rabbit-horn".

The existence of the world is equated to this!! Can anyone assimilate this? Why not concede that the universe exists? The sky won't fall. It does not pose a threat to the stability of Awareness.

Prakasam: cognition: The light of the sun, moon, fire, electric bulbs etc. shows-up— throws light on – things around. But the awareness has a difference ...it cognizes the darkness also (*Proudhanubhuthi* p426). It is a light that shows up darkness..(also). It cognizes the presence and also absence.

•• 'If the existence of a thing or being is not known by itself ...or by others, how can it exist ...where does it exist? What is the proof of its existence? When a thing exists, it exists in the awareness that knows its existence. Where else can it exist? The world (universe) exists only in the sky of awareness—space of awareness. Time and space exist only in the Awareness that lends reality to time and space. Time and space exist because of your Awareness. Awareness is the substratum on which stand the time and space'...(and for further explanation to Maya, see...p118 *Gowdapada Darsanam* ..Mal.) 'And so, nothing is born ..nothing exists. ...If anything exists, it is Maya...not real'. But Maya is the creation of mind. When and how did the mind come in? — 'Like mirage in a desert!'

•• But the world exists ... as a continuum...with all its minor pleasures and major horrors. And that is its reality... That makes it real.

* If you don't recognize me...my existence, does it mean that I don't exist?
* If the United Nations do not recognize a nation, does it mean that that nation doesn't exist?
* If a word is not found in a dictionary, does it mean that the word doesn't exist?
* If my name is not in the Government's list, does it mean that I don't exist? How do I extinguish

Ch.4 Confusions & Conflicts

myself...nullify myself...vanish?...by declaring myself 'Maya'? Then again, what will I do with myself? Where will I hide myself? Because ...I remain!

* You ignite some gun-powder. It blasts, even if it be a rock that constrains it. Laws of physics work. The universe answers to the laws of nature. (not to anything else...probably.) If it is a shadow (unreal) it will not bleed ...but here it bleeds.

•• See that the vast space extends into the pot-space. Don't see the other way round—that the pot-space expands/unites/joins or assumes the form of...endless space.

"The comparison ...(no, the equating $Đ_n$) ...of waking to dream is due to a confusion. All cognitions are empty of content? The dream has the dreamer's mind as its locus. What is the locus for waking experience? Emptiness? – if the world and the body are non-existent...Maya?" (Dr Radhakrishnan)

Another argument is that—

* With the eyes you cannot hear.
* With the ears you cannot see.

Each is endowed with a different capability. All the instruments of perception have their limitations. We know only what they present us. (To highlight this argument, Swamy Ram Tirtha presents a dramatic story of a blindfolded man -- in an eye hospital — licking a glass to know its colour!)

•• All these arguments perhaps sound good. But to my mind, these do not suffice fully to neutralize/evaporate/dissolve the body (BMI) and the universe.

These are – to my mind – not logical reasoning (*tarkam*), but *ku-tarkam* (illogical).

I am tempted to understand that <u>in</u> the Real <u>me</u> (<u>the Awareness,</u> eternal), <u>there is no body</u>. Body is only a superimposition ...like the colour of hibiscus flower on a glass-cube. Glass cube is colourless, though it appears red. Then the 'how' and 'why' of the body? ... Bury these questions ...deep. It has no real relevance to You..the Awareness Eternal. Be happy...and in peace, absolute. If you start digging for answers, you can end up digging....and digging, with no result. There are various theories explaining the 'how' and 'why' of this body. Some are very plausible; but in a closer analysis, useless.

Karma theory is a jungle:

Where from is the first karma? Has anybody ever got an answer? Awareness has no involvement in karma....then the karma belongs to the body? Sankaracharya has answered it with an emphatic 'No". Karma is for the 'jiva-bhavam' – the body-mind-intellect-Awareness-combine! Agreed. But how and why and where did it originate? What for? It leads to the first creation. That is attributed to— (1) Leela, (2) Maya, (3) to avoid boredom – all these are not satisfactory explanations. That is why I said: Bury these concerns ... deep. And be happy. *"Sadho, vismaranam varam".* (Vasishtam). Better is to forget all these.

•• Awareness gets condensed into matter ...'*prakrthi*' ...universe? Aware gets condensed into non-awareness? That too into a nasty universe ...red in tooth and claw? Why not something better ...more peaceful, pleasurable, enjoyable, acceptable?

One more doubt. If awareness gets condensed, that is a transformation. After a transformation, the original does not exist. A gets transformed into B. Thereafter A does not exist; only B exists. Here, after condensing into non-awareness, the awareness co-exists with the universe?

Ch.4   Confusions & Conflicts

•• The world exists only in the mind? Then, where is the mind located?

Sage Ashtavakra prefers to face this jungle with his back.'-

नाना मतं महर्षीणां साधूनां योगिनां तथा
दृष्ट्वा निर्वेदमापन्नः को न शाम्यति मानवः ॥

(Asht.Gita IX 5)

nana matam maharsheenaam
sadhunam yoginam thadha
drshtva nirveda'maapanna
ko na shaamyati maanava?

Having observed the diversity of opinions among the great seers, saints and yogis, why don't people become indifferent and attain quietude?

How valuable are the siddhis?

There are very many god-men and god-women all round the world. They all seem to show only gimmicks. There occurred a tsunami in central Kerala. The waves washed away many lives at the very doorstep of one such. Why didn't this personality foresee the calamity and forewarn the people living on the shore? When everybody came out for rescue, they too came out with rescue work. Their siddhis were of no use ...no life is saved. When a severe earthquake struck Gujarat, and demolished two big towns totally, a big god-man was living in south India with a huge empire built up. And when the recent tsunami struck Japan, this godman was still living. No help was possible of him. Not even a timely warning. Don't they have this foresight?

So they are all gods of small things?

•• "janm'aushadhi'manthra'thapa : samadhija siddhaya:" says Patanjali in Yogasutras enumerating the sources of siddhies. (Birth, herbal potions, incantation of manthras, penances, meditations.)

•• Also in Yoga Vasishtam, sage Vasishta says the same words to Sri Rama; and in the same breath adds: "Those who abide as the self in the self ..steeped in the peace and contentment of the self will not run after siddhies. Of what use is siddhies for them?" In one verse sage Vsishta shuts up the curiosity of Sree Rama on sidhies.

"Siddhi-s are for immature minds. A hindrance. Unimportant. To be burnt off". (Prof GB in *Bhagavatha Hrdayam* p.437)

Nisarga Datta was asked: 'Can you enter into the mind and heart of another man and share his experience?
NM: "No. Such things need special training". (I AM THAT P257)

Sankaracharya says, siddhies develop to those who have done heinous crimes such as killing one's own mother, killing a realized person (Brahma hathya) and so on ...because people who have made some progress along the spiritual path are stalled by siddhies from progressing further.

Knowledge of the future:

Even the way-side palmist comes out with very close ...why very close?...exact .. predictions.

Once one such palmist told me such-and-such a thing would happen to me on the third day. And it did happen. It is his trade...and its secret. Small and big ...Everything is a trade. When you understand it...Oh! It was so simple!? The awe and wonderment is gone. And you start wondering why the others don't know it.

All these (siddhies) are in the world ...in respect of the world and your body ...related to the five elements .... Past, present, future...aakaashik records, spiritual world ...all. (related to *prapancham*, in its various forms). And you are '*nish-prapancham*' (without *prapancham*) in reality. There is only one sky...space...akasha for the real You, ..and that is *chid*-akasha—the sky of consciousness.

•• "Through utter ignorance, man takes pride in his knowledge. He offers to carry others to knowledge and freedom, while he himself is whirling in *samsara* under delusion. It is like the blind leading the blind". (Mu.1.2.8)

•• "These spurious/adulterated yogas are of no use". (*Arul Mozhikal* p.283, Poojappura Gopala Swami).

5

SOME RELATED THOUGHTS

Brahman who is existence, consciousness and infinity is the Reality. Its being Iswara (the Omniscient Lord of the world) and Jiva (the individual soul) are superimpositions by the two illusory adjuncts (Maya and Avidya, respectively). Brahman is called Iswara and Jiva according to the functions it performs. (*Pancadasi* III.37)

Brahman is called the individual soul (Jiva) when It is viewed in association with the five sheaths, as a man is called a father and a grandfather in relation to his son or his grandson. (*Pancadasi* III.41)

A man is neither a father nor a grandfather when considered apart from his son and grandson, so Brahmam is neither Iswara nor Jiva when considered apart from Maya or the five sheaths.(*Pancadasi* III.42)

This power (Maya) appears as 'conscious' because it is associated with the reflection of Brahmam. And because of the association with this power, Brahmam gets Its omniscience. *(Tat-sakti-upathi samyogat Brahmaiva Iswaratvam vrajet)* (*Pancadasi* III.40)

As the *Akasa* in a pot is concealed by the *Akasa* reflected in the water with which the pot is filled, so too Kutastha is obscured by Jiva. This principle is called mutual obscuring or super-imposition. (*Panchadasi* VI.24 Swami Vidyaranya)

***   ***   ***

karthrtwam na cha karmaani.....
"na karmaphala samyogam"   *(Bh.Gita V.14)*

na karthrtvam na cha karmaani
lokasya srjati prabhu..   *(Bh.Gita)*

God does not prescribe a course of action for you (*karma*) nor a doership. Ensuring that you face the consequences of your actions – good or bad – is also not God's look-out.... (*na karma'phala'samyogam*) This is Gita that says. People don't usually see this.

•• **Gita XIII. 20:** The Cause and Effect and the Causation (doership) are said to be in *Prakrthi* (Nature); while in the experiencing of happiness and misery, the *Purusha* (our awareness) is said to be the cause. The *Purusha* residing in *Prakrthi* experiences the gunas born of *prakrthi*. XIII. 20, 21. Note it: Gita also points out that the cause and causation are in Nature.
(*Karya-kaarana—karthrthve hethu: prakrthiruchyathe*)

The following four more verses from *Bhagavath Gita* also very clearly demarcate the roles of *prakrthi* and *purusha*, without any confusion. Those who specialize in confusing should look at these with wide open eyes:

(1) पुरुषं प्रकृतिंचैव
विद्ध्यनादी उभावपि
विकारंश्च गुणांश्चैव
विद्धि प्रकृति संभवान् ॥   *(Bh.Gita XIII.19)*

purusham prakrthim'chaiva
viddhi'anaadi ubhaavapi
vikaaramscha'gunaamschaiva
viddhi prakrthi'sambhavaan.

Know both *Prakrthi* and *Purusha* to be beginningless, and know the evolutes and the gunas as born of *Prakrthi* (nature).

(2) मयाध्यक्षेण प्रकृति सूयते सचराचरं

*mayaadhyakshena prakrthi
suyathe sachara'acharam* (Bh.Gita IX.10)

'In my presence (lit. presided over by me), Prakrthi brings forth the world of moving and unmoving things'.

If our earth were not exposed to sunlight, there would not have been any living beings here. If the temperature were too hot or too cold also there would not have been any living beings.

(3) न च मां तानि कर्माणि निबध्नन्ति धनञ्जय
उदासीनवदासीनं असक्तं तेषु कर्मसुः ॥ *(Bh.Gita IX.9)*

*na cha maam thaani karmaani
nibadhnanthi Dhananjaya
udaaseenavad'aaseenam
asaktham theshu karmasu.*

These acts (of creation etc.) do not bind me, who remain unattached to them like one indifferent.

(4) न कर्तृत्वं न च कर्माणि
लोकस्य सृजति प्रभु

*na karthrthvam na cha karmaani
lokasya srjathi prabhu.*

God doesn't produce, or prescribe a course of action to the world.

Ch.5 Some related thoughts

In the blooming of a lotus in the morning, or in its folding up in the evening, the sun has no interest; and yet its presence is a must for this to happen.

***   ***   ***

•• "The indivisible Bodham alone is the Reality. And the multiplicity is not at all existent[1]. This is the one thing to be understood. In the ultimate analysis, the appearances in Bodham are also Bodham. This is the second thing to be understood. Firm up these two things by repeated contemplation. If these two things are firmed up, then there is nothing else to gain in this life. Nothing else to know. You will gain limitless peace and tranquility.

"All these appearance is brought about by Maya. How can you assert that? Maya means, whatever brought about by it is also Maya – unreal – non-existent. Mere magic, hallucination. The things that are shown by a magician are really not there. (and the word Maya itself means 'that which is not there'). This is the one thing that we have to get convinced first. How can we be sure that it is not there? How can you say that this mike is not there. The sun is not there. The phenomenal universe, the endless millions of galaxies which the physical scientists watch and wonder at and try to extract the truths, are not there? How can we be sure?

"Think, how can they be existent, except in the all-pervading Bodham / awareness? And perhaps we have not grasped that Awareness fully as of now." (This is from a class-room talk by a big teacher / guru)

Another Professor challenges: "Can you show me one person in the whole world who is capable of showing me this universe without the help of Bodham (awareness)?"

---

[1] I prefer to add here : '….not at all existent in me, the Awareness'.

246 The Eye of the Universe

(Prof. GB) I don't consider this an argument. This is negative-argument (*ku-tarkam*).

"I — the Consciousness — am there, and the universe is there. I am not there, the Universe is not there (?) Therefore I am the universe myself. If the sea is there, the waves and bubbles will be there. If there is no sea, no waves, no bubbles" (Prof GB). Awareness alone exists; nothing else. Whatever else, if you find, is also awareness; nothing else. This is the doctrine of Adwaitha Vedantha ... 'non-dualism'.

•• Vedant-ists (vedantin) repeatedly assure us that the burden of Vedanta is not to prove the non-existence of the world (Maya), but to assert the Reality of Brahman. But in reality (in practice) I find , 80 to 90 percent of the volume of teaching is devoted to the subject of Maya.

With this whole book, my attempt is to assert the Reality of Brahmam / bodham /awareness, and define its role; and in this, I don't find any need to negate the world!

"The repugnance of the Advaitin to admitting the reality of Nature is due to his firm faith in the absolute attributes of God, in His infinitude, eternity, unchangeableness, absolute intelligence and indivisibility. He thinks that the admission of the reality of Nature amounts to a denial of these attributes. If finite things really exist, do they not form so many limitations of the Infinite, which in that case ceases to be infinite?

"......Again to say that the Absolute Reality changes, that it becomes what it was not before, means that it is subject to the law of causation and is therefore no Absolute at all. To say, as the Parinamavadin says, that God assumes the form of the world, that He Himself becomes the various objects of the world, animate and inanimate, is to say that the Infinite

Ch.5 Some related thoughts

One divests Himself of His infinitude, ceases to be infinite – a doctrine which is absurd on the face of it, and which makes all spiritual exercises, all efforts to attain unity with the Infinite utterly meaningless. The Vivarthavaadin therefore concludes that objects in time and space, including finite intelligence, or to speak more correctly, all things that make intelligence appear limited, are only appearances and not realities and the power by which God projects these appearances is like that by which a magician performs his wonderful feats......" (p.xxxi Introduction: 112 UPANISHADS).

I see some confusion in all this. How will the world become unreal ...by saying that it really does not exist? If at all there is a doubt about the existence of the world, leave it for science to settle. *Awareness does not create the world* ...**awareness only shows up the existing world.** In preceding chapters I have quoted enough of statements from Upanishads and all, that supports this view.

Vivekachudamani 232: 'satyam yadi' .."If the universe, as it is, be real,

1) the Atman would not be Infinite
2) the scriptures would be falsified, and
3) the Lord Himself would be guilty of having spoken an untruth. *

None of these three is considered either desirable or wholesome."

This doesn't impress me: (If we want the Truth, we will have to side-step these .. forget these. If this causes inconvenience to some line of thinking, forget it; we cannot

---

* Bhagawan Sri Krishna, in Geetha, declares more than once, that the world is just a projection ...with no factual reality.

sacrifice the Truth. We cannot simply disown the real world. Like some people disown the parent-hood of their own children, where it causes inconvenience ...embarrassment.)

1. Athman would still be infinite and eternal. The existence of the universe doesn't pose a threat to awareness. In fact Awareness is a reality that lends reality to the universe. The universe ...*prakrthi* ...evolves, changes, dissolves and gets reborn; ....and Awareness stands changeless and eternal ..unaffected by whatever that happens to the world ...*prakrthi*.

2. Look at all that I have quoted in this book from scriptures ....They support my view that the universe is real. Look at the scriptures with a clear vision.

3. This is not a serious objection. Bhagawan at times shirks the responsibility of his statements by adding that 'so say the experts' (*kavayo viduh*). [And Sage Vaishta lends us the courage to question everything that is questionable. ..."Accept the truth even if it comes from a child; and reject the untruth even if it comes from Brahma (...*vachanam baalakaadapi*) – *Yoga Vasishtam*]

*** *** ***

"It is in ignorance that the universe exists. In reality, you are the only One. There is no individual Self or the Supreme Self other than You.

"So long as the universe exists, the Self is conceived in two aspects—individual and absolute. In the individual aspect it is transmigratory, samsaarin, passing through rounds of births and deaths. In the absolute aspect it is eternal and unchanging. But the universe exists only through ignorance. In reality, the Self is One; universe does not exist. So the distinction between the individual and the absolute aspects of the Self is *ipso facto* unreal. The Self alone is."

Ch.5 Some related thoughts   249

This much I quoted from Ashtavakra Gita (XV.16) for anyone to take advantage of the thought process...if it becomes possible. ..though I don't subscribe to the view that the universe does not exist. "through ignorance alone the universe exists" etc.

* "Prathyagathma', 'Brahma" bhedam (differentiation)
* 'Jeeva' 'Brahma' bhedam.
* The individual Self, the Supreme Self differentiation
* Jivaathma, Paramathma differentiation

This is the Duality that should end. This is the differentiation that should end. ...a differentiation that is actually not existent. **Where is the big difficulty in this? Pot-space, vast space. These are not two. Space is only One ...vast endless space. Remaining vast and single (one only), the space occupies the pots also.**

***   ***   ***

'The power of Creation vests with God; not in vyashti (individual) nor in a Siddha'. (P.138 *Vedanta Prabodh*) I have discussed elsewhere that ...when the thought proceeds along the proper line, God vanishes. God-hood is imposed on Brahmam (seemingly) while it is in association wirh Nature ...in conjunction with *Prakrti*. Like red colour to a glass cube, while it is on a hibiscus flower. The power comes from Nature ..*prakrthi*. So, no confusing. 'You' are not powerful, siddha is not powerful, Brahmam is not powerful, God is not powerful. (Don't be afraid; sky won't fall). 'The efficiency...(omniscient, omnipotent etc.) manifests only through upadhis': that is the usual talk. *(Tath-sakthi-upathi samyogath Brahmaiva Iswaratwam vrajeth) (Pancadasi* III.40)

"A Siddhan / knower of Brahman/ Jnani is not omniscient and omnipotent etc". (p.98 *Veda. Prabodh*). (Sidha = a person who has attained what has to be attained. One who has become Brahmam—one who knows he is Brahmam.)

'*Brahmavith Brahmaiva bhavathi*' asserts the Upanishads.

If the 'power' is not in siddha, it prompts me to conclude that this power is not in Brahmam either—Brahmam and the Siddha being the same—nothing different, nothing separate, nothing less or more (minus the BMI).

•• "Brahmam is the cause,...not the effect". (p.82 *Ved. Probodh*) Here I see a confusion. Brahmam, Athma, Bodham, Awareness, your own awareness – Do you see these on an equal footing, or a bit differently ...in a descending order, with a diminishing status ...with Brahmam at the top rank and 'your awareness' at the lowest end? This is the thing to be firmed up; this is where we lose our grip on the right understanding. These are synonyms of one and the same word – nothing different, nothing separate, nothing less or more. If we firm it up (without *smrthi, vismrthi, bhraanthi*) the job is done. That is the end. If this is firmed up ...your awareness cannot cause the universe; you know that pretty well. So Brahmam also cannot cause[+].

Then what is wrong in concluding that '*Prakrti*' (nature) is not caused by anything outside *Prakrti* ..it is its own cause ...nature has its own cause in-built, intrinsic?

Like power (electricity) and the computer.

Electricity ..and computer. Made for each other. Computer is useless without electricity. Electricity is not computer; computer is not electricity. In conjunction ...put together, they work. In the context of Brahmam and Prakrthi

---

[+] It can reveal the universe ..show up the universe ..when it exists; ...not create.

Ch.5 Some related thoughts 251

...the situation may be something like this, though not exactly. *Prakrti* may work, at least to some extent ...without anyone knowing it ..without even *Prakrti* knowing it! Electricity has its independent standing; computer is built up all-right with all capabilities, but is simply useless without electricity. No use to itself, no use to others.

(*upadana kaaranam* and *nimittha kaaranam*—both these roles are usually attributed to Brahmam. Out of these, *upaadaana*....(material cause) is the one that provides the material of the universe.)

There are other pointers that aid a clearer vision:-

sthavaram jangamam vyaaptham
yath kincith sa-characharam

It pervades everything, movable and immovable; yet it is not having (nor holding) everything in it.

So, Brahmam is clean, pure. Think.

Here we come close to one thought: ...that Brahmam (awareness) is one thing, and nature another; but working in conjunction, in a mix-up (seemingly mixed up ...seemingly, because Brahmam has independent standing). Brahmam (awareness) is independent, and seemingly mixed-up at the same time. This is the Maya ...Maya should be understood this way; not through the voluminous confusions presented to us so far. Independent Awareness, seemingly mixed-up with the Nature ...still retaining its one-ness and independence. That is good enough; we don't have to make the universe non-existent, unreal.

•• For Bhagawan who is *kevala ananda* — Bliss Absolute — and with no desire to be fulfilled, what for is a *shakthi* as Maya? No logical answer is available to this question. (Prof.GB in *Bha. Hrd.*)

Sankhyam analysed:

If Brahmandam (the cosmos) is there, that is a combination of five elements. Elements can be traced back to Mahan Atma, Mahan Atma to Prana,

> Prana to Avyaktham (not falling under the senses)
>
> Avyaktham to Kaalam (time) ...
>
> Prakrthi (Nature) merges into Time
>
> Time into Jeevan
>
> Jeevan into Atma
>
> Atma abides in its Own Form.

If this idea is solidified—firmed up....then where can darkness stay when the sun rises? (Prof.GB P421 *Bha. Hrd.*)

•• Time. space and causation – all fall under the ambit of Creation. Why, when, where was this Creation done? No logical answer is possible for such questions. Even the question "why did the Jeevas originate?" remains unanswered. (Prof GB P307 *Bha.Hrd.*)

'The atoms, fundamental particles, molecules are all modes of frozen energy. The entire universe is formed by the integration and differentiation of energy. Matter is also another form of energy like light, heat, magnetism and electricity. In the unending expanse of universe the only thing real is the energy frozen in different stages'.

This is an answer to the doctrine of Maya (that the world has no reality). **But the energy has no eyes.**

"World has Awareness as its eyes." ...Upanishad. Awareness is not a product of the body or body/brain chemistry. If it is, it should end with the body and brain. But it is not found to end with the death of the physical body. It continues in the astral body. Any doubt? Can you think of an astral body /astral being without awareness? A by-gone ancestor without awareness? A God without awareness?

The world appears as Vivartham—like snake in a rope!

This is the view of non-dualistic Vedanta. That means, a snake is really not there; non-existent. If someone tries to photograph that snake, rope alone will be there in the photo, no snake. If the world is *vivartham*, it should elude the physical laws and test-beds. But we don't see that. Maya theory is also similar.

The thing to be understood is—

In you the Reality / Bodham / Awareness, there is no universe. You are pure. Flawless. There is no dirty world in you, and you are not contaminated by the dirty world. Like the space is not contaminated by the flying of a crow with a stinking dead snake in its beak. The air is of course contaminated, but not the space. There is no scope of contamination in space.

Thripudi mudinju thelinjidunna deepam (Mal) (Narayana Guru)– A light that shines bright, subsiding the thripudi (the division into Jiva-jagat-Easwara). When the triad subsides, then Bodham alone remains – being not-big not-small – not having any necessity to be All-knowing, All-powerful — as Pure Awareness, *Shuddha Bodham*.

•• *Prapancham* (Nature), *Shakthi* (power—power of the Omnipotent)—Where are these from—then? Are they from Brahmam? Why should it not be from Nature (*prakrthi*)? *Iccha shakthi, kriya shakthi, jnana shakthi*—these are usually attributed to *Prakrthi* and *Maya*. (Out of this *Jnana-shakthi* I cannot attribute to *Prakrthi* — it is inert. Similarly, *iccha shakthi* also). *Kriya shakthi* (power of action) it can have. But is the presence of Awareness necessary for this? Intelligent probing is necessary in this area.

Why not look at it this way?

Take the case of electricity.

.. All equipments are energized/ activated by electricity.

.. All equipments are made, with electricity in view – for electricity to activate.

Similarly, Nature can have/ may have its own laws of working. Water flows downwards. Air expands with heat; causes winds and whirlwinds. So heat creates many of the havocs (not God)—tsunamis, earthquakes. Thunder is another very powerful /ferocious thing that the primitive man looked at with awe (We, even today, find it awesome). The thunder has its chemical/physical natural reasons.

So, electricity is one thing; equipment another. Electricity need not be intrinsically, integrally in the equipment. Electricity need not be inside the computer. Electricity can exist without the computer. But for the existence of computer to be meaningful, it requires electricity. Awareness does not need the body for its existence.

Nature has its intrinsic efficiency.

Brahmam/ Bodham/ Awareness has its intrinsic efficiency.

Are they mutually complementary...? I think it will be a wrong conclusion if we think so. Awareness is complementary

Ch.5 Some related thoughts

to the universe; that is apparent. (Awareness lights up/ shows up the working of the universe[1]).

Awareness is complementary to the Universe; but universe is not complementary to Awareness. For the Awareness to be complete, the universe is not necessary. The Awareness is Self-Existent[2]. You are You....with or without the body and the universe. That is reason enough to be in Peace. All the rest? Let it be what it is...existent, non-existent, seemingly existent, transcient. If anyone can find the answers, find it. Even if you find the answers, it is not going to affect Your Reality. Only if You are there (Awareness), the existence or non-existence of other things is known. All the living organisms—whatever that respond to stimuli — have awareness, plants also. You are this Awareness — and Eternal too. That is good enough. You can relax—rest in Peace.

na bhumi'rapo na ca vahnir'asthi
na ca'anilo'mae'asthi na ca'ambaram ca   ...(etc)

No earth, no water, no fire in me, nor any air, or space.

One who knows me thus—as pure Awareness, as the witness of all, as shining in the intellect—alone comes to realize my real form. (*Kaivalyopanishad*)

Beyond that whether it plays any conscious, willful role— it is doubtful. It needs investigation.

With the help of sunlight / in the presence of sunlight / because of sunlight (caused by sunlight) many things happen

---

1&2. The universe also may be self-existent—minus Awareness it runs on, on its own wheels (the universal laws governed by physics and chemistry , gravity, heat and the like). And awareness also may be playing a role, by its mere presence. Like the sunlight playing a role on the earth   ...like the role of spring in the flowering of trees.

on earth. The growth of plants, chlorophyll, the production of oxygen – our dependence on them – and so on. But can we conclude that the sun does all these? The sun may not even be knowing the existence of the earth.

•• 'Because of Its association with this power (Maya) Brahmam gets Its omniscience. (III.40 *Pancadasi*)

•• Athma ...minus *upadhi* ..is neither male, nor female nor neutral. (*Swethaswathara Upa.*)

•• Those who live ignoring the call of *athman* are reborn in the world of the materialist and sense-bound creatures; they commit spiritual suicide, as it were. (Isa. 3, Ke.2.5, Br. 3.8.10, Bh. 11.21-27-28.

*** *** ***

•• There are grades in Swargam (heaven) ...as there are different levels of punya ...and differing durations. *Pancadasi* also corroborates this.

•• "Vedas, puranas, Brahma and all, and Iswara – all these have no perpetual, eternal, absolute Reality" !!!

(*Swasamvedyopanishad*; Upa-108, p832)

Illusion

"Then I began to enquire into the nature of the objective world; what is the cause of this world, and who is aware of it? (who knows it?) Surely the one infinite consciousness alone exists. The firmament, earth, air, space, mountains, rivers, east-west etc. are all the same indivisible consciousness (space-like)(?). They exist as notions in the consciousness. These are not mountains, nor is this the earth, or space. This is not 'I' either. All these are appearances that arise in pure consciousness." (in p.658 SUPREME YOGA / Vasishtam)

"Brahmam is the pure, spontaneous self-experience which is the one consciousness that dwells in all substances.

Ch.5   Some related thoughts   257

It is the seed of all seeds, it is the essence of this world appearance. It is the greatest of actions. <u>It is the cause of all causes</u> and it is the essence in all beings, <u>though in fact it does not cause anything</u> nor is it the concept of being and therefore cannot be conceived. It is the awareness in all that is sentient, it knows itself as its own object, it is its own supreme object, and it is aware of infinite diversity within itself.

"<u>It is the consciousness in all experiences, but it is pure and unconditioned. It is absolute truth and therefore not truth as a concept.</u> It is not limited in the definitions of truth or falsehood. It is in fact the very end (terminus) of the supreme truth, or the primordial reality. It is pure absolute consciousness, nothing else. Yet it itself becomes coloured with desire or attraction for pleasure. It itself becomes the experiencer of pleasure and the impurity caused by it. Though it is like the space – unconditioned and undivided – soon it becomes limited and conditioned. In this infinite consciousness there have been millions of mirages known as world-appearance and there will also arise millions more such mirages . Yet nothing really has come into being independent of the infinite consciousness: light and heat seem to come out of fire, but they are not independent of fire.

"This infinite consciousness can be compared to the ultimate subatomic particle which yet hides within its bowels the greatest of mountains. It is eternity as well as a fleeting second also. It is subtler than the tip of a single strand of hair, yet it pervades the entire universe. No one has seen its limits or boundaries.

"<u>It does nothing</u>, yet it has fashioned the universe. Sustaining the entire universe, it does nothing at all. All substances are non-different from it, yet it is not a substance.

Though it is non-substantial, it pervades all substances. The cosmos is its body, yet it has no body. It is the eternal 'now', yet it is the tomorrow. Often apparently meaningless sounds become meaningful while communicating with one another; even so that infinite consciousness is and is not. It is even what it is not. All these statements about what is and what is not are based on logic, and the infinite consciousness goes beyond truth, beyond logic.

'It is this infinite consciousness that makes the seed sprout with the help of water, earth, time etc. and become food. It makes flowers blossom, and makes the nose smell their fragrance. In the same way it is able to create and sustain." (all from SUPREME YOGA / Vasishtam)

Where does the efficiency of nature *(prakrthi)* end, and where does the efficiency of awareness begin? This needs closer investigation :

(i) Someone is lying unconscious. Life did not ebb out ...he breathes. 'Prana and apana' work, it seems. Some functions will go on ...but how long?

(ii) In nature, if there is water it will flow downwards ..without the presence of awareness.

If the consciousness itself creates, will it create things and situations unsavory? ...It will choose to create pleasantries.

Till we get some clue to understand this enigma and double-talk, we have one course open – in this single talk: Let the world of objects be real or unreal ...keep aside that question to settle. ...Awareness is a greater reality, and awareness is not affected by the reality or un-reality of the world.

"In this body, thoughts and notions generate action in the light of this very consciousness. Surely, but for this consciousness you will not see even an object which is immediately in front of you. The body cannot function nor exist but for this consciousness. It grows, it falls, it eats. This consciousness creates and maintains all the movable and immovable beings (things) in the universe. The infinite consciousness alone exists ...nothing else". (p.381 *Supreme Yoga*)

The paragraph below, from the same text, does not confuse as the last two sentences of the above paragraph. It is clean:-

"The Lord fit to be worshipped is indeed the one who upholds the entire creation, who is beyond thought and description , who is beyond the concepts of even the 'all' and the 'collective totality'. He alone is referred to as 'Lord' who is undivided and indivisible by space and time, whose light illumines all the objects, who is pure and absolute consciousness. It exists everywhere like the essence in a plant. That pure consciousness which is in you, in me, in all the gods and goddesses, that alone is God. ...That God is not distant from anyone, nor is He difficult to attain. He is for ever seated in the body and He is everywhere like space. He does everything, He eats, He holds everything together, He goes, He breathes, He knows every limb of the body. He is the light in which all these limbs function and all the diverse activities take place. He dwells in the cave of one's own heart. He transcends the mind and the five senses of cognition; therefore he cannot be comprehended nor described by them – yet for the purpose of instruction He is indicated as 'consciousness'. Though it appears as though He does everything, <u>he does nothing,</u> <u>he does nothing</u>. That consciousness is pure and seemingly it engages itself in the activities of the world, to the same extent as the spring does in the flowering of trees".

       ***   ***   ***

•• "*Rajayoga* is meant for persons whose minds have become relatively quiet, whose *'vasanas'* have been relatively exhausted. Others whose minds get agitated, who again and again fall into the mire of the flesh and again and again indulge in sensuality, have to practice *Hadha Yoga* first which helps to reduce the *'tamasic vasanas'*, and then come to these fifteen steps called *Raja Yoga*."

(किञ्चित् पक्वकषायाणां हठयोगेन संयुतः)

(kincith pakva kashaayaanaam hadhayogena samyuta)

(*Aparokshanubhuti* 143; Swami Chinmayananda's commentary)

•• "For those who are not qualified for gaining true knowledge through enquiry, Sri Vidyaranya recommends the yoga of meditation (dhyana yoga)." *Pancadasi* p.xix

•• *Karma yoga* ... is there such a yoga? Any possibility of yoga through karma? I have my strong doubts.

•• *Saguna dhyanam* is capable of giving siddhis (*anima* etc); and *nirguna dhyana* leads to samadhi. (*Yogatatwa Upanishad* 105)

(सगुणं ध्यानमेतत्स्यादणिमादिगुणप्रदं ।
निर्गुणध्यानयुक्तस्य समाधिश्च ततो भवेत्

sagunam dhyanamethathsyad
animaadi guna pradam
nirguna dhyana yukthasya
samaadhischa thatho bhaveth..)

•• Samaadhi is only one; the six categorisaton is only a guideline ...*sabdanuviddha* ...*drsyanuvidha* ...*savikalpa* .... *nirvikalpa* etc. (for further elucidation please look up '*drk-drsya vivekam*' commentary by swamy Tejomayanana)

•• I have known for a long time that some of the Realised personalities around here used to spend the nights, alone, in cremation grounds. Now I have read in an Upanishad that this is done to wipe off the vestiges of body-consciousness and the attendant fear of death.

Maya:

It is revealing ...and also a great relief to me ..to note that Shankaracharya's first charge against Maya is that it puts up a differentiation between Brahmam and Jivan. (in the opening verse of *Maya Panchakam*): ...*khadayathi jagadisha jiva bhedam.* All its other mischiefs are secondary ..including the existence of the universe.

Kick off the universe to the background and take care of this Jiva-Brahma *bhedam.* There is absolutely no confusion in dealing with this duality ...and solving it.

•• उपादानं प्रपञ्चस्य ब्रह्मणोन्यन्य विद्यते
तस्मात् सर्व प्रपञ्चोयं ब्रह्मैवास्ति न चेतरात् ॥ *(Proudha. 45)*

upaadaanam* prapanchasya
brahmanonnanya'vidyathe
thasmaad sarva'prapanchoyam
brahmaivaasthi nachetharaath.

Brahmam alone is the cause of the universe; no other cause is seen. Therefore, the whole universe is Brahmam ...and nothing else.

---

* upadanam: it denotes material cause.

•• "The universe stands superimposed on Brahmam and appears real. The reality of Brahmam is superimposed on the universe, and it appears existent though non-existent". (ref: lost)

'Be it noted that separately they (Brahmam and Maya) are neither the material cause nor the efficient cause. It is only in conjunction that they are both. In fact they are not two, but one, ...functioning differently though jointly. (Pancadasi p.96)

•• "In absolute knowledge—super consciousness—there is no trace of creation nor the memory thereof." (*Pancadasi* p99, *Brhadaranyaka Upa*.1.4.4)

•• "The latency of the world in Brahmam before creation does not mean its real existence. Such description is a concession to the beginner who cannot conceive the world or avidya to be causeless."

•• "Mind is Maya; whatever seen through it is also Maya (non-existent) ...inclusive of gods and goddesses." (heard from somewhere).

Panchadasi 2.60: The first modification of *Maya* is aakaasa.

(आद्यो विकार आकाश: *aadyo vikaara aakaasa*)

•• Aakaasa derives its existence from Brahmam, its substratum.

•• When it is said that aakaasa exists, it implies that the property of 'existing' which resides only in Brahman, is transmitted / transposed/transfixed to akasa. The existence of the snake too in the illustration is not different from this existence.

•• The nature of Brahman is existence only. Brahmam is space-less; but *akasa* has both space and existence as its nature. (*Pancadasi* 2.61)

Akasa has the property of sound (conveying, communicating), which is not in Brahmam. (*Pancadasi* 2.62)

So it tries to point out that 'something' can come out of 'nothing'! 'Something' was there in the 'nothing' in seed form ...dormant? No, that cannot be. This is a right pointer in the wrong direction.

••   *'na bhoomir'aapo na cha vahni ...*
    na cha'ambaram cha':

'space, air, fire, water, earth are not in me' ... says *Kaivalyopanishad*.

Continue to think along this line... In the seed there is no leaf.... No wood for furniture or firewood. It has its potentialities hidden in it. They work in conjunction with contributory factors like rain, sunshine, nutrients.

Perhaps these parameters apply only to the seed, and not to Brahmam. Brahmam is not a seed, holding the universe in It; we have seen enough of Upanishadic statements that It is '*nirgunam*'.

[Doubts/questions....that may lead you to answers ....perhaps right, perhaps wrong—to be amended later on].

Two plus two is four. (2 + 2 = 4). Anything else is wrong. Wrongs can be many .

All the paths lead to one destination?   Absurd.

••   आकाशात् पतितं तोयं यथा गच्छति सागरं
    सर्व देव नमस्कारं केशवंप्रति गच्छतिः

> *aakaasaath pathitham thoyam*
> *yadha gacchathi saagaaram*
> *sarva deva namaskaaram*
> *Kesavam prathi gacchathi*

All the rain-water that fall move towards the ocean—whatever be the route it takes. The salute to all the gods go only to Kesava. This is written in **BOLD** letters. The multitude sees it ..and quote also. This is convenient for the multitude. But Kesava stands up and declares—

> यान्ति देवव्रतान देवान् पितृन् यान्ति पितृव्रताः
> भूतानियान्ति भूतेज्या यान्ति मद्याजिनोपिमाम् ॥ *(Gita IX.25)*

> *yaanthi deva'vrathan devaan*
> *pithrn yaanthi pithr vratha:*
> *bhoothaani yaanthi bhoothejya*
> *yaanthi madyaajino'pi maam.*

The devotees of devas (deities) reach their respective deities; those that are devotees of the (*pithr* ...forefathers) by-gones[+], reach the bygones, those who follow the bhuthas (black spirits) reach them, and those that follow me reach me.

Note: if all the paths lead up (in the case of a peak), probably these may reach the pinnacle. There also, if any impassable precipice ...forbidding blockage ... is encountered, one has to retrace to the starting point. If the path leads to the sides or even downhill how will anyone reach the top? If your destination is the airport at Ananthapuram, you have to go westward from the centre of the city. If you choose to go

---

+ *Pithr*: human souls/spirits in various stages of high maturiiy ... sometimes holding the positions of karma devatha-s and upwards also ...and what not!

Ch.5 Some related thoughts 265

eastward, after a long long journey you will reach Kanyakumari. And realizing the futility of having chosen that path, will have to take a detour to the starting point, and restart in the right direction. Whereas, one who chooses to move westward will, in a few minutes, reach the airport.

Mulla - distance

Mulla Naziruddin was running a small wayside shop. Some one came in a car and asked him "How far away is the temple that is somewhere around here?"

Mulla: "Oh! It is very very far off. You may reach or may not reach. Road may be there; or may not be there".

Visitor: "Why...someone said it is somewhere here within half-a-kilometre."

Mulla: "True, if you turn back and take the proper road." Think.

Bhakthi:

Bhakthi is projected as one of the sure paths for *mukthi* (liberation). For the majority, bhakthi consists of beggary... spreading hands in front of God-s. And then there are nine different forms of *Bhakthi*...it is said. Enmity is also a form of *Bhakthi*! (The examples of Sishupalan and Ravanan are cited). (Narada bhakthi sutram p.127). Sensual, sexual lust towards god (or incarnation) is also *Bhakthi* (eg: Gopikas). Fear and hatred are also projected as routes of *Bhakthi*!! (eg: Kamsa)

To me it is not a fragrance that wafts out of this *bhakthi* ...it stinks. Multitudes prefer to follow   only this. They are not open to knowledge—the path of Knowledge (*Jnanam*)*

---

* The pronunciation of *jnanam* cannot be reproduced with English letters.

Right sign-boards to the wrong direction:

'Whatever you hear in the world is Om....inside you and outside. ...the chirping of birds, the croaking of toads, the sound of the waves, the wind, the thunder and so on. There is the unchanted chant (*ajapa-japam*) of Om going on inside you.. the universe chants Om' ...and what not!

•• **It seems all these channel-gods – godmen and godwomen – 99 per cent of them — are avowed to keep their followers away from seeing the light** ...away from the 'Aham Brahma Asmi' idea ...eternally. They want to bury THATH TWAM ASI. They want to bury 'Brahmavith Brahmaiva bhavathi'. They ask: "how can you be THAT? You are only a slave of THAT. And how will a 'knower of Brahmam become Brahmam? Impossible. In that case there will be clashes if many people become Brahmam-s — clash of Brahma-s". This is the limit of understanding of *bhakthi* yoga ....and that is why **Vivekananda laments:-**

"To teach dualism was a tremendous mistake made in India and elsewhere, because people did not look at the ultimate principles but only thought of the process which is very intricate indeed. To many these tremendous philosophical and logical propositions were alarming. They thought these things could not be made universal. ...But I do not believe at all that monistic ideas preached to the world would produce immorality and weakness. On the contrary I have reason to believe that it is the only remedy there is. If this be the truth, **why let people drink ditch water when the stream of life is flowing by?** Why not at this moment teach it to the whole world? **Why not teach it with the voice of** thunder to every man that is born ...to saints and sinners, men and women and children, to the man on the throne and to the man sweeping the streets? ...We have listened to words of weakness from our childhood." (SV Vol.2 p199)

Sage Vasishta also attaches little value to *Bhakthi:* Listen from the great sage the secret of *Bhakthi* / devotion:

शास्त्रयत्नविचारेभ्यो मूर्खाणां प्रपलायिनां ।
कल्पिता वैष्णवी भक्ति: प्रवृत्त्यर्थं शुभस्थितौ ॥ 5 ॥ *(5-43-20)*

1667. Devotion to God Vishnu is invented for the sake of the progress (or employment) in the auspicious state (of Self-Knowledge) of fools running away from scriptural injunction, effort and investigation. (*Vaasishta Darsanam* - SAMATA BOOKS)

सर्वस्थैव जनस्यास्य विष्णुरभ्यन्तरे स्थित:
तं परित्यज्य ये यान्ति बहिर्विष्णुं नराधमा: ॥ 7 ॥ (5-43-25)

1669. Vishnu is situated in the inner space of quite every one of these living beings. Those who set out for Vishnu externally, discarding him (seated within), are the lowest among men. (*Vaasishta Darsanam* - SAMATA BOOKS)

*** *** ***

Nature: has its rules. Rules (principles) of heat, electricity, magnetism, gravity...and so on.

Water flows down...not up ..under the compulsion of gravity. Torrential flows form whirlpools. If you happen to get drawn to them ...no hope. Water has no intention to kill you,..but it kills ...without knowing that it kills.

Electricity: If you work with an open-coil-heater in the kitchen, you have to be extremely careful that nothing spills over to the open live coil...It can give a deadly shock. Even if you pray, it will not spare you.

Fire, water, electricity. They are of great use. Cannot shut out. Use them...but let them not use you. Use the world; but don't let the world use you up...fully.

***   ***   ***

Let the universe ... and therefore also your body ... remain in Awareness ..get mixed up with Awarenes. That cannot in any way pose a threat to Awareness. Can the waves do any harm to the ocean? The pots and rooms and caves cannot threaten to contain the endless space? !

So the 'fearlessness' guaranteed by the Upanishads will not be shaken if Vedantha grants a 'reality' status to the universe.

***   ***   ***

'Brahmam (bodham / awareness) alone exists' ...they swear. 'And if you see anything else, it is unreal'. There is no transformation, no evolution. It is *vivartham* ...meaning, appearance without any reality. Like snake in a rope.

In a rope we can see a snake by mistake; but we cannot see an elephant. Can we? The rope has no power to project an elephant.

•• *neela vastradi yogena sphatiko yatha*: (glass cube and blue cloth) To provide blue colour to the cube, blue cloth has to be there ...an existent blue cloth? The cube will not simply assume a colour.

From mud the potter can make a pot ...but not a woman for him. Mud has its limitations. This is called *vasthu swabhavam*. ...material properties. This is another argument. So the abominable universe and your pitiable body is the 'material property' of Brahmam ...that is material-less and property-less? If at all it has these properties, why not better properties?

I don't find that these lines of thought can lead you to anything worthwhile. I don't find any way out of this jungle, (as of now) .. using their paths.

The Upanishads throw some bright light on the path when they say that there is no *sajaathiya-vijaathiya-swagatha bhedam* in Brahman. When you understand that, the above arguments and confusions evaporate. NOTHING COMES OUT OF BRHMAM. Brahmam remains *avikaari* – immutable, changeless.

The existence of the universe ...and your body ...does not militate against the awareness. The awareness serves as the eye of the universe (*prajna-nethro loka*). The eye does not militate against the body. Here there is no question of fear from this duality (*dwaithath vai bhayam bhavathi*). Such an antagonistic duality is not here. It is a helpful – complementary – duality. The eye is a help and strength to the body. And eye has no fear of the body.

Moreover, awareness is not concerned about the world, either. The sun is not concerned about the planets. The existence or non-existence of the planets pose no threat to the sun!

***   ***   ***

•• In the spirit world revealed by Dr Michael Newton's research, souls are produced as in an incubator or as in a tissue culture set-up, and grown in nurseries – pigeon holes – and planted and replanted several times on the earth and in other near-earth situations/surroundings – grown through rain and shine ... the souls are subjected to tests and trials and hardships and miseries – undergoes acid tests...and finally purified and matured....And ultimately what? What for? Stacked up...it seems..somewhere. And new souls are still produced. What is the big idea behind? Ultimate Absolute Peace is not found anywhere there.

•• To the discriminating, the whole world is a stage of tragedy, since the modifications are antagonistic to the *summum bonum* through the vexations of the various forms and of anxiety and of impressions self-continuant.

•• अस्ति भाति प्रियं नाम रूपं चेत्यंश पञ्चकं
आद्य त्रयं ब्रह्मरूपं जगद्रूपं ततोद्वयं

*(asthi bhaathi priyam naama'roopam
chethyamsha'panchakam
aadya'thrayam brahma'roopam
jagad'roopam thatho'dwayam)*

Existence (Reality), Awareness, Bliss, Names and Forms ...five such components / constituents. Out of these, the first three constitute Brahmam, and the next two form the *Jagath*/ universe.

Look at this...closely. There is a connotation ....*dhwani* ...indication... that Brahmam and Jagath are two...not one.

In the view of Jainism:

•• 'The whole universe of being consisting of mental and material factors has existed from all eternity, undergoing an infinite number of revolutions produced by the powers of nature without the intervention of any external deity'.

Ch.5 Some related thoughts   271

'Strictly speaking, there is no room for devotion or *bhakthi* in the Jaina system' (Indian Philosophy p331, Dr S. Radhakrishnan)

•• "Truly speaking, the essence of all jivas is consciousness." (writes Dr S.Radhakrishnan in INDIAN PHILOSOPHY)

"The liberated jiva freed from matter is called the Athman. The Athman is pure consciousness untainted by matter. It excludes all space and externality. It is the jiva purified and raised to its highest spiritual status, which is mere formless consciousness." (p335 Indian Philosophy. Dr Radhakrishnan) *Moksham* is said to be eternal upward movement. (*nithyordhvagamanam mukthi*) ? (Jainism) No let-up, rest, relaxation, peace? $\mathcal{D}_n$

***   ***   ***

Permanent atoms ?!

Theosophic Society says that 'some people are able to hold their permanent atoms' ... ie, to sit up somewhere beyond and watch the world, eternally. Is it not a boring situation? Who wants to sit like that? If you watch, you may land up in a necessity to react..respond...intervene. Without having to watch...is a better situation, I think.

•• NM: "All this is temporary, while I am dealing with the eternal. Gods and their universes come and go. Avatars follow each other in endless succession, and in the end we are back at the source (?). I talk only of the timeless source of all the gods with all their universes, past, present and future".

I prefer to see it as 'the eye' of the universe. — not as 'the source'. Think.

•• *Nirmalaya prasanthaya niralambaya thejase:*

Clean, peaceful, independent *thejas* (light) If It has the duty and power to create preserve and destroy the world, then it cannot be said to be *nirmalam* and *prasantham*.

***   ***   ***

"When the intellect takes after or resembles *Purusha*, its intellection ceases. It may be said that from the practical standpoint then *Purusha* looks like intellect while he looks like himself as well. That is the state of *kaivalya* or oneness with the absolute. *Kaivalya* thus means to remain '*kevala*' one alone, in his integral state on the part of *Purusha*, in whom intellection ceases altogether. Hence in the state of *kaivalya, Purusha* does not undergo any transformation but in him intellect undergoes complete dissolution". (words of AC Sastri of Calcutta University in his introduction to *Yogasutras* of Patanjali)

***   ***   ***

The murderer ...washed the dagger, washed the hands. The dagger gets no punishment, the hands get no punishment, nor even the body. The punishment is to the consciousness. If the person is unconscious, he is not punished; even if he is out of his wits, he is not punished. Here also the view that you are really the consciousness, is upheld.

***   ***   ***

Whatever exist, exist:

The theory of Maya negates the existence of the world ...and your body. (My thoughts on this are discussed elsewhere in this book).

Ch.5 Some related thoughts   273

I don't believe in the cult of negating anything that exists. I don't think we have a right even to negate the existence of Astral Beings.

Astral beings exist: If human beings have astral body and astral existence, why not the other beings, which are thought to be existing ...known to be existing for ages? Very many people have experienced the existence of astral beings. If you have not experienced it, that is not reason enough to negate. Your grand father had a father. Just because you have not seen him, can you argue that grand-father had no father?

Suppose someone comes to your house and asks for you. And someone in the house (to whom you are a *persona non grata*) tells him that you are not there, ...not living there any more ...or even that you are no more ...passed away long ago. And you hear it. What will be your feeling? Spirits exist ...and you negate. This is a crime ..hurting the feelings of the bygones and all (who are interested in your well-being, mind you) . ..and that too, very deeply. Think.

Do you see my voice? No.

Do you see the fragrance of the flower? No.

There are things we cannot see also.

Astral beings: (Words of Narayana Guru):

Just as there are millions of varieties of creatures in the physical world we see, there are millions of varieties of beings in the astral world also. And we now and then get proof of this existence (...he cites the occasions, circumstances). And there cannot be any argument against it ...it is unquestionably clear. They are unseen, but when they approach, the presence is marked by heat sometimes, sometimes cold, some smell sweet, some stink. "I am not elaborating these here" says

Gurudev himself. Some are pleased with milk, some like ghee, some like honey, some like paayasam, some like fruits, some like roots (tuber crops), some like incense, some like manthra, ..thanthra, yanthra, ...dance, music, musical instruments ..and some like all these. Some like meat, some like blood, liquor ... ... Some are huge in size, some small. Some are white, some are black, some are yellow, some are strange-colored. Some are tall, some are short. Some ride on ox, some fly on eagle, some on peacock. Some have horses to ride. Some travel all over without obstructions; some are seen at many places at the same time. Some have heads of birds, some have horse-heads, some have the hoods of serpents. Some live in clean regions, and some in unclean. Some have white clothing, some have yellow. Some wear torn clothes, some wear *kaupeenam*. Some are naked. Some have *jata* (matted hair), some have shaven heads. Some are peaceful, some are violent. Some are harmless, some have the power to kill. Some can create. Some can destroy. Some have *damshtra-s* (canine teeth). Some are beautiful, some have fearful looks.

... Narayana Guru proceeds with their impingements into the human world, interactions, ...outcomes, good and bad ...the overall desirability of keeping away from them and seeking the help of helpful clean astral powers (devas) ...Those interested may look up 'complete works of Sree Narayana Guru' for more details (I have reproduced a few things from here and there from his exposition. I have reason to believe that he has written this from his first-hand experience. I have heard of stories of someone seeing him in conversation with a horse-head in the night in an island in a lake near here.) Astral body has no obstruction from closed doors and walls and pillars ...it moves through and through, it seems.

Ch.5   Some related thoughts   275

But that too has environs to deal with. Too much of heat, cold, and noise affect them – says Narayana Guru.

***　　　***　　　***

And it can be a reality that god-s and goddesses also exist.

And the common denominator — the Awareness .. exists in every being — humans, gods, demons, animals ...worms ..and all sorts of other astral beings.   And because of this Awareness they know their existence ...and because of this Awareness you say you don't know their existence.

But ...the gods and goddesses ..if they exist ...why don't they go all-out to support their dependants ...those who beg for assistance? To my reckoning, the vast majority of prayers for help go unanswered. (a statistics is needed in this matter). Gods are not supposed to intervene in the working of karma; may be that is one reason.

***　　　***　　　***

••   World is unreal. (?) Everybody choose to explain things in their own individual styles. Wild wild explanations are also given.   But do these original words have no meaning and content of their own? Yes, they do have ...the one intended by their writer. <u>Push aside all the commentators, and see the original meaning</u>. Have a look at this one verse   ..from *Ashtavakra Gita* (XIII.1)

> *akinchana bhavam swasthyam*
> *kaupeenathwepi durlabham.*

Swami Chinmayananda stretches the explanation to the peace gained from abidance in the Self. (ref. p181) Swami Jnanananda Saraswathi accepts its simple meaning ...

"*swasthyam*" in the sense we normally use it in common parlance. I too see it this way only. In my assessment, the context demands only that much. This much is the meaning he sees in it: Without possessions, one is peaceful. Even the possession of a loin cloth disturbs the peace[1].

•• "*Thath Twam Asi*"[2] p49: "Vedas degenerated into Brahmanas, Brahmanas into puranas, puranas into fables and fairy tales ...and finally into loss of memory. Indian spirituality has lost its direction and content. The eyes that have sighted the fundamental light (*thejas, jyothis*) dimmed down. One who has mistaken a firefly for a sun, eventually lost the efficiency to look at the sun and ended up with the firefly." (Sukumar Azhikode). I now see this in the people who throng in their thousands in front of the numerous TV-channel god-men and god-women in this country that is Bharath. (Revelling in light? !)

SOME STRAIGHT THINKING:

"When the duality of the knower and the known comes to an end, what remains is the Self". (*Pancadasi* Verse X.26 p433) When the 'duality ends', when the 'thripudi ends' ..are the usual sayings. Even when these remain, if the 'drk ...the seer' knows his status, (like the boss in an office) he (It) is supreme in all situations ..and without situations! Think.

---

[1] There is a story to drive home this idea: A sanyasi had a loin cloth ...in the wilderness. He used to hang it out to dry. A rat started gnawing at it a bit daily. To solve this, he brought a cat. Then there was the necessity to find milk for the cat. So he bought a cow. Then he had to find a person to take care of the cow ....and then to buy a piece of land for fodder for the cow. Then the cow-keeper had to be married ...and so on.

[2] A book by Sukumar Azhikode, in Malayalam.

Ch.5 Some related thoughts

sarva'shaktham (all-powerful) ?

Not at all. As if the breath will stop if we do not believe that Brahmam is all-powerful and all-knowing (in the sense it is a vast mass of information). If you cannot stop with this peaceful, tranquil Brahmam, ..then you have to go in search of a Brahmam that is all-powerful, all-doer. Then you will find 'you are not that'. But Upanishads guarantee you 'YOU ARE THAT'. Where will you bury this deep – this priceless Mahavakya YOU ARE THAT?

"The power of creation of the universe vests with God alone – not in a siddha or individual". Says Vedanta Prabodh p.138. As is usually done, here the word 'God' is used as a synonym of 'Brahmam' ...and then the Great Saying 'Aham Brahma Asmi' is at stake ...under challenge.

"Brahmavith becomes Brahmam Itsef" ... To put it precisely, 'Brahmavith is Brahmam itself' ...no need of a 'becoming'. Then why and how is this diminution as a 'powerless' *vyashti* (jiva) and siddha? I am not willing to bury...I find no reason to bury 'Aham Brahma Asmi'. One who upholds the above view will have to concede that Brahmam also does not have this power ...Brahmam, siddha, jiva all being the same ...nothing different, nothing separate, nothing less or more. (Those who see it differently, don't see the reality.) Then we come to the conclusion that the power of creation *prima facie* is in Prakrthi (nature). (Glass cube + flower) Prakrthi+Brahmam = Prakrti+God. The power of prakthi is seemingly transposed onto Brahmam, giving Brahmam a semblance of God.

And if one thinks closely about God ... in this background ...God vanishes. Brahmam remains, seeing (..as the eye) ...with the Power retained by *Prakrthi.* Think.

Are you the body?

Are you the mind?

Are you the intellect?

Are you the *praana*?

I am none of these. (see Vivekachoodamani, Nirvana shadkam etc where all these are negated)

Are you the astral body?

No, being the seer of the astral body.

Are you part of God?

No, God has no parts.

Are you God?

I am nameless.

***   ***   ***

"The beater and the beaten are the same" says Vedanta Prabodh. In the literal sense I cannot understand this. Can anyone understand? If beater and beaten are the same, how can beating take place? How can I pick up a pointed knife and stick it into my own flesh without any feeling? Can your mouth attempt at a bite at your own thigh for a chunk of flesh when you are starving? You will better starve to death. Consciousness is the common factor in the beater and the beaten. (That way alone it is the same). The awareness of the beater does not take on the suffering of the beaten. Awareness stands as the witness in both these adjuncts/ *upadhis*. It is not affected by the event. Here then the fact that 'consciousness' is a 'witness' proves its validity.

... The SPACE provides space for the existence of everything.

... SUNLIGHT .. you know what all it does for everyone ...everything ..alike.

Ch.5 Some related thoughts

... WATER in the oceans and on land provide sustenance to every living being — although some beings are hostile to others.

... AIR ..is available to all alike. The prey breathes frantically to run and escape ..the predator breathes hard to run faster to catch the prey.

Similarly ...Awareness is the sustainer (of both the beater and the beaten ..even in the process of beating) – and still neutral. The beater and the beaten ...both are sustained by awareness alike.

To my mind, this is a great clue. This explains many things. Think.

The towering consolation and hope is that this Awareness ...your Awareness ...is ETERNAL.

Here you will ask for proof:

1. Awareness is there in the (with the) physical body.

2. It continues in the astral body. (Many people all over the world have had occasions to realize this.) Astral beings, and dead humans presently in astral bodies ...all have their awareness. They show up their vibrant awareness.

3. When we analyse the physical body, we don't find awareness as an integral part of the body. (Remember the neti-neti process ...and Nirvana shadkam ...*mano-buddhi....na aham* and many such.)

•• When we analyse the astral body also, awareness is not found as a part (*vaagaadi pancha, sravanaadi pancha, pranadi pancha' bhra,mu'khaani pancha, buddhya'davidya'-pi'cha kaama karmani ...puryashtakam sukshma sarira'maahu.*) The components are laid bare; but 'awaress' is not one among them. Awareness stands apart; like electricity to a computer

...so to say. They are different, but work in unison ...as if it is an integral whole. So awareness is in the physical body and in the astral body ...and still it is beyond these bodies.

"Awareness stands as the 'seer' of the astral body also" (*Vedantha Prabodh* p.117). The awareness that does not end with the physical body, does not end with the astral body ...where does it end? Here we can safely believe ...it is eternal ...as the ancient Upanishadic seers assure you.

***   ***   ***

•• "The efficiency...(omniscient, omnipotent etc.) manifests only through *upadhis* (equipments)" (p.214 *Vedanta Prabodh*). What is the difficulty if the efficiency remains in the *upadhi*?

***   ***   ***

•• Act on in this world vibrantly like a motor[1] ...if your circumstances demand ...but always keeping the bottom of your mind rooted in your Reality ... A L W A Y S.

Some un-related thoughts:

•• Life situations change 'kaleidoscopically' ...as Swami Bodhananda puts it.

••   *ma kuru dhana jana youvana garvam*
       harathi nimeshath kaalam sarvam
          ...warns Sankaracharya. *(Bhajagovindam)*

Don't gloat over your riches, manpower under command, or the youthfulness of the body; time can take away all these any moment.

---

[1] The simile used in Yoga Vasishtam is the burr-r-r-r of the peacock tail in dance. Sage Vasishta asks Sri Ram to divide his mind, and use the upper half to deal with the world, and the bottom half to be immersed in his Reality always.

0 x million = 0

Sky diving, walking on sky-high long-distance tight rope, ..and many such dare-devil acts ...the rat races to get into the Guinness book and all. These challenges are like zero in front of your eternal reality. Multiply a zero by a million – still you get only a zero. When you know what you are, you can be in peace.

The bull story: Let me tell you an incident that occurred to a friend of mine. He used to handle an ox (bull), shifting it from place to place for grazing ...as a 7-year old boy. One day he gave it a blow with a stick. It did not like it. The bull bent its head close to the ground, scratched the earth with the legs (the preliminaries of charging) ...but held back, and remained in that pose for a long time! And the boy utilized the time to run away. It thinks, it loves, it forgives. It knows what will happen to the boy if it flips its horns. A living, loving, feeling, thinking, tolerant ox ...you call it beef .. and you want it in a plate three times a day! ...Suppose one day the tables are turned, and you get a turn to become beef and mutton in their plates?

I have seen some impassioned appeals for life in our Malayalam poetry:

1) Please, please don't kill me. After discarding the bones, skin, feathers, beak, wings, legs and all, you may get or may not get a little of my flesh to eat. (In Nalacharitham Tr.in Malayalam:- when Nalan caught the swan). Swan continued: "If you leave me alive, I can introduce you to Damayanthi, the most beautiful maiden I have ever seen. I can be the messenger between you both." (The swan was released; and it made the marriage between the two possible.)

2) A firefly appeals to a bird that is about to eat it: "Please don't mistake me for a golden grain and eat. I can

stay in your nest, giving company and my light to your young ones when you fly about."

Life is the dearest thing for every creature; and we are ready to barter anything – anything short of life – to live one more day.

Cockroaches: I have been hearing from my early childhood that some people eat big worms. Never believed it. But now I see in TV channels that people in High Society eat all sorts of worms, cockroaches, tarantulas, black-widows, ….even larvae of flies!. Is civilization moving forward, or backward towards barbarianism? From the way it looks, a member of this high society can any day get an itch, … temptation …challenge …spirit of adventure to taste his own shit …fried, half-fried, and raw. Challenges and adventures … upside down.

One language: While I was in Kovalam, an Italian lady talked to me for five minutes in her language …<u>and I did not get a word of it</u>. There was not even one word in English. Someone watching this, told me that she was complaining about someone charging her more for a bottle of soft-drink. This sort of communication is no communication. So everyone should learn a world language. Who knows when you have to get out of your country for some compelling reasons …treatments and all, if not for pleasure travel. But for the ugly intolerance of the God of the Old Testament, we would have been speaking one language all over the world …remember the Babel incident. My childhood guru, Swami Brahmasuthan, had a Utopian vision that the whole world must have one language!

Apples well-preserved:

A friend of mine working in the gulf reported that someone known to him died of eating apples. Apples nowadays are well-preserved with injection inside and chemical coating outside. This represents the whole food preservation. How long are we going to get along with this? Even while the kings ruled this country, no-one dared to do such preservation.

Noise pollution

•• If someone brings a dog to his house, the peace of the neighbourhood is disturbed, in the dead of night.

•• About the appearance of Beatles in England, someone wrote: "thereafter, the world has never been peaceful as before" (TRADING FAITH).

•• Music is made pollutant noise and convulsive movements with the arrival of Michael Jackson.

•• Someone introduced a diesel auto-rikshaw (tuk-tuk) on the roads; and the roads have become a hundred times more noisy than before.

•• Don't build abodes for the Almighty that builds the universe-s. Build abodes for human beings. (said Swamy Brahmasuthan).

Each new aboard (place of residence - devaalayam) built for God/gods contributes its share of noise pollution; and those who are weak of heart in the neighbourhood will have to think of migrating to some peaceful place. Studies of youngsters in the neighbourhood are geopardised. How can you concentrate with mikes blaring into your ears? And how do the gods take it? Any idea? Think. (Remember what Narayana Guru said: "Too much of noise affects the astral beings"). May be, they slip out and go for a walk!?

Man is the greatest of creations?

Big big gurus say that man is the greatest of creations. They point out the grandeur of the brain, the eyes etc. But

... Some octopus species has eight brains! Some spiders have four pairs of eyes. Some sharks have eyes four times more powerful than man's...with a reflective layer behind the retina. A shark can smell a drop of blood from 5 km away in sea water. What is man's status in this respect? Most wild animals can smell the presence of man from 5 km away. Can we smell it even if it is on the other side of the tree? Our arms and legs are barely able to do some minimal things; they are not fit for fight or flight against animals. Any new-born mouse will out-run a full-grown man. A human baby can stand up on its feet only after a year-and-a-half after birth, whereas all other creatures stand up instantly. To the human infant everything has to be taught .. swimming and the like; while the animals do these instinctively, naturally. Animals most often smell poison in the food. Once someone left poisoned food for some monkeys, to get rid of their nuisance. A senior monkey first smelled it ..all the monkeys went into the forest, ate some anti-poison, came back and ate up the poisoned food.

Remember the recent (July 2012) 'elephant story'...drama in real life – where wild elephants attended the funeral of a human 'friend of elephants' ...walking in two groups over 12 hours through the bushes. Nobody informed them of his death, but they knew. ('Elephant Whisperer' related).

Where lies the great superiority of human beings?

Anthropologists know (perhaps) what made man superior.....The long gestation period of the human infant called for closer social connections, evolution of language and so on...perhaps. (You know better).

6
CONCLUSION

The awareness is not a product of the body or body chemistry or brain chemistry. It survives the body; continues with the astral body. It is in these bodies, and outside also – like the space. Space is in the pots, outside the pots also. Space is one, single, whole – the limitless, borderless entire vast space. Same is the case with awareness also.

The duality of (1) the Awareness and (2) the universe and your body, does not pose a threat to Awareness. The existence or non-existence of the planets around is not a cause of concern to the sun!

Someone asked Buddha: "How many people have you been able to lead to Nirvana so far?". Buddha said: "I am going to give you an assignment before answering your question. Go about this village, meet every occupant, and ask them what their needs are. Compile that, and come back to me." Hardly a hundred houses were there in the village. He met everyone in t

he village and compiled their needs and requirements and desires. More land for farming ...a healthy body ...a beautiful life-partner, more comforts, luxuries, vehicles and so on ...These were the lookout of everybody; and no one mentioned Nirvana. All the items listed were invitations to more and more mental agitations ...and not providing any peace. He came back to Buddha; and Buddha said "This ..your finding ..is your answer".

The ultimate aim and purpose of life is to know what you really are ..and thereby put an end to this cycle of births-

and-deaths. Nothing else is worthwhile. Don't let the golden opportunity slip away this time. Who knows when we will get the next chance?[1]

How long do you want to continue with this death-and-birth cycle ...eternally? Is it so enjoyable? The balance sheet of life in the majority of cases is very grim. Even for those who had a smooth sailing throughout, death is not that pleasant! Birth is also not pleasant, it seems. The babies become unconscious sometimes, in the trauma of birth.

Life situations often change kaleidoscopically. Everything always do not progress as we plan.

Death stays with you all along ...from the time of birth. Like a filled-up balloon moving among thorny bushes, you live on ...till a prick of a thorn bursts the balloon.

Is life all enjoyment? Childhood is spent in forced-studies. No breathing time is allowed.[2] In the middle of life – a few years – are good ...if everything goes well. There also you cannot have all that you want! Social, financial, physical constraints ...thousands. And if you live through to old age, then it is hell. A few moments of flickering happiness, and all the rest is misery.

Unless you see the light of reality, and get away from this cycle, you have to continue eternally in the cycle of rebirths. And there is no certainty that you get a human body every time; the theory of 8.4 million *yonis* in which one

---

[1] Even Devas yearn for a physical body (*'surair'abhivancchitham*) to reach this ultimate goal of liberation. (This is one theory. Suthra Bhaashyam says Devas are also eligible for Brahmavidya).

[2] A very large percentage of school-going children in India nowadays are obese. Do the parents see it? Do they think of the unnatural life imposed on them in the rat race?

can suffer, cannot be brushed aside lightly. This situation ...possibility ...is usually referred to as an ocean riddled with dangers (*bhava saagaram*). And you are in it ...not on the bank ..on the land. And you continue your struggle in this ocean ...with no end; eternity is in front of you. There is no cessation even on the dissolution of the universe. When the universe unfolds again, the soul will continue its journey picking up from where it had left off earlier. You continue until you see the light of reality. When you see this light, you will cover this ocean with one foot, like the water collected in the foot-print of a cow that can be covered up if you place one foot on it! Choose what is good for you. Don't wait for severe blows ...to change the course.

The treasure

A beggar sat at the foot of a tree for six years. He became sick, disabled, immobilized. ...and lay down there ...dirtied the floor for a few long days ...and died. The people of the locality disposed of his body, and tried to clean the spot by scraping the floor. As they scraped the ground, from four inches below the surface where he used to sit, a treasure was unearthed! The beggar was not lucky to get the treasure that was four inches away from him. Your treasure is not even four inches away – nor even one inch. No distance absolutely ...you are that ...YOU ARE THAT.

If you choose the path for your good ...then don't get entangled with endless doubts and confusions. In the field of Self, there are no questions, no confusions, no scope for any confusions. Only in the field of BMI and *prapancham* (the world) there is scope for all questions and confusions and differing opinions and explanations. And even in the field of scientific enquiry, the conclusions are often revised.

Leave everything other than the Awareness to their course, and be happy. Atman (Brahmam/Awareness) is not affected by the existence or non-existence – reality or non-reality — of the universe.

The body that died never knew that it lived. Think. And the one who knew, never died.

The absolute non-duality of Advaita Vedanta is a confusion – a half-truth. How can anyone negate his body and the world around? When it speaks about the Self, it projects your Self in dazzling brilliance; but where it speaks about Maya ..non-existence of the world / body-mind-intellect, there it is confusion ...half-truth or no truth. Why not substitute it with a real world with real existence ...and see how well it fits! Brahmam has no threat from this duality. (The Upanishadic dictum 'out of duality arises fear' is inoperative in this context.) World and Awareness are not at all two factors in conflict. The co-existence of the universe is not a threat to Awareness. The snake wriggling round the neck is not a burden to Lord Siva ...but an ornament! Think.

There are no questions in the Self—only peace — undisturbed, undiluted. Questions are related to BMI and the universe. There is no scope in the Self for further dissection — search and research, because there are no *swagatha-sajathiya-vijathiya bhedam* in the Self/ Brahmam. There is no *swagatha bhedam*; understand it correctly – this is a great pointer.

.. Nature works; God (or rather Awareness /Brahmam) looks on—witnesses – as the EYE OF THE WORLD. Does God regulate? In that case things would have been different, smooth, fair. No *jivo jivasya jeevanam*. No geological cataclysms ...no cosmic collisions.

Omniscient, omnipotent

"*Prajnanam Brahma*" : At least in this one Great Saying I don't find any shade of power or energy or the latent power to activate/prompt or the power of creation, preservation and destruction. *Prajnanam*—simple; awareness. **Awareness doesn't have to produce anything or destroy anything. Not that awareness becomes awareness only if it has power, energy etc.**

Awareness is awareness and see it as such, clearly—without confusing, without infusing all sorts of qualities and attributes.

Electricity energises ...activates electrical equipments, machinery, gadgets. It heats (in oven), cools (in cooler), it rotates fans, turns a lathe, activates an electric chair for execution also. But electricity cannot be considered to be cooling or heating; it is the equipment that is cooling or heating or killing. The energy alone is provided by electricity. This analogy doesn't fit well with the situation in regard to Awareness; but in a way it comes closer to our point of discussion, because, we are trying to describe what is considered to be indescribable. Words cannot fully express certain things—and more so in the description of the Reality. Why—you cannot fully express in words a simple thing as the taste of sugar to a person who has never known sugar. You cannot make a blind man understand what the beauty of a lotus is, or what the sunlight looks like.[+] There is a classic saying in Upanishads:

[+] The story of milk, white like a crane.

"*Vaachoditham thath anrtham*"

किं भद्रं किमभद्रं वा
द्वैतस्या वस्तु नः कियत्
वाचोदितं तदनृतं
मनसा ध्यातमेवचः॥

kim bhadram kim'abhadram va
dwaithasya vasthu'na kiyath
<u>*vaachoditham thath anrtham*</u>
manaso dhyaatham'eva'cha.

All that is expressed in words can be only untruth. in the context of describing the indescribable …because words cannot fully project the true picture of Reality. To show you the star 'Arunthathi' which is a minute one in the constellation of 'saptha-rshi-s' one will have to point to some star bigger and brighter close by, and tell you that Arunthathi is the one close by.

So, in the analogy of electricity there is some power …energizing impulse in electricity (it is called power, nothing else) and it manifests differently in different equipments. But in Awareness in "Prajnanam Brahma" (Awareness is Brahmam) no such power or energy is discernible—not even a shadow of it; it can be safely negated.

When I read all the four Maha Vakyas together, I don't think it conceals the power or energy. I don't find anything explosive —the power to create, the power to destroy the universe, the power of big bang. *Prajnanam* (awareness) is definitely not explosive. Brahmam—people confuse it; refuse to see it straight.

When we use the '*neti neti*' process and get rid of every thing that can be got rid of, what remains is the Seer, the awareness— pure and simple. You don't suddenly become all-knowing and all-powerful. Don't worry on that score. It is so. You are in peace—perfect peace, peace absolute. In this context Swami Chinmayananda asks: "If you get perfect peace, what else do you want?" He also reassures you, you don't have to look beyond for anything further. Why get confused about not becoming omniscient and omnipotent? That is a wrong reading of the situation. What are you looking for, really? Absolute Eternal Peace...or omnipotence?

The mind in agitation is the world; the mind subsided is Brahmam. Prof GB also corroborates this. Don't complicate the simple. Show the courage to accept the simple. Be satisfied with the simple and pure.

Muster the courage to understand Brahmam as a very simple thing ...as your awareness. Nothing else. Don't get frightened by the tall talks of teachers who have not understood what It is ...and themselves groping in darkness. Brahmam has a simple meaning that will not frighten you – Brahmam is something big ...limitless; and is capable of making others also big, limitless. The Awareness ...consciousness ...cosmic consciousness (all are not different, but one) has endowed you with the power of cosmic consciousness ..being your consciousness ...making you also endless, limitless, eternal.

Brahmam becomes easy and clear to understand if It is rid of omnipotence. Try to concede that all this potentiality is in Nature; and it is transfixed on to Brahman while they commingle. The power of the Nature fuses with Brahman, seemingly (not really). Like glass cube and the colour cloth. How peaceful and clear it is to understand this ! Think.

- पत्रस्य पुष्पस्य फलस्य नाशवद्-
  देहेन्द्रियप्राणधियां विनाशः
  नैवात्मनः स्वस्य सदात्मकस्या-
  नन्दाकृतेवृक्षवदस्ति चैषः ॥ *(Vivekachudamani 460)*

  pathrasya pushpsya bhalasya naasavath
  dehendriya prana dhiyaam vinaasa
  naivaathmana swasya sadaathmakasyaa-
  'nandaakrthe vrkshavadasthi chaisha.

The loss of the body, organs, *prana* and *buddhi* is like the fall of a leaf or flower or fruit to a tree. It does not affect the Athman, the Reality, the embodiment of Bliss—which is one's true nature. That survives like the tree.

- न निरोधो न चोत्पत्तिर्न बद्धो न च साधकः
  न मुमुक्षुर्न वै मुक्त इत्येषा परमार्थतः ॥

  na nirodho na chothpatthi'r
  na baddho na ca saadhaka
  na mumukshur'na'vai muktha
  ithyeshaa paramardhatha   *(Vivekachudamani 574)*

There is neither death nor birth, neither a bound nor a struggling soul, neither a seeker after liberation nor a liberated one – this is the ultimate truth.

- आचक्ष्व शृणु वा तात
  नानाशास्त्राण्यनेकशः
  तथापि न तव स्वास्थ्यं
  सर्वविस्मरणादृते ॥   *(Asht.Gita XVI.1)*

  aachakshwa srnu va thaatha
  nana sasthranyanekasa

*thathapi na thava swasthyam
sarva vismaranadrte.*

You may hear various scriptures – you may speak upon various scriptures; but you cannot abide in your Self unless you forget all.

• • क्व माया क्व च संसारः क्व प्रीतिर्विरतिः क्व वा
क्व जीवः क्व च तद् ब्रह्म सर्वदा विमलस्य मे ॥

*kva maya kva cha samsara:
kva preethir'virathi: kva va
kva jiva kvva cha thath Brahma
sarvada vimalasya mae.   (Asht.Gita XX.12)*

Where is illusion and where is the world of change? Where is attachment and where is detachment? Where is jiva and what is Brahmam for me, who is ever Pure?

• • क्व प्रमाता प्रमाणं वा   क्व प्रमेयं क्व च प्रमा
क्व किञ्चित् क्व न किञ्चिद्वा   सर्वदा विमलस्य मे ॥

*kva pramatha pramanam va
kva prameyam kva cha prama
kva kinchith kva na kinchidva
sarvada vimalasya mae.   (Asht.Gita XX.8)*

Where is the 'knower' and where is the 'means to knowledge'; where is the 'object of knowledge', and where is the 'objective-knowledge'; where is 'anything' and where is 'nothing' for me who is ever-Pure?

One who knows his reality abides eternally in the Self, as the Self —

- *upadhi*-less (no adjuncts/containers/limiting factors)
- absolutely pure

- in perfect peace
- doing nothing (having to do nothing) ...action-less
- in saturated ecstasy ...

Ashtavakra continues, like a torrent, to tell you that in front of your eternal Reality everything fades into insignificance:-

- where is the world and where is the aspirant?
- where is the contemplator, where is the man of knowledge?
- where is the soul in bondage, where is the liberated soul?
- where is creation, where is destruction?
- where is knowledge, where is ignorance?
- where are the elements, where is the body?
- where are the organs, and where is the mind?
- where is concentration, where is distraction?
- where is knowledge, where is delusion?
- where is joy, and where is sorrow?
- where is activity, and where is inactivity?
- where are instructions, and scriptural injunctions?
- where is existence, where is non-existence?
- where is unity, where is duality?

"What need is there to say more? Nothing emanates from me" Thus concludes Ashtavakra. (Ashtavakra Gita also concludes with these words.)

•• *aananda bhddhi purnasya*
   mama dukkham katham bhaveth?

In me the fullness of consciousness and saturated bliss, how can there be any misery?

•• The bliss of Brahmam he who knows, **fears not at any time.**

(आनन्दं ब्रह्मणो विद्वान न बिभेति कदाचनः)

(änandam Brahmano'vidwan
na bibheti kadachana.)   (Taitiriya Upa. II.4)

•• Athmajnani's death..never happens.
How can eternal awareness die!?

What Dr Michael Newton's research into spirit world reveals is your existence as a limited eternal entity; but Upanishads present your existence as a totality in eternity ...without limiting factors ...without any challenge from any quarters ...not depending on anything ...standing on your own foundation.

***   ***   ***

Lion story

A fully pregnant lioness jumped over a gorge to catch its prey; but fell down and died. While dying it gave birth to a male cub.

A shepherd coming that way took this lion cub and brought it up in the midst of his sheep. It grew up with the goats, eating grass and bleating like goats.

When it grew up for six months, it was bigger than the goats around; and a big male lion saw it from a distance. It decided to tell him his reality – to correct his understanding. It lay in wait for several days, and after many unsuccessful attempts, one day caught hold of the cub; and told him with great love and compassion that he was not a sheep; he was a lion. The cub did not believe it. Then the lion took him to a water-hole and asked him to look into the stagnant water. When the cub looked he realized that what the big one said was true. Then the big lion said that lions don't eat grass; and don't bleat but roar. He showed him how to roar. Then the small one tried and succeeded in roaring, and the lesser animals in the jungle were afraid of the roar of the lion cub also.

Here a sheep did not transform into a lion; only a mistaken identity is corrected. Similarly, we think we are the bodies; whereas in Reality we are …… birthless, deathless, infinite, eternal Awareness – THE EYE OF THE WORLD …THE ETERNAL EYE OF THE UNIVERSE.

Correcting the mistaken identity …is the help of proper teachers .. and proper texts. And this book should help the ripe student to reach the goal like an arrow.

So many public preachers end up their daily talk by telling the hearers/viewers to seek a proper Guru. This book should unmistakably serve the purpose of a proper guide to one and all who have not seen the light of Reality.

A blanket does not produce heat; it gives back your own heat. We say: 'Ah, what a good blanket'. Similarly the guru points out your reality …does not give you anything new from outside. If a book can serve this purpose …that is good enough. This is my strong view; Prof GB also has expressed this view on many occasions. Upanishads contain a huge amount of knowledge …and nobody cares to use it properly.

Almost all the teachers in the field of spirituality ask their followers …disciples …to purify their minds first. And almost everyone knows it is not easy. It is not workable that way. I believe that, one should try to see the reality first; and in the light of reality things happen as they should. Swamy Chinmayananda used to cite an example: One digs up a water hole ...and the hole is filled with muddy water. Don't get impatient; wait and see. Slowly clear water displaces the muddy water.

***   ***   ***

To those who grope in the dark, truths can be many. But to those who see things in broad daylight, truth can be only one.

Two plus two is four (2 + 2 = 4). Anything else is wrong. Wrongs can be many. All the paths lead to one destination? Some great personality (a siddha) from South India (Tamil Nadu) once said: "saying that all paths lead to the same destination is like saying that there is no path."

•• When you see the entire space, the pot-space vanishes (even while it exists).

•• To see a burning lamp, do you have to light another lamp? ..asks Sankaracharya in *Vivekachudamani.*

•• Your awareness is your closest, most intimate experience (*swaprakaasam, aparoksham*; —self-shining, nothing indirect). You don't have to go about in search of your awareness.

•• 'The light that sees the darkness. The power that perceives the darkness. The fire and all such don't have this capability. Cognition has two aspects: cognizes that a thing exists if it exists, and that a thing does not exist if it does not exist. These two cognitions happen in awareness. Fire and such show up things depending on space and time. Bodham is something that cognizes even the space and time. Bodham is something that lends reality to time and space...by its cognition, recognition. If Bodham does not cognize, then where do space and time project their existence? Where will time and space mark their existence? And how? Awareness is something (a light) beyond time and space. A power that perceives the darkness[+]. With this, it becomes clear that Awareness / Athma is the ultimate cause of the universe. A self-shining, supreme Reality'. (Prof.GB in *Proudhanubhoothi* p.426)

'Ultimate cause of the universe'? How lightly he calls it 'cause of the universe'! Not only GB, you know that hundreds of teachers call It the 'cause of the universe'.The light that shows up a thing ...throws light on a thing ...that brings a thing to light; does that cause it ...create it!? It is like saying that the mirror created the moon in it. If it is only with this much intention ...without attaching any seriousness to it ...using it only as a figure of speech that it is said that Brahmam is the cause of the universe, (meaning simply that It reveals the existence of the universe) ... OK there is no contention. But if those who say it mean it seriously — in its literal sense ...caused, created — then all the repulsion remains ...unsolved. I don't have a brain that accepts this hypothesis. It resists ...repulses.

•• Is it that the Atma activates the BMI or the BMI get activated in the presence of Atma? Is it that the sun rays activate the earth or the earth gets activated in the presence of sunlight?

In the case of sun rays – on both the alternatives – it is not a conscious activity. The nature works, naturally. *Jadam/*

[+] Till this Prof. GB has been giving a profound lead to reality ...but at the end he confuses me, by saying 'cause of the universe'.

matter works. (It has its laws, its forces...like gravity, electricity, magnetism, heat).

In the case of Atma, if it activates, it is then a conscious activity. The Brahmam / the Atma / the Self is definitely emphasized to be '*nish-kriyam*' (inactive)—so that cannot be the case; It does not activate, the other part (partner) ...prakrti ...nature... gets activated.

•• 'The Self is the universal experience of all living beings; and hence it is not void. By realizing the Eternal, one is liberated from all bondages. Thereafter one lives gloriously, victoriously'.

•• 'To those who are searching in vain in the desert of spirituality, thirsty and exhausted, Brahmavidya is an ocean of Nectar.....which is Sathchidananda. The final result of such a spiritual Self rediscovery is a total liberation of the mortal individuality from all its physical mental and intellectual entanglements. *This is called liberation, Self-Realisation or God Realisation'.*(Swamy Chinmayananda ..last page, Chinmaya Vivekachudamani ... big vol.)

•• कालत्रये यथा सर्पो रज्जौनास्ति तथा मयि
अहंकारादिदेहान्तं जगन्नास्त्यहमद्वयः॥

*kaala'thraye yadhaa sarpo
rajjau naasthi thaha mayi
ahamkaaraadi dehaantham
jagannaasthyaha'madwaya.*

Just as the snake does not exist in the rope in the three periods of time – past, present and future—the universe down to the I-ness *(ahamkaram)* and the body does not exist in Me. (*Atmaprabodha-Upanishad* 2.29)

•• That which is real and your own primeval Essence, that Knowledge and Bliss Absolute — which is beyond form and activity — attaining That, one should cease to identify with the false bodies, like an actor casts off his assumed role and the related costumes. (*Vivekachudamani 292*)

•• The conviction of the Truth is seen to proceed from reasoning upon the salutary counsel of the wise, ...and not by bathing in sacred waters nor by helping the poor, nor by a hundred *pranayamas. (na snanena na daanena praanaayaama shathena va)*. (*Vivekachudamani 13*)

•• 'Prathyagathma', 'Brahma" bhedam (differentiation)

'Jeeva' 'Brahma' bhedam.

The individual Self, the Supreme Self differentiation

Jivaathma, Paramathma differentiation

— This is the duality that should end. This is the differentiation that should end. ...a differentiation that is actually not existent. Where is the big difficulty in this? Pot-space, vast space. These are not two. Space is only One ...vast endless space. Remaining vast and single (one only) the space occupies the pots also.

•• That which beholds all, but which no one beholds ...that which illumines the intellect, but which the intellect does not illumine—That is This. (*Vivekachudamani 127*)

•• That which pervades the universe, but which the universe does not pervade. (*Vivekachudamani 128*)

•• By whose *very presence* the body, the organs, mind and intellect keep to their respective spheres of activity. (यस्य सन्निधिमात्रेण *yasya sannidhi mathrena*) ....I AM THAT. (*Vivekachudamani 129*)

Ch.6 Conclusion

∴ Advaita-jnanam (knowing the non-duality) is also a state of the mind. (*mano-vrthi*).

∴ Brahmatma-bhavam (I-am-Brahmam attitude) is also an attitude...state of the mind. -- One should reach a state-less state.

Mind in action = ...is the samsaara, worldly life, universe.

Mind inactive = ...is Brahmam ...mukthi ...liberation.

∴ निश्चलतत्त्वे जीवन्मुक्ति

nischalathathwe jivan'mukathi

— in stillness, is liberation-in-life (*jivanmukthi*).

∴ Universe is a reality; it is apparent. **But you — as the Eternal Awareness –- are a far Greater Reality than the universe.** *You are a Reality that lends reality to the universe.*

All these pointers—

> ➢ Like salt dissolves in the sea
> ➢ Like pot space merges into vast space[+]
> ➢ Like rivers flow into the ocean and become the ocean
> ➢ Like the essence of all the flowers mix into honey
> ➢ Like light merges into light

— Singly, they may not give you a correct grasp of the position ... of the reality; but put them all together and churn them in your mind ...and the correct understanding will emerge ...like

---

[+] Pot-space does not merge; there is no room to merge; space is always single ..THE END-LESS SINGLE SPACE OCCUPIES THE POT ALSO.

the rising sun ...making it as clear as day-light that Your Awareness is the Cosmic Consciousness ...the eye of the world; and YOU ARE THAT. Not a part of THAT ...nothing different, nothing separate, nothing less ...the very same single Absolute Reality ...AWARENESS / *bodham* ...THE EYE OF THE WORLD.

•• When someone points to a star, don't stop short with the finger-tip, try to find the star.

•• "I am Brahmam" (*aham brahma asmi*); not 'I am part (a spec) of Brahmam as all other schools teach. When you come to this cross-roads follow the pointer provided by Vedas — the Four Maha Vakyas:

- Prajnanam Brahma
- Ayam Athma Brahma
- Thath Twam Asi
- Aham Brahma Asmi.

See their meaning clearly, churn them in your mind; and you will see the light of Reality ...an auspicious, brilliant, glorious, eternal Reality ...before which the universe fades out[+] even while it exists.

•• With this much, the Reality should be known. ...Beyond this nothing worthwhile remains to be known.[++]

•• All that is needed is a paradigm shift ...shift in the point of view. Shift from *shavohum* to *shivohum*.

[+] Fades into insignificance.

[++] Look at what Schopenhauer said ...about the philosophy that points out to you "YOU ARE THAT": "Human mind has not conceived anything so brilliant anywhere else in human history".

•• श्रवणादिभिरुद्दीप्त ज्ञानाग्निपरितापितः
जीव सर्वमलान्मुक्त स्वर्णवद् द्योतते स्वयं ॥

sravanaadibhir'uddeeptha
jnana'agni parithaapitha
jiva sarva malaan muktha
swarnavad'dyothathe swayam. (Athmabodham 66)

Burnt in the fire of '*sravanam –mananam-* etc.' the impurities of jiva are removed, and it shines like burnished gold. (ref: Ch III in this book)

•• A frail flower braves the midday sun when it is rooted ... supported ... sustained by the mother plant. If the connection is cut, it wilts in minutes. Be connected with your Eternal Awareness always. Don't think *shavohum* ...be *shivohum* always.

•• निमिषार्थं न तिष्ठन्ति बुद्धिं ब्रह्ममयिंविना
यथा तिष्ठन्ति ब्रह्माद्या सनकाद्या शुकादयः

nimishartham na thishtanthi
budhim Brahma-mayim vinaa
yatha tishtanthi Brahmadya
Sanakadya Sukadaya.   (Vasishtam)

Even for a split-second, don't shift from the Brahmam-attitude (Brahma bhavam). Brahma-Vishnu-Mahesa, and Deva Rshis such as Sanaka and human Maha Rshis such as Suka ..are all in this *bhavam* always. Always be in this *bhaavam* (mental attitude) ... I AM REALITY-AWARENESS-BLISS ABSOLUTE ...without *smrthi-vismrthi-bhranthi*. Dont see it as anything different from you ...YOU ARE THAT ...nothing different, nothing separate, nothing less. ….SHIVOHUM …SHIVOHUM …SHIVOHUM.

> "He who knows It as separate from himself knows It not; while he who knows It as his Self knows It in truth. He who sees his consciousness as separate from It, is ignorant of consciousness itself."

.. एकस्मिन्नव्यवयेशान्ते चिदाकाशेऽमले त्वयि
कुतो जन्म कुत कर्मः कुतोऽहंकार एव चः ॥

(Asht.gita XV.13)

*ekasmin'avyaye'santhe chidakase'amale'tvayi
kutho janma kuthah karma kutho'hamkara eva ca?*

In you – the Single, immutable, serene, uncontaminated Pure Consciousness – how can there be birth, activity, and ego-sense? [+] *(Asht.gita XV.13)*

> All the karmas are in the sphere of body-mind-intellect. Not in me …not related to me …not binding on me — the Awarenesss. (This verse is in 1st Chapter also, & repeated here in last chapter end).

Stillneness of mind is not the ultimate aim … purpose …*prayojanam* of spirituality. Know what you are … through Brahma jnanam …and stay in Brahmaakaara vrthi … in 'I am

---

[+] ego-sense = the feeling that 'I am an individual' – the Awareness, by mistake, thinks it is individuated.

Brahmam' attitude (Nobody can have any problem with this) and get stabilised, solidified, in that conviction, without *smrthi-visnrthi-bhranthi* (without having to remember, without forgetting, without confusing to be something else). This is the ultimate state. The Brahma-bhavam becoming in-born ...natural, *sahajam*. If you are a man, you don't have to be reminded that you are a man, you will never forget that you are man, you will not get confused whether you are a man, woman or animal or something else. Similarly. At this stage the question will not arise as to whether you have to keep remembering or not – it becomes natural, in-born.

•• Get intoxicated with the best of intoxicants—your Self ... the eternal awareness, your reality; not with anything less.

•• अहो अहं नमोमह्यं विनाशो यस्य नास्ति मे
ब्रह्मादिस्तम्बपर्यन्तं जगन्नाशेऽपि तिष्ठतः ॥

aho aham namo'mahyam
vinaaso yasya naasthi mae
Brahmaadi sthamba'paryantham
jagan'naase'pi thishtatha

I salute me, the deathless end-less me – who remain even after the dissolution of the universe and its creator (Brahma).

•• Jiva loses its jivatwam (jiva-hood) and Easwara (God) loses His God-hood – and the *jagath* (world /universe) also dissolves ...vanishes ...gets obscured – and the Self—your

Self ...Atman (your own awareness $\mathcal{D}_n$) alone remains[+] ......

- body-less
- mindless, thoughtless
- organs-less (*anangam*)
- aprameyam
- adwithiyam
- formless, nameless
- aheyam
- anupaadeyam
- not connected to anything
- not related to anything
- not attached to anything
- anaakhyam
- vishuddham
- vijnana-ghanam
- niranjanam
- nishkalam (indivisible)
- aadyantha viheenam
- avyayam
- shaantham
- nithyam
- sukham
- nishkriyam (action-less)

  - apraano'hyamano'shubhra
  - motionless, filling everywhere
  - existing in and out ...like space
- Ayameva hrdaakaashas'chidaadithya swaroopavaan
  (I am the sun in the firmament of perception.)
  - Sarva heena swaroopohum
    - Shuddha Bodha swaroopohum
      - Sthimitha gambhiram.[++]

[For meanings of unfamiliar words above, please refer p90-93]

I end this book with a verse Swami Chinmayananda has chosen to adorn his commentary on ATHMA BODHAM.

[+]   (p.161 *Vedanta Prabodh*)

[++] Sit up and think of the stature of your awareness. Its grandeur is stunning ...*sthimitha gambhiram*.

प्रातःस्मरामि हृदि संस्फुरदात्मतत्त्वं
सच्चित्सुखं परमहंसगतिं तुरीयं ।
यत् स्वप्नजागरसुषुप्तमवैति नित्यं
तद्ब्रह्म निष्कलमहं न च भूतसंघः ॥

praatha smaraami hrdi samsphurad'athma thathvam
sath-chith-sukham paramahamsa gatim thuriyam
yath swapna'jaagara'sushuptha'mavaithi nithyam
thath Brahma nishkalam'aham, na ca bhuthasamgha:

In the early hours of the day I meditate upon the Essential Self clearly experience-able in the heart-cave—that which is Existence-Knowledge-Bliss —that which is the Supreme Goal, the *Paramahamsa* state—the fourth plane of Consciousness – which constantly illumines all experiences in the dream, waking and deep-sleep—I am that part-less[+] Brahmam—not (this) assemblage of matter-vestures.

nishprapanchaaya shaanthaaya
niraalambaaya thejase.[++]

jyotishaam jyothi ...

SHIVOHUM ...I am SHIVAM ...I am AUSPICIOUS ...
I am the deathless, eternal, AUSPICIOUS AWARENESS...

I AM THE EYE OF THE WORLD.

SHIVOHUM ... SHIVOHUM ... SHIVOHUM

[+] partless = not made up of parts—components....that cannot be dismantled into parts or pieces....one, single, whole.

[++] nish-prapancham = devoid of prapancham
shaantham = peaceful
niraalambam = not dependent
thejas = light

Appendix-1

Tejobindu Upanishad Ch.III. 1 to 11
(112 Upanishads Vol.1 p.505)

परब्रह्मस्वरूपोहं परमानन्दमस्म्यहम्
केवलं ज्ञानरूपोहं केवेलं परमोस्म्यहं १
केवलं शान्तरूपोहं केवलं चिन्मयोस्म्यहं
केवलं नित्यरूपोहं केवलं शाश्वतोस्म्यहं ॥२
केवलं सत्वरूपोहमहंत्यक्त्वाहमस्म्यहं
सर्वहीनस्वरूपोहं चिदाकाशमयोस्म्यहं ॥३
केवलं तुर्यरूपोस्मि तुर्यातीतोस्मि केवलः
सदा चैतन्यरूपोस्मि चिदानन्दमयोस्म्यहं ॥४
केवलाकाररूपोस्मि शुद्धरूपोस्म्यहं सदा
केवलं ज्ञानरूपोस्मि केवलं प्रियमस्म्यहं ॥५
निर्विकल्पस्वरूपोस्मि निरीहोस्मि निरामय
सदाऽसङ्ग स्वरूपोस्मि निर्विकारोहमव्ययः ॥६
सदैकरसरूपोस्मि सदाचिन्मात्रविग्रहः
अपरिच्छिन्नरूपोस्मि अखण्डानन्दरूपवान् ॥७
सत्परानन्द रूपोस्मि चित्परानन्दमस्म्यहं
अन्तरान्तररूपोहं अवाङ्मनसगोचरः ॥८
आत्मानन्द स्वरूपोहं सत्यानन्दोस्म्यहं सदा
आत्मारामस्वरूपोस्मि अहमात्मा सदाशिवः ॥९

आत्मप्रकाशरूपोस्मि आत्मज्योति रसोस्म्यहम्
आदिमध्यान्तहीनोस्मि आकाशसदृशोस्म्यहम् ॥१०
नित्यशुद्धचिदानन्द सत्तामात्रोहमव्ययः
नित्यबुद्धविशुद्धैक सच्चिदानन्दमस्म्यहम् ॥११

P.505 *Atmaanubhavam* (Experience of the Self)

Parabrahma swaroopoham paramaanandamasmyaham
Kevalam jnana'roopoham, kevalam paramosmyaham (1)
Kevalam shantha'roopoham, kevalam chinmayosmyaham
Kevalam nithya'roopoham, kevalam saaswathosmyaham. (2)
Kevalam sathwa'roopoham, aham tyaktvaahamasmyaham
Sarvaheena swaroopoham, chidaakaasa'mayosmyaham (3)
Kevalam turyarooposmi turyaatheethosmi kevala
Sadah'chaitanya'rooposmi chidananda'mayosmyaham (4)
Kevalaakaara rooposmi shuddha rooposmyaham sadah
Kevalam jnanarooposmi kevalam priyamasmyaham (5)
Nirvikalpa swarooposmi nireehosmi niraamaya
Sadah asanga'swarooposmi nirvikaarohamavyaya (6)
Sadaika rasa rooposmi sadah chinmaathra vigraha
Aparicchinna rooposmi, akhandaananda'roopavaan (7)
Satparaananda rooposmi, chitparaananda'masmyaham
Antharaanthara roopoham, avaangmanasa'gochara.(8)
Aatmaananda swaroopoham, sathyaanandosmyaham sadah
Aatmaaraama swarooposmi , aham aatma sadasiva (9)
Aatmaprakaasa rooposmi atmajyothi rasosmyaham
Aadimadhyantha'heenosmi aakaasa'sadrsosmyaham(10)
Nitya'shuddha'chidananda'satthaamaatro'hamavyaya
Nitya'buddha'visudhaika satchidananda'masmyaham.(11)

Tejobindu upanishad: Chapter-III   (Upa-112   p509)

(By the time you reach here you are expected to gain the proficiency to read this portion of the Upanishad in Sanskrt directly, without the distortions contributed by the English script; and should be able to follow the meaning also, without anybody's support. So no English script.)

अहं ब्रह्मास्मि मन्त्रोयं दृश्यपापं विनाशयेत् ।
अहं ब्रह्मास्मि मन्त्रोयं अन्यमन्त्रं विनाशयेत् ।६०
अहं ब्रह्मास्मि मन्त्रोयं देहदोषं विनाशयेत् ।
अहं ब्रह्मास्मि मन्त्रोयं जन्मपापं विनाशयेत् । ६१
अहं ब्रह्मास्मि मन्त्रोयं मृत्युपाशं विनाशयेत् ।
अहं ब्रह्मास्मि मन्त्रोयं द्वैतदुःखं विनाशयेत् । ६२
अहं ब्रह्मास्मि मन्त्रोयं चिन्तादुःखं विनाशयेत् । ६३
अहं ब्रह्मास्मि मन्त्रोयं बुद्धिव्याधि विनाशयेत् ।
अहं ब्रह्मास्मि मन्त्रोयं चित्तबन्धं विनाशयेत् ॥ ६४
अहं ब्रह्मास्मि मन्त्रोयं सर्वव्याधीन्विनाशयेत् ।
अहं ब्रह्मास्मि मन्त्रोयं सर्वशोकं विनाशयेत् । ६५
अहं ब्रह्मास्मि मन्त्रोयं कामादीन्नाशयेत्क्षणात् ।
अहं ब्रह्मास्मि मन्त्रोयं क्रोधशक्तिं विनाशयेत्॥ ६६
अहं ब्रह्मास्मि मन्त्रोयं चित्तवृत्तिं विनाशयेत् ।
अहं ब्रह्मास्मि मन्त्रोयं संकल्पादीन् विनाशयेत् ॥ ६७
अहं ब्रह्मास्मि मन्त्रोयं कोटिदोषं विनाशयेत् ।
अहं ब्रह्मास्मि मन्त्रोयं सर्वतन्त्रं विनाशयेत् ॥ ६८
अहं ब्रह्मास्मि मन्त्रोयं आत्माज्ञानं विनाशयेत् ।
अहं ब्रह्मास्मि मन्त्रोयं आत्मलोकजयप्रदः । ६९
अहं ब्रह्मास्मि मन्त्रोयं अप्रतर्क्यसुखप्रदः ..७०

अहं ब्रह्मास्मि मन्त्रोयं ज्ञानानन्दं प्रयच्छति
सप्तकोटिमहामन्त्रं जन्मकोटिशतप्रदं ॥ ७३
सर्वमन्त्रान्समुत्सृज्य एतं मन्त्र समभ्यसेत्
सद्योमोक्षमवाप्नोति नात्र सन्देहमण्वपि ॥ ७४

Tejobindu Upanishad (contd.) p506 Upa112/I

देहभावविहीनोस्मि चिन्ताहीनोस्मि सर्वदा
चित्तवृत्तिविहीनोहं चिदात्मैकरसोस्म्यहं ॥१४
सर्व दृश्यविहीनोहं द्रग्रूपोस्म्यहमेवहि
सर्वदा पूर्णरूपोस्मि नित्यतृप्तोस्म्यहं सदा ॥९५
स्वयमेव स्वयं भञ्जे स्वयमेव स्वयंरमे ।
स्वयमेव स्वयंज्योति स्वयमेव स्वयंमहः ॥२३
स्वस्वात्मनि स्वयं स्वात्मन्येव विलोक्ष्ये
स्वात्मन्येव सुखासीनः स्वात्ममात्रावशेषकः ॥२४
स्वचैतन्ये स्वयं स्थास्ये स्वात्मराज्ये सुखे रमे
स्वात्मसिंहासने स्थित्वा स्वात्मनोन्यन्न चिन्तये ॥२५
सर्वदा सर्वशून्योहं ....
अहमेवह्रदाकाशचिदादित्य स्वरूपवान्
आत्मनात्मनि तृप्तोस्मिः अरूपोस्म्यहमव्ययः ॥२८
आकाशादपि सूक्ष्मोहं आद्यन्ताभाववानहं ॥२९
सर्वप्रकाशरूपोहं पारावारसुखोस्म्यहं ....(३०)
सत्तामात्रस्वरूपोहं ..
सर्वशून्यस्वरूपोहं सकलागमगोचरः
मुक्तोहं मोक्षरूपोहं निर्वाणसुखरूपवान् ॥४०
सत्यविज्ञानमात्रोहं सन्मात्रानन्दवानहं
तुरीयातीतरूपोहं निर्विकल्पस्वरूपवान् ॥४१

Deha bhaava viheenosmi chinthaa heenosmi sarvadah
chittha'vrtthi viheenohum chid'athmaika rasosmyaham (14)
Sarva drsya viheeno'ham drg'roopo'smyahameva hi
Sarvadah purna'ruposmi, nityatrpto'smyaham sadah. (15)
....
Swayameva swayam bhanjo swayameva swayam rame,
Swayameva swayam jyoti swayameva swayam mahath.(23)
Swasya'atmani swayam swatmanyeva vilokye
Swa'atmanyeva sukhaaseena swa'atma'maatra'-avaseshaka
Sarvadah sarva'sunyoham... (27)
Aakaasaadapi sukshmo'ham, aadyanthaabhaavavaanaham.(29)
Sarvaprakasa roopoham paaraavaara'sukho'smyaham'... (30)
...bhumanandamayo'smyaham...
Ekame'vadvitiyam sad brahmaivaaham na samsaya
Satya vijnana'maatro-ham sanmaatraananda'vaanaham
Ayameva hrdaakaasaschidaadithya swaroopavaan
*Turiyaatita-rupoaham, nirvikalpa swarupavaan.(41)*Vol.I, P507

I am bodiless, mindless, thoughtless, ... always in *chid-athma-eka rasam* ...I am the seer ...I am without all objects ...I am happy and contented always ...I am subtler than the space ...I am beginningless and endless, eternal. I am self-awareness.

I am the sun in the firmament of perception *(chid-akasam)* ...in saturated ecstasy *(bhumanandam)*.

I am the primeval consciousness alone, the partless non-dual essence ...I am of the nature of the all-void   ...of one beyond the fourth (state).

(Tejobindu is not only this much. Only essentials are reproduced here.)

GLOSSARY

aadithyan	=	sun
ajnaanam	=	ne-science / ignorance /non-apprehension of reality.
amrtham	=	It is a legendary thing – in liquid form, drinking which one is supposed to become immortal. Elixir, nectar, ambrosia are closer words in English, I think.
aparoksha.	=	*Aparokshaanubhoothi* (Sankara)
arani	=	flint wood
athma-jnani	=	one who knows what Athma is.
athma-puja	=	worshipping yourself
avathar	=	incarnation of God (star coming down)
Bh.	=	*Bhaagavatham*
bhaavam	=	attitude
bhaavana	=	conceptualisaion, imagination
bhedam	=	difference
bhraanthi	=	confusing to be something else — seeing one thing as another
BMI	=	Body, Mind, Intellect
buddhi	=	the determinative faculty
Bha. Hrd.	=	*Bhagavatha Hrdayam* (Malayalam) by Prof GB
Ch.	=	*Chandogyopanishad*
chid-aabhaasan	=	Awareness seemingly limited and contained in the body.
chid /chith	=	bodham / awareness
chid'aakaasam	=	the sky (firmament) of awareness
$\mathcal{D}_n$	=	Devesan

E	=	English
GB	=	Prof G.Balakrishnan Nair
jagrath	=	waking life
jivan-mukthi	=	liberation in life (while in the body; not after death)
jiva	=	a being with life impulse in it.
jivathwam	=	individuation
Kailas	=	(Kailas Ashram, Rishikesh) Isaadi Dwadasa Upanishads commentary by Swami Vidyananda Giri
Ma.	=	Mandukya Upanishad
Ma. Ka.	=	Mandukya Kaarika
maha vaakyas	=	Great (profound) statements. (four of them. THATH TWAM ASI etc.)
Mu.	=	Mundakopanishad
mukthi	=	liberation
Mal.	=	Malayalam (language of Kerala)
nirguna	=	without guna-s (qualities) ..adjective.
nirgunatvam	..	noun form of 'nirguna'.
NM	=	Nisargadutta Maharaj
OET	=	Objects-Emotions and-Thoughts
paamara jnanam	=	knowledge of the illiterate
paayasam	=	a sweet semi-fluid food-stuff (south Indian)
PFT	=	Perceiver-Feeler-Thinker
prapancham	=	whatever is formed of five elements (the universe)
Prou.	=	Proudhanubhoothi…..a composition by Sankaracharya …commentary by Prof GB in Malayalam
Q	=	Quoted in
roopam	=	form

roopavaan	=	one with the form
samsara	=	recurrence of births and deaths
shakthi	=	power, ability
shavam	=	dead body
shivam	=	auspicious
smrthi	=	remembrance
states (3 states)	...	waking, dream, deepsleep
SV	=	Swami Vivekananda (speeches & writings in 8 volumes)
swaroopam	=	own form (natural/original form)
swa'kandha'-abharanam	=	ornament on the neck
thri-guna	=	three gunas: The three ingredients of prakrti (nature) viz. sattva (calmness), rajas (activity) and thamas (inertia), with which the whole universe is constituted
Thrisikhi	..	*Thrisikhibrahmanopanishad*
upathi	..	Container, limiting factor, adjunct (body, universe)
U-108	=	108 Upanishathukal (a publication in Malayalam) Prasanthi Publishers, Tvm.
U-112	=	112 Upanishads (a publication in English) Parimal Publications, Delhi
Ve. Pra.	=	*Vedantha Prabodh* (in Hindi) by Swami Paramanand Bharathi
VC	=	*Viveka Choodamani*
vismrthi	=	forgetfulness
vivekam	=	the ability to discriminate ..to discern the difference
vrtthi-s	=	movements, activities, vibrations, pulsations, attitudes

Some responses from the participants of the BRAHMAVIDYA MEDITATION:

— An American lady (72) who was following Vipassana meditation for 22 years – out of curiosity – came in for my meditation. At the end of the meditation, she sat up; and tears rolled down her cheeks; and she assessed this meditation in one word: "AMAZING!" And thereafter she came in for this meditation all through the days of her stay in the resort (some 23 days).

— Another person said after the meditation: "NOW I KNOW WHY I CAME TO INDIA'. (Dagmar Bettin)

— Another response: "I THINK I HAVE HAD A RE-BIRTH in this last hour".

— YOU ARE A GIFT TO HUMANITY. (Dr Heinrich Zeeden)

— "I am reaching my retirement age. I have been hearing and reading Indian spirituality so long; ...so far I was confused. But through your words everything becomes clear" (Dr S. Radhakrishnan Nair, Professor – Linguistics, Kerala University)

Appreciations are numerous. Only a few samples are given here.

U<small>The eye of the</small>NIVERSE
प्रज्ञानेत्रो लोकः

- ➤ A spirituality acceptable to the sharpest of intellects

- ➤ Packed with the power to explode all spritual mis-conceptions

- ➤ Maya seen from the correct angle

- ➤ Brahmavidya meditation -- a highway to Self-Realisation

ISBN 978-93-5126-755-3

www.ingramcontent.com/pod-product-compliance
Lightning Source LLC
Chambersburg PA
CBHW070546050426
42450CB00011B/2742